Wrestling with the Ox

Wrestling with the Ox

A Theology of
Religious Experience

by

PAUL O. INGRAM

CONTINUUM NEW YORK

1997

The Continuum Publishing Company
370 Lexington Avenue
New York, NY 10017

Copyright © 1997 by Paul O. Ingram

Printed in the United States of America

Library of Congress Cataloging-in-Publication Data

Ingram, Paul O., 1939–
    Wrestling with the ox : a theology of religious experience / Paul O.
Ingram.
        p.   cm.
    Includes bibliographical references and index.
    ISBN 0-8264-1040-5 (pbk.)
    1. Experience (Religion).   2. Postmodernism–Religious aspects.
3. Religious pluralism.   4. Christianity and other religions–
Buddhism.   5. Buddhism–Relations–Christianity.   6. Kʻ uo-an, 12th
cent.   Shih niu tʻ u.   7. Ingram, Paul O., 1939-   .   I. Title.
BL53.I59   1997
291.4'2–dc21   97-20365
                                                              CIP

Contents

Preface

ONE OF THE MANY LESSONS I LEARNED FROM MY FATHER HAPPENED ON A CAMPING trip deep in the High Sierras at a lake near Mount Whitney. I was trying to make a cinch strap by braiding a rope to repair a saddle for our pack mule. We covered twelve miles that day, most of it up hill, and the saddle had slipped off the mule about a mile before we made it to the lake. So we had to unload the mule, leave our supplies, hike in with the mule and our own backpacks to our camping sight, tether the mule, go back down the trail to fetch everything else, and haul it back up to where we set up our camp for the next four days. I was determined that we would not go through that experience again so far from civilization, so after supper I began braiding a rope strap to replace the leather one on the pack saddle.

I was angry at the day and was having trouble braiding the rope.

"Here, let me show you," my father said.

"You already have," I grumbled. "I'd rather do it myself."

"No one ever makes anything alone," he said. So I let him instruct me again on how to braid a rope strong enough to repair a broken cinch strap, and learned a lesson in the process. From braiding cinch straps to writing books, "no one ever makes anything alone." This lesson my father taught me long ago became particularly evident in the process of writing *Wrestling with the Ox*, and I wish to acknowledge with thanks the special persons who helped me as I struggled to "make this book."

Frank Oveis at the Continuum Publishing Group was instrumental in convincing Continuum's editorial board to publish *Wrestling with the Ox*, and he has also been an extremely capable and patient editor. Several colleagues from the Society for Buddhist-Christian studies were especially helpful. Paul Knitter offered criticism and encouragement of this book in its earlier stages. He has also done more than any other working theologian to help me focus on the interrelation between the practice of interreligious dialogue and liberation theology. Sallie B. King, whose work on Buddhist social activism, now referred to as "Buddhist social engagement," is the foundation of much of my reflection on this topic in dialogue with Christian liberation theology. Rita M.

Gross has been my primary teacher in the area of feminist thought. David Chappell, "founder" of the Society for Buddhist-Christian Studies, created a space for my theological reflection as a historian of religions. Frederick J. Streng's friendship and scholarship still influence not only my understanding of Buddhism but my continuing theological evolution. John B. Cobb, with whom I studied Whitehead as a student at the Claremont School of Theology, offered strategies for my wrestling match with religious and cultural pluralism—the "ox" with which we both wrestle in our own particular ways.

I could not have written key chapters of *Wrestling with the Ox* without the aid of several colleagues from the Department of Religion at Pacific Lutheran University. Douglas E. Oakman, who is a New Testament scholar-teacher, gave me much needed help and criticism as I was writing chapter 2. In fact, I could not have written this chapter without him. Lyman T. Lunden read most of the chapters of this book from his perspective as a Lutheran systematic theologian and forced me to take seriously the issue of the particularity of universal religious claims as well as the issues of philosophical-theological relativism. His critiques of my ideas and conclusions still haunt me like a Chinese hungry ghost, and I am grateful for this since his interest in my work has led me to more clarity than I otherwise would have achieved. Mary Jane Haemig, who teaches Reformation history in particular and church history in general, was especially helpful in encouraging me not to give up when several publishers decided they could not publish this book. She personified the advice I used to receive from Willis W. Fisher, a Hebrew Bible professor during my seminary days: "Keep on keeping on." I am very glad I listened to Mary Jane. My colleague in philosophical theology, Nancy R. Howell, not only sharpened my sense of the issues in feminist theology but stimulated my reflection on ecological issues and liberation theology. She was particularly helpful in the writing of chapters 5, 6, and 8. Patricia O'Connell Killen offered invaluable conversation and critique that served me well as I wrote chapters 3 and 4. Finally, two colleagues from the Department of English deserve to be singled out. Audrey S. Eyler is a wonderful composition and literature teacher, as well as a first-rate scholar of Irish and English literature. She has read most of what I have published over the past fifteen years, including the chapters of this book. Her gracious, generous, and hard demand that I write with clarity and style is deeply appreciated. All writers need readers, and she is particularly good at both. Jack Cady, who I think is one of the most creative American novel and short fiction writers now living, has been my mentor in my own attempts at fiction writing. He was especially instrumental in helping me understanding the power of story and personal narrative. What he has taught me has influenced every chapter of this book.

My wife, Regina, is the center of all that I do, and she certainly has played a role in my teaching and scholarship. She too is theologically trained, a sharp reader, and a good critic who helps me think ideas through before I present them publicly in print or orally in lectures. I don't know where I'd be without her, and I don't want to think about it. Finally, I wish to dedicate *Wrestling with the Ox* to my father-in-law, Robert R. Inslee. His work in church architecture over the past fifty years continues to inspire up-and-coming practitioners of this art, as well as churchgoers throughout the Southwest, particularly California. He is an artist whose wise theological understanding has inspired his son-in-law in more ways than either of us at the moment probably understands. I am grateful for how the grace of his life flows into mine.

Pacific Lutheran University, 1997
The Year of the Ox

Wrestling with the Ox

MY APPRENTICESHIP AS A HISTORIAN OF RELIGIONS BEGAN IN THE ACADEMIC
year 1960–1961, six and a half years before the Claremont Graduate School
granted me journeyman standing in the community of scholars and teachers
of my chosen field. I was struggling to complete my undergraduate degree in
philosophy and had enrolled in a "world religions" course that, in those days,
"counted" as an elective for completion of my major. I was not pleased with
having to take this course. In those days I thought "love of wisdom" and religious studies were completely unrelated disciplines.

I also remember being restless and uncertain about what I was going to
do after graduation. In spite of my love of philosophy, it did not seem a very
practical means for earning a living in the world I was about to enter. Now I
know better. "Love of wisdom" is its own reward, but I was unable to perceive
this truth then. I was in a "waiting state," as mystics sometimes put it—uncom-
fortable, anxious, and quite insecure.

It is in such states that we sometimes encounter grace, in my case in the
form of the course's instructor, Ronald M. Huntington.[1] He was an artist of a
teacher, and a teacher who *was* an artist; he was living proof that not only
does something come if you wait, it pours over you like a waterfall, a tidal
wave. But waiting must be natural, without expectation or hope, empty and
translucent. Then that which comes rocks and topples you; it shears, looses,
launches, winnows, grinds. Worlds never imagined will discover you as you
discover them.

Professor Huntington introduced me to these worlds with a Hindu text
and a Buddhist art form. The Hindu text was a tantric Hindu saying he shared
with us during the first class meeting. It was the bait that hooked me into history of religions: *nadeva devam arcayet,* "By none but a god shall a god be
worshiped." The lesson of this ancient text, he said, is about what is now called
"religious pluralism": the deity one worships is a function of one's own state
of mind, which means that it is a product of one's history and culture. Roman
Catholic nuns do not normally have visions of the enlightened Buddha, nor
do Buddhist nuns normally have visions of the risen Christ.

1

The ancient fact of religious pluralism, which first took root in my consciousness thirty-six years ago, is fast becoming part of humanity's "postmodern consciousness," and provides the context for the particular theology of religious pluralism described in this book as "primordial theology."

"Postmodern consciousness" means the experience that religious faith must be played out in full awareness that all images, teachings, and practices, all symbols of the Sacred, are local ethnic ideas, historically conditioned metaphors, and must be recognized as transparent to transcendence. So the question is, How can we live a centered religious faith that accurately reflects reality, "the way things really are," in the midst of the universal relativity that postmodern consciousness implies? How can we know that the practices, symbols, and metaphors of our particular religious faith correspond to the way reality is, instead of merely corresponding to the way we desire reality to be?

I received help with these and other questions when, toward the end of my first "world religions" course, Professor Huntington introduced me to the Ten Ox-Herding Pictures of Japanese Zen Buddhist tradition. I have wrestled with this ox ever since, searching for clues that might help me find unity within the diversity and relativity of humanity's religious Ways, while avoiding ahistorical attempts to explain away the diversity in the unity I perceive.

The Ten Ox-Herding Pictures are a kind of picture book. Originally dating from the twelfth century, they function both as teaching aid and object of Zen Buddhist meditative practices, which they graphically portray as a ten-stage process of self-realization culminating in what Buddhists call "enlightenment." Each stage is represented by a simple black ink drawing in a circular frame that depicts distinct modes of existence and experience that the seeker of enlightenment encounters on the way to discovering the "True Self that is No-Self" or the "Empty Self." The ox is the symbol of the "True" or "Empty Self" being sought, while the man searching for his ox symbolizes the seeker in quest for the True Self he has never lost.

Since I have appropriated the ox of these pictures as a running metaphor symbolizing the interrelation between the Sacred that is encountered in the religious Ways of humanity, and the wrestling match with the Sacred required of human beings for achieving authentic selfhood, a brief discussion of the nature of metaphorical language is in order.

Metaphorical language stands in contrast to literal language. I mean by "literal language" the standard use within a given language system to convey agreed meanings, which may or may not be recorded in a dictionary. Thus the literal meaning of a word is, roughly, its dictionary meaning. To speak literally is to intend to be understood in this standard dictionary sense.

In distinction from literal language, metaphorical language occurs when a speaker's or a writer's meaning differs from dictionary meaning. The precise way in which metaphorical meaning and literal meaning differ is difficult to locate, and in fact has never been defined by linguists in any generally accepted way. However, the central idea of metaphor is indicated by the derivation of the word from the Greek *metaphorein*, meaning "to transfer." Metaphors always involve a transfer of meaning in the sense that a word is illuminated by attaching to it some of the associations of another. The result is that a metaphor is a figure of speech in which we speak of one thing in terms of another.

In this sense, metaphorical meaning is generated by the interaction of two sets of ideas. This is what happens when we speak, for example, of a running nose, or an ideological smoke screen, or when Christians speak of God the Father, Mary, the Mother of God, the Father who begot the Son before all ages, the Bride of Christ, St. John of the Cross's dark night of the soul, or Herman Melville's version, the dark November of the soul.

Thus, if I speak of life as a "journey," I am applying to the experience of living the associations of journey that most persons share and am thereby highlighting certain aspects of the experience of living. Life is *like* a journey because it is a process through time, with a beginning and an end; as on a journey, the moments of our lives move from stage to stage; new and unexpected experiences and interruptions occur; one can proceed on a planned route; one can get lost.

In spelling out the similarities between "life" and "journey," I had to translate a metaphor into literal language. Yet this does not exhaust the metaphor's meaning. No literal translation of a metaphor can exhaust its meaning, because there are no fixed boundaries to a metaphor's range of similarities that can occur to different people in different contexts. Since these similarities can activate an indefinite range of varied associations, there is always an indefinable aura of meaning to a metaphor. Consequently, while a metaphor's central point can be literally translated, its overtones and emotional colors cannot because they are variable and changing. This fact constitutes metaphor as a different kind of speech-act, more akin to poetry than to literal translation of meaning. Like poetry, metaphorical language is not fully translatable into literal, discursive prose.

Even so, however, part of a metaphor's effectiveness depends on a common reservoir of shared associations. In this sense, metaphors function to promote community by creating a sense of familiarity or intimacy between speakers and their shared world. In fact, this is why people living in the same community speak metaphorically almost as much as they speak literally. Language, both literal and metaphorical, is highly plastic and its use is an art.

Since this book assumes that religious faith must today be lived and metaphorically expressed within conditions imposed by a postmodern world, further comment about the nature of postmodern consciousness is in order before I summarize the contents of this book's chapters.

Postmodern consciousness is the major form of my ox, and, therefore, is a major contributing factor to my sense of selfhood. I also believe it is the primary form of selfhood experienced by most contemporary human beings living in highly technological and competitive societies. I have learned to accept this form of the ox, have sometimes tamed and ridden it home, and on occasion have experienced non-duality with it. I have loved it, hated it, been gored by it, been sometimes indifferent to it. But I have never been apart from it. It follows me everywhere I go, for Paul Ingram *is*, in part, the ox, and the ox *is*, in part, Paul Ingram.

The beginning of wisdom for contemporary religious people, then, is confronting and understanding postmodernity. Although my confrontation and understanding have been engendered by my studies in history of religions, postmodernism is a nearly universal phenomenon. Consequently, there are kindred spirits—malcontents across scholarly disciplines who are critical of the reigning methods in their fields—from whom one can receive important aid. One such malcontent, Kenneth J. Gergen, professor of psychology at Swarthmore College, has recently published a reader-friendly effort to make sense of postmodernism entitled *The Saturated Self: Dilemmas of Identity in Contemporary Life*.[2]

Gergen argues that romantic and modernist conceptions of the self are still alive but are being overtaken by new postmodernist attitudes. This takeover changes our personal lives and conceptions of selfhood and society in profound and little-understood ways. For example, during the romantic era, people believed in inner joy, moral feeling, and loyalty. Then modernity gave precedence to logic, reason, and observation—the great values of Western culture's Enlightenment. In contrast, postmodernity is characterized by multiplicity, variety, and change. The self is no longer coherent, and we have different selves for different roles. Our relationships are played out through technologies—like faxes or computer bulletin boards—that allow us to reach across the world cross-culturally without looking into the eyes of those to whom we daily "relate."

In short, postmodernity causes a condition Gergen calls "multiphrenia." Sometimes it can be too much and results in confusion over what is important, how to be sincere, or whom to believe. In the process, we are stretched out all over the place, like runners panting from a race we can never win, much less finish. Even so, like Gergen, I remain nostalgic for what was good about the "good old days" of romanticism and modernity. So even as I welcome variety and pluralism and celebrate them, I also refuse to apologize for seeing a positive side either to relativism or my "modern"—some would say "romantic"—primordial attempt to write a book that affirms a Sacred reality unifying the diversity of humanity's "postmodern" experience of religious pluralism.

It is in light of the preceding discussion of metaphor and postmodern consciousness that the structure and contents of this book should be read and understood. All chapter titles are taken in sequence from the Sung dynasty Zen master Kuo-an Shih-yuan's (Japanese, Kaku-an Shi-en's) commentary on the ten pictures and point to that chapter's topic, although the actual pictures used in this book are from a version given to me by Professor Masao Abe some twenty-eight years ago. Thus, while this book is not specifically about the Buddhist experience of enlightenment, each chapter begins with a commentary on its picture as a springboard for wrestling theologically with that chapter's topic.[3] For this reason, chapters 1 through 10 are introduced by a reproduction and description of its particular Ox-Herding picture.

Chapter 1, "Searching for the Ox," responds to a number of questions raised by the facts of postmodern experience of religious pluralism by means of a typological analysis of the structure of interreligious dialogue. Its thesis is that interreligious dialogue now assumes two major types, each with several nuanced epistemological themes and variations: a "theology-of-religions" model and a "primordial" model. After summarizing the main ideas of several important representatives of each model, I specify and defend a specific "primordial" model of interreligious dialogue as the most adequate theoretical model through which to encounter and interpret contemporary postmodern experience of religious pluralism.

"Seeing the Traces" is the title of chapter 2. Its topic is how the primordial model of interreligious dialogue described in chapter 1 might help us see the "scriptural traces" of humanity's religious story, here illustrated by means of interpretation of selected passages from the New Testament. The experience of cultural and historical relativism continues in this chapter as an important epistemological issue.

"Seeing the Ox" is the goal of chapter 3. It is concerned with the relationship between "seeing" and what is "seen" in humanity's various encounters with the ox. Its operating thesis is that what human beings have seen are images of the Sacred, not the Sacred as such. That is, the various religious Ways of humanity are taken to be ways of "seeing" a single "relatively inaccessible" Sacred reality through the lenses of culturally and historically conditioned metaphors that symbolically point to, but never capture, the ox. The issue of chapter 3 is, accordingly, the nature of the Sacred and its relation to the world as "seen" from the primordial point of view developed in chapter 2.

"Catching the Ox," the fourth picture and the title of chapter 4, focuses on how human beings, by means of humanity's religious Ways, have tried to capture the Sacred and domesticate it through myth, ritual, and doctrine. The experiences of the Sacred as either a nonpersonal or personal reality are compared, after which I argue that both forms of experiencing the ox accurately catch the character of the Sacred.

In chapter 5, "Herding the Ox," I apply the primordial perspective to the interrelation between self and nature. My major assumption is that every thing and event at every moment of space-time is what it is, and what it can become, because of how all things and events mutually interrelate and interpenetrate. This assumption seems confirmed not only by the natural sciences but also by many meditative religious traditions East and West. While the structure of this process can be analyzed from a number of points of view—my view is informed primarily by Whiteheadian process philosophy—reality *is* a process of interrelationships. One important theological implication of this view, as portrayed in the fifth Ox-Herding picture, is that self, world, and the Sacred are interdependent. That is, *how* we experience the ox, or perhaps *whether* we experience the ox, is interdependent with *how* we experience nature, and vice versa. Given chapter 3's notion of the Sacred, then, this chapter compares traditional Christian, Buddhist, and Chinese understandings of nature as a means for suggesting a more adequate primordial understanding of the ecological issues engendered by human interaction with nature than is found in either traditional Christian, Buddhist, or Chinese views.

The elements of a primordial environmental ethic, the goal of which is the "liberation of life," is the theme of the sixth picture and also chapter 6, "Coming Home on the Ox's Back." Chapter 6's thesis is that the "liberation of life" is the foundation for other forms of liberation taken up in chapters 7 and 8.

The seventh Ox-Herding picture, "The Ox Forgotten, Leaving the Man Alone," also the title of chapter 7, in its proper Zen context portrays the initial blissful experience of enlightenment, but not enlightenment's full attainment. What is still needed is understanding that the self's ultimate transformation and liberation cannot be attained apart from the transformation and liberation of other selves. Accordingly, chapter 7 begins a dialogue with the forms of liberation of other selves that is mutually bound up with one's own self-liberation by concentrating on women's liberation. The thesis of this chapter is that the liberation of women engenders other forms of liberation taken up in chapter 8, "The Ox and the Both Man Gone Out of Sight": human liberation from political, social, and economic forces of oppression. Consequently, chapters 7 and 8 are concerned with, to employ a Western theological category, outlining the main features of a primordial theology of liberation.

The eighth Ox-Herding picture, "The Ox and the Man Both Gone Out of Sight," is an empty circle. In Mahayana Buddhist teaching, Emptiness (*śūnyatā*) does not mean that things and events are nonexistent. Emptiness means that nothing exists independently of other things and events, that every thing and event at every moment of space-time is interdependent with all things and events. So nothing is substantially permanent, including our experiences of self and world and self and community. Chapter 8's thesis is that in an interdependent universe—here symbolized by an empty circle—our religious quest and experience do not separate us from the world but throw us into wrestling with the world's suffering rough-and-tumble in order to work for peace and justice, because whatever else enlightenment or salvation may be, it always involves both mutual transformation and liberation of the self and the world in which the self must dwell.

The point of the ninth Ox-Herding picture, "Returning to the Origin, Back to the Source," is that as we apprehend reality, "the way things really are," we discover that oneself and the world with which the self interacts have never been lost or defiled. Where before we could not apprehend clearly the relationship between self and world, we now can live in harmony with the myriad of forms reality can assume. According to the Zen perspective, this experience is a hair's width away from the attainment of full enlightenment. Or, in more generic language, we are close to achieving what Frederick J. Streng called the "mutual transformation" of self and world.[4]

Consequently, the topic of chapter 9 is "soteriology" or "salvation." My thesis is that all religious Ways are about "final liberation" or "salvation" because all religious Ways are "means of ultimate transformation."[5] Chapter 9 is therefore concerned with the plurality of conceptions of "salvation" that have evolved from the almost universal human desire to transcend the finality of death. More specifically, this chapter's problem is whether it is reasonable, from a primordial theological perspective, to hope for final liberation from death, since how one views this issue conditions how one views the liberation of life (chapters 5 and 6), the liberation of women (chapter 7), and the liberation of humanity from political, social, and economic oppression (chapter 8).

Finally, chapter 10, "Entering the City with Bliss-bestowing Hands," seeks to summarize the unity I see underlying postmodern religious experience of the Ox. However, unlike the tenth Ox-Herding picture, I have not attempted to portray the final stage of enlightenment. Instead, this chapter seeks to share ideas, perhaps even occasional insights, while identifying new, "far-off countries" not thought about before the change in consciousness engendered by the writing of this book. In other words, chapter 10 is about loose ends that I hope to tie together in a way that will allow the thoughts and imaginations of others to range freely in new and more challenging directions beyond the specific conclusions this chapter summarizes. Since I have not attained the enlightened consciousness of the man portrayed in the tenth Ox-Herding picture, chapter 10 should be read as an initial, groping effort to describe primordial hints of what I think this stage of consciousness might be like.

Some Reflections on Method

Scholarly discourse in religious studies more often than not exhibits what Alfred North Whitehead called "the fallacy of misplaced concreteness": the tendency to persistently abstract universals or essences out of material conditions and particular matters of fact by turning away, often in great abhorrence and fear, from concrete existence. The error is not with abstract thinking as such. Thinking is always a process of abstracting the universal character out of the plurality of particular concrete matters of fact. Certainly, this book engages in such an enterprise. Yet, ideally, abstract thinking and practice ought not turn their backs on the sources of human life and experience, from matter, from bodies, from the particulars of history. This is why writers should demonstrate how their arguments and claims are entangled in and reflect their own local social, political, and religious contexts. Intellectual honesty and integrity require it.

Too often, however, writers fail to connect their arguments and conclusions with the hard facts of the concrete material existence of their lives. Accordingly, in the interest of avoiding the fallacy of misplaced concreteness as much as possible—I suspect it can never be completely avoided—I will seek to be as clear as I can about the local situation that is reflected in the arguments and conclusions of this book.

First of all, I am a white Anglo-Saxon middle-aged male living in the Pacific Northwest who teaches history of religions in a liberal arts university affiliated with the Evangelical Lutheran Church in America. I am a member of this church body, as are seven of my ten colleagues in the department of religion. Most Lutherans with whom I teach or who are part of my local synod's hierarchy regard my published work as theologically suspicious. I suppose this is a typical reaction many historians of religions working in church-affiliated colleges have encountered. We are, after all, mostly trained to look at religious traditions historically and culturally, including our own, and therefore are not often disposed to absolutizing the Christian Way or any other Way as the final means of human redemption. In my case, at least, I am very prone to take any claim to final truth with a great deal of salty suspicion—especially the claims of ecclesiastical bureaucrats.

That my work as a historian of religions has somewhat marginalized me within the Lutheran form of the Christian community is not, however, the main fact of my local situation. This book also reflects my rebellion against certain aspects of my academic training. Traditionally, historians of religions are trained by their graduate studies to seek an "outsider's" understanding of religious phenomena in distinction from the "insider" understanding of those who participate in a particular religious Way. The goal of outsider understanding is "objective" descriptive knowledge of what religious people do—the totality of their religious lives in community—without passing normative theological or philosophical judgments about whether what they do corresponds to reality. Issues of normative truth are not generally regarded as the scholarly concern of historians of religions.

However, as helpful and interesting as accurate, descriptive knowledge of what religious persons do undoubtedly is, it is not enough because it is only half the story of humanity's global religious history. Any historian of religions who has taught university students knows this; normative questions do not go away as students gain clearer descriptive awareness of religious phenomena. The opposite is more likely. The more students objectively encounter and understand the global facts of humanity's religious experience, the more they are energized to explore normative theological and philosophical issues that are raised by historical studies. In their experience, and in my own, exposure to "what *there is* to be believed and practiced" quickly evolves into "*what ought I* believe and practice?" Student's normative questions keep coming, questions about meaning and truth, all wrapped up in differing levels of emotional and intellectual intensity, in an astonishing variety of forms—as they did for me thirty-six years ago when I first stepped foot inside Ronald Huntington's history of religions course. Furthermore, once normative questions start coming, they never seem to go away.

What can the religious Ways of other people teach us about our own religious faith and practice? Is any one religious Way the sole means of salvation, and if so, how can we determine which one? In a religiously and culturally plural world, can any particular religious teaching and practice be truer than another, and if so, how can we know which one? Or are we stuck in a debilitating relativity in which no religious claim is truer than another because the truth of all claims is merely a function of their historical and cultural contexts? Is it necessary, or even possible, to remain exclusively loyal to only a single religious Way?

So as I earn my living confronting students with the descriptive facts of the history of religions, theological-philosophical questions always emerge as I try to help them think critically about religious faith, their own and that of others. For this reason I find myself wearing two "methodological hats," as Rita Gross described it, in every undergraduate course I teach and in every essay and book I write.[6] When I function as an outsider, I wear my historian-of-religions hat. Wearing this hat transforms me into a comparativist whose academic specialty is Japanese Buddhism and who tries to train students to see the world through the eyes of religious persons who participate in religious traditions other than their own as objectively as possible. When they ask me to help them reflect on normative questions regarding the adequacy or truth of what they have descriptively understood, I switch hats and become theologian and philosopher.

Sometimes I wear both hats simultaneously, as I did when I wrote this book, with apologies neither to my colleagues in history of religions nor to those in theology. It seems that I have become primarily a historian of religions writing a theology of religious pluralism. As historian, I intend to present descriptive accounts of particular religious matters of fact as objectively as I can in order to avoid the fallacy of misplaced concreteness as I reflect as theologian on the normative truth issues descriptive historical understanding engenders. As theologian, my goal is to arrive at a coherent resolution of the normative issues these descriptive facts raise, at least for me. Therefore, this book should be read as a "thought experiment" whose analyses and conclusions are not presupposed to be the only possibilities, even though I think they are interesting and worth arguing for.

A second way I have tried to avoid the fallacy of misplaced concreteness is by employing autobiography as an element of my methodology. I have learned much from Mark Kline Taylor in this regard. "Putting autobiographical elements into theology," he writes, "is one way to redress the often lamented distance of theology from peoples' religious culture and political experience."[7] In following Taylor's lead, I have included memories of past experiences throughout these chapters while trying to avoid pointless self-reflection on my own subjectivity, as if such self-scrutiny can in itself yield theological knowledge that can be a model for the reflection of others. Still, if employed with sensitivity, autobiography can be an important means of avoiding the fallacy of misplaced concreteness in theological discourse.

Accordingly, I have interwoven historical and theological reflection with my personal story throughout this book, while trying hard to avoid narcissist individualism or pious fabrication of my particular spiritual journey into what fundamentalist Christian groups call "testimony." To prevent this, I have tied bits of my personal story to specific issues and historical contexts on the premise that theology without self-reflection is lifeless, just as self-reference without specifying one's entanglement in cultural and political contexts creates an exaggerated universalism. Theological discourse should avoid both errors.

Notes

1. Shortly after writing these pages, I learned of Ronald Huntington's death early in 1994.
2. Kenneth J. Gergen, *The Saturated Self: Dilemmas of Identity in Contemporary Life* (New York: Basic Books, 1991).
3. See D. T. Suzuki, *Manual of Zen Buddhism* (New York: Grove Press, 1960), 129–44.
4. Frederick J. Streng, "Mutual Transformation: An Answer to a Religious Question," *Buddhist-Christian Studies* 13 (1993): 121–26.
5. Frederick J. Streng, *Understanding Religious Life* (Belmont, Calif.: Wadsworth Publishing Company, 1985), 2.
6. Rita M. Gross, *Buddhism After Patriarchy* (Albany: State University of New York Press, 1993), 305–17.
7. Mark Kline Taylor, *Remembering Esperanza: A Cultural-Political Theology for North American Praxis* (Maryknoll, N.Y.: Orbis Books, 1990), 2.

1

Searching for the Ox

MUCH CONTEMPORARY RELIGIOUS SCHOLARSHIP IS ENTANGLED IN THE SAME situation as the man portrayed in the first Ox-Herding picture. Religious pluralism, one aspect of the ox with which many wrestle, is often approached as "phenomenal data," as a reality apart from the scholar giving chase, to be studied with Cartesian objectivity through the collective methodological lenses comprising the field of religious studies. But like the man searching for his ox, scholars who remain at this stage often seem confused, and desire for gain and fear of loss burn like fire. The poem for this picture reads:

> Alone in the wilderness, lost in the jungle, the man is searching, searching;
> The swelling waters, the far away mountains, and the unending path;

Exhausted and in despair, he knows not where to go.
He only hears the evening cicadas singing in the maple woods.[1]

This chapter responds to a number of questions raised by postmodern experience of religious pluralism through a typological analysis of the structure of interreligious dialogue.[2] My thesis is that contemporary modes of interreligious dialogue have evolved into two major types, each with several nuanced epistemological themes and variations: a "theology of religions" model and a "primordial" model. Issues here become extremely complicated, as can be illustrated by the well-known Buddhist metaphor of Indra's net.

In the heavenly abode of the great Indian god Indra, there is a wonderful net hung in such a way that it stretches out in all directions. The clever weaver of the net has set a single jewel in each eye, and since the net is infinite in dimension, the jewels are infinite in number. If we look closely at a single jewel, we discover that its polished surface reflects every other jewel in the net. Not only that, each of the jewels reflected in the one we are looking at simultaneously reflects all the other jewels, so that there occurs an infinite reflecting process.

Mahayana Buddhists are particularly fond of this image for the way it symbolizes the cosmos as an infinitely recurring series of interrelationships coexisting among all particular entities. It illustrates, in other words, what Buddhists call the principle of "dependent co-origination" (*pratītya-samutpāda*): the relationship between each thing and event in the universe at every moment of space-time is one of mutual identity and intercausality.[3]

Indra's jeweled net is a marvelous metaphor for imaging the interrelationships that constitute the reality of religious pluralism and for figuring out whatever unity there might be in the diversity of humanity's religious Ways. Dialogue between the religious faiths of humanity seems an absolute necessity in the present era. But like the universe mirrored in Indra's net, interreligious dialogue is a complex and controversial problem. Its cross-cultural loci—contemporary religious and secular pluralism—are sources of extremely difficult sociological, political, psychological, and epistemological issues. As never before, religious persons are now dragged—often kicking and screaming—into confrontation with ancient, perennial questions. While the questions may not be new, the global postmodern context in which they are asked gives them an urgency never before experienced.[4]

What is the generic nature of religious experience? Are there generic features common to all historical and cultural forms of religious faith and practice? If so, why is there so much diversity in the religious Ways of human beings? What does religious pluralism tell us about human nature? What does religious pluralism tell us about the Sacred? How do religious faith and practice influence art, politics, economics, literature, ethics, and history? How do aesthetic, political, economic, ethical, biological, and historical factors influence religious faith and practice? In a world in which the fact of modern pluralism highlights the problem of relativism as never before, which religious Way is best? Or is this question meaningful—or important?

As I noted earlier, Western scholarship on religious pluralism has engendered two modes or models of interreligious dialogue: a theology-of-religions model and a primordial model. Since current Buddhist–Christian dialogue is the most active and systematic illustration of interreligious dialogue now occurring globally, I will demonstrate my thesis within the setting of this encounter by (1) specifying and comparing important Christian examples of the theology-of-religions model with leading examples of the primordial model; (2) describing how humanity's religious story is read by each model; and (3) summarizing the structural differences and similarities between each model. But first, some preliminary assumptions and definitions.

The Structure of Interreligious Dialogue

That interreligious dialogue has emerged in the last decade as a primary topic of discussion in religious studies is beyond question. While the goals of interreligious dialogue still evoke debate, extensive agreement exists about its structure. A convenient starting point for reflection on this structure is the process the Catholic theologian John S. Dunne calls "passing over" and "returning."[5]

According to Dunne, the structure of dialogue is "Socratic." It demands a twofold realization by those participating that they are ignorant of the "truth" and thereby wish to undertake the risky search for this "truth," which is simultaneously the first step toward "wisdom." Awareness of ignorance and the beginning of wisdom merge when we are pushed into dialogical encounter. Once we are pushed, dialogue takes place within two polar movements: (1) "passing over" to the faith and experience of another human being; and (2) "returning" to the "home" of our own standpoint, now deepened and enriched by the "odyssey" of the encounter.

But much depends on the perspective from which the odyssey begins and ends. Normally a Christian begins and ends with the Christian Way, a Muslim with Islam, or a Buddhist with the Buddhist Way. It is this form of interreligious dialogue that I call the "theology-of-religions model."

There are, however, a number of religious persons engaging in interreligious dialogue who find themselves unable to return to the home of their original religious Way. They are deeply influenced, perhaps overwhelmed, by the reality of modern religious pluralism and the relativizing of religious faith and belief this reality occasions. Such persons include scholars as well as simply well-read individuals trying to make sense of postmodern existence. They may wear the labels of a particular religious Way, or they may be committed secularists. But they have no "religious home," as Dunne puts it, to which to return after the odyssey of their dialogue. For them, the odyssey is never finished. Not fully at home in any particular religious Way, grasped by the relativization of all religious claims implied by religious–and secular–pluralism, interreligious dialogue means "passing over" from relativity to the religious Ways of humanity and "returning" to relativity. It is this form of interreligious dialogue that I call the "primordial model."

But whether a theology-of-religions model or a primordial model, the general consensus is that the goal of interreligious dialogue is renewal of our own living standpoints. Otherwise, why bother with dialogue at all? Consequently, as Donald K. Swearer has written, four conditions must be present before meaningful interreligious dialogue can occur.[6]

First, ulterior motives must be excluded. Approaching another person's religious standpoint with ulterior motives provides only limited results. For example, comparatively studying Buddhist faith and practice, with the dogmatic intention of comparing it to Christian faith and practice in order to increase Christian awareness of the "uniqueness" or the "superiority" of the Christian Way, undermines the integrity of Buddhist–and Christian–faith.

Second, interreligious dialogue requires being engaged by the faith and practice of persons dwelling in religious standpoints other than our own. Nothing important emerges from interreligious dialogue unless our own perspectives are genuinely challenged, tested, and stretched by the faith and practice of our dialogical partner. Approaching persons of other religious Ways as advocates of our own faith, or absolutizing our own religious Way as the only true or valid Way, replaces genuine dialogue with a series of monologues. The truth we seek is not found because we have not looked for it; religious imperialism replaces creative transformation.

Third, interreligious dialogue demands clear, critical, and empathetic comprehension of our own religious Way. Part of the openness of engagement with others includes being engaged by the truth claims of our own religious Way. Without a point of view, dialogue can be only a formless sharing of ideas in which we merely state what we believe while another person reciprocates in kind. Nothing is achieved. We need to hear the "music" of our own religious Way before we can hear the "music" of the religious Ways of others.

Finally, the truth we seek is relational in structure. Those practicing dialogue through a theology-of-religions model will find this requirement especially difficult. For example, the Christian understanding of incarnation more often than not has been reduced to a set of unchanging doctrinal propositions better serving the needs of the institutional church than the needs of Christian persons. But "truth"—whatever label it wears—can have no institutional or confessional boundaries in a universe which the natural scientists are now picturing as governed by universal relativity and probability. This surely implies that Christians, as well as other religious persons, can share their faith without presupposing the inferiority or falsehood of their, for example, Buddhist colleague's faith and practice. Interreligious dialogue must grow out of our common humanity as persons whose sense of what it means to be human expresses itself through different, yet valid and real encounters with the Sacred. But truth is falsified into half-truth when we approach one another merely through abstract labels like "Christian," "Buddhist," or "Muslim."

The Theology-of-Religions Model

In *Theology and the Philosophy of Science*, Lutheran theologian Wolfhart Pannenberg defines and defends a generic notion of theology as "the science (*Wissenschaft*) of God" whose object is "the self-communication of the divine reality." Consequently, Christian theology is the study of the Christian tradition's encounter with the self-communication of the divine reality in the life and death of Jesus as the Christ. Likewise, Islamic, Jewish, Hindu, or Buddhist theology is the study of the self-communication of the divine reality within these traditions by their theologians. As subdisciplines of the general science of God, each specialized form of Christian theological reflection—systematic theology, biblical theology, practical theology—must be grounded in "theology of religions." He writes:

> The investigation of religions, and therefore of Christianity, has a theological character only when it examines religions to see to what extent their traditions provide evidence for the self-communication of a divine reality. Religions can be investigated from other points of view . . . but the characteristic of theological investigation of religious traditions is that it looks at the specifically religious intention in religions and investigates the self-revelation of a divine reality in the various religions and their history. . . . A theological investigation of historically given religions operating on these principles would examine how far the conception of reality as a whole expressed in the religious tradition in fact takes account of all the currently accessible aspects of reality and is therefore able to identify the God described and worshiped in the religion as the all-determining reality. The traditional claims of a religion may therefore be regarded as hypotheses to

be tested by the full range of currently accessible experience. They are to be judged by their ability to integrate the complexity of modern experience into the religion.[7]

Because theology of religions is the foundation of "the science of God," Pannenberg spent considerable effort elucidating its meaning and task. In fact, his formulation of theology of religions is the primary model assumed, either explicitly or tacitly, in the work of most Protestant theologians now engaged in interreligious dialogue.[8]

The key that unlocks what Pannenberg means by theology of religions is his criticism of Adolf Harnack's claim that the study of Christian religion is sufficient for knowledge of religion in general.[9] Harnack's claim, says Pannenberg, is a "political illusion" because today Christian theology must emphatically distance itself from "imperialist and colonialist obsession with Europe. The need today is to engage in a dialogue with other religions, which is impossible if the premise that the Christian religion possesses sole validity is declared in advance to be not open to discussion."[10]

Consequently, Pannenberg argues that the "science of religions" (*Religionswissenschaft*), or what is called in America "history of religions" or "comparative religions,"[11] is the foundation of theology of religions. But before history of religions can become the underpinning discipline of theology of religion, two constraints—one theological and one methodological—must be abandoned.

First, the task of history of religions should never be the study of non-Christian religious Ways for purposes of gathering information required for Christian missionary activity. Here Pannenberg enunciates the distinctive principle now governing the work of historians of religions. Nevertheless, the point continues to require emphasis within the disciplines of Christian theology. "The importance of any single religious Way or its particular stage of evolution can be grasped only within the framework of a history of the religious Ways of the world." History of religions, therefore, is the "appropriate framework for the practice of Christian theology in all its disciplines."[12]

Accordingly, history of religions is methodologically crucial in the study of the history and systematic self-understanding of the Christian Way itself. Pannenberg writes:

> Only a dogmatic view of Christianity, which separates the Christian faith as knowledge of revelation from the world of religions, which it dismisses as merely human projections, could treat religions as a phenomenon so external to Christianity as not to require consideration until missionary work makes Christianity look outward.[13]

Now as currently studied and practiced, history of religions is a collection of methodologies—social-scientific, psychological, historical, ethnological, philological, and anthropological—which individual scholars try to integrate into their studies of the religious experience of humanity. The usual goal of science of religion is "phenomenological," meaning accurate description of the effects of religious experience on the social and individual lives of human beings. Accurate phenomenological description requires suspending normative judgments about the truth or value of these effects, along with normative judgments about the "object" or "sacred reality" to which these experiences might or might not refer. Therefore, sharp distinctions are usually made between the proper goals of theology and history of religions. In Pannenberg's words, "the 'object of the science of religion' is not identical with the 'object of religion.'"[14]

The "object of religion" is a "sacred power," but the "objective reality" of this sacred power is not the object of historical inquiry. Therefore:

> A mere phenomenology, psychology or sociology of religions cannot come to grips with religion's specific object, and the claims of such investigations to be sciences of religion and religions must consequently be described as problematic.[15]

By methodologically ignoring the "object" of religious experience because it is beyond the capability of "objective" phenomenological analysis, history of religions remains incomplete. "Science of religion" must be supplemented by theology of religions.

What, then, is the methodological core of theology of religion, according to Pannenberg? First, it must be critical theology that does not "produce an interpretation of religions on the basis of a previous religious position."[16] It must remain free from "dogmatic premises."[17]

Second, theology of religion should focus on constructing a theoretical framework for understanding the generic nature of religious experience. And third, within this theoretical framework, it should treat the beliefs of all religious Ways, including the Christian Way, as hypotheses about the Sacred that require testing and confirmation of their validity.[18]

Pannenberg's vision of theology of religion is clearly a dialogical methodology similar to the movements John Dunne poetically named "passing over" and "returning." That is, in dialogue, Buddhists or Christians encounter religious persons whose faith and practice are other than their own from the perspective of their circle of faith and practice. In so doing, no dogmatic assumptions about the superiority of the Buddhist or Christian Ways must be allowed to influence the dialogue's outcome. This requires "bracketing off" in phenomenological suspension all dogmatic assumptions so that they remain operationally ineffective during the dialogue. Indeed, Pannenberg's notion of theology of religion requires the assumption that every religious Way possesses truth and validity and is worthy of respect because, in Christian language, "God has not been without witnesses."

Accordingly, the beliefs of one's own religious Way and the beliefs of religious Ways other than one's own should be treated as hypotheses about the Sacred; the validity of these hypotheses must never be assumed prior to "testing" by the theoretical framework provided by one's understanding of the generic nature of religious experience established by the "evidence" of history of religions. We should enter dialogue as Buddhists or as Christians, "pass over" into religious Ways other than our own, approach the beliefs of these Ways and our own Way as a collection of hypotheses whose validity must be tested, never dogmatically assumed, and then "return" to our own religious Way.

On the surface, Pannenberg's theology of religions seems thoroughly free from the traditional Christian claim to absolute validity. Christians should enter into dialogue with the worldviews and claims of non-Christians as well as with the plurality of Christian teachings as hypotheses to be tested and measured, trusting the dialogical process itself to adjudicate which hypotheses most accurately represent reality and which do not. But in fact, Pannenberg does not practice what he preaches because he fails to apply the genuine openness of his theology of religions to non-Christian traditions. What prevents him from doing so is his insistence that Christ is the final manifestation of God as the power of the future.

> The saving character of the universal relevance that belongs to Jesus' figure is determined by whether Jesus is to be understood as the *fulfillment* of the hopes and deep longing of humanity. There is no salvation that is not related to the needs of those to whom it is imparted. . . . When we say that ultimately through his resurrection from the dead the true man, the real human being that is the destiny of us all, has appeared in Jesus, then we can only mean that in him the hopes of men are fulfilled.[19]

For Pannenberg, then, Christian faith in Jesus as the final manifestation of God as the power of the future working to fulfill all of humanity's hopes is not a hypothesis to be proved. It is an assertion of an absolute requirement for Christian faith and possesses absolute validity, for both Christians and non-Christians.

Consequently, as open to non-Christian faith and practice as Pannenberg's theology of religions seems to be, it turns out to be a very traditional form of Christian theological exclusivism: the absolute truth of humanity's encounter with the Sacred is, when all is dialogically said and done, to be found in Christian faith in the historical Jesus as the Christ—the single, final,

and ultimate manifestation of God drawing all creation to that future fulfillment Christian theology calls the Kingdom of God.

By far the boldest Roman Catholic example of the theology-of-religions
model of interreligious dialogue is represented by the thought of Hans Küng,
whose theology of religions is an example of theological inclusivism. Partly as
a critique of Karl Rahner's notion of "anonymous Christianity,[20] Küng argues
that the world religions, by which he means religious Ways other than Roman
Catholicism, should be viewed as "extraordinary ways of human salvation."
The Catholic Church, however, is the "ordinary way." Individuals may attain
salvation through the particular religious Way available to them in their
unique historical and cultural circumstances, since God, whose fullest self-
revelation is through Christ, is also at work in the extraordinary ways of non-
Christian faith and practice. Accordingly, non-Christians, says Küng, should
seek God within whatever religious Way is available because all religious Ways
are "ways of salvation in universal salvation history."[21]

But compared to Roman Catholicism's "ordinary" Christian way of salvation, the salvation offered by non-Christian faith and practice appears, while
"extraordinary," less comprehensive. What God generally offers to human
beings through non-Christian religious Ways is most fully available through
conscious participation in the faith and sacramental system of the Roman
Catholic Church. Hence, the Church should engage in missionary efforts to
convert the world to Christian faith, while simultaneously granting full recognition to the profound truths of non-Catholic faith and practice.

If "extraordinary" in Küng's perspective simply means "majority," his version of the theology-of-religions model entails little more than that most people
are saved outside of institutional incorporation into Roman Catholicism. However, Küng intends much more than this. In his view, the extraordinary ways of
salvation are only interim measures. Non-Christians may have the "right and
duty" to seek God within their own religious Ways. But this right and duty are
valid only until they are directly confronted with the revelation of God through
Jesus Christ. Non-Christians, he says, "are pre-Christian, directed toward Christ.
. . . The men of the world religions are not professing Christians, but, by the
grace of God, they are called and marked out to be Christians."[22] Sooner or
later, non-Christians must become Christians. But meanwhile, non-Christians
should not be condemned, because the gospel has not yet reached them in a
form capable of overcoming their existential ignorance of the full truth of salvation preserved and offered in Roman Catholicism.

Küng's application of the theology-of-religions model clearly presupposes
a dogmatic stance that Pannenberg asserts we should not presuppose, even
though in fact Pannenberg does presuppose it: a stance that John Hick calls

a "Ptolemaic" view of modern religious pluralism.[23] Küng situates Roman Catholic faith and practice at the center of a religious universe around which all other religious Ways must necessarily revolve, and according to which all must be interpreted. Thereby, his conception of interreligious dialogue finally leaves no more room for dialogical encounter with non-Christians than the Catholic doctrine of no-salvation-outside-the-Church (*extra ecclesiam nulla salus*).[24] In fact, his understanding of modern religious pluralism is a "liberal" application of this doctrine to the world religions, although with none of the overtly chauvinistic overtones of traditional Catholic—and Protestant—approaches. That is, Küng does not think non-Christian religious Ways are different yet fully valid alternatives to Christian faith and practice. They are primarily "preparations for the gospel."

The most coherent—and radical—application of Pannenberg's concept of theology of religions to interreligious dialogue is found in the work of the process theologian John B. Cobb., Jr.[25] Cobb's encounter with the religious Ways of humanity, particularly the Buddhist Way, also pushes trends initiated in modern Protestant theology by Ernst Troeltsch's famous essay "The Place of Christianity Among the World Religions" to their most logical conclusions.[26]

According to Troeltsch, Christian faith is bound up with Western culture and the "Western spirit." Therefore, for Westerners, the Christian Way is the final form of religious truth. But the religious Ways of Asia are also bound up with their respective cultural versions of the "Eastern spirit." Furthermore, the religious Ways of Asian cultures are the final forms of religious truth for them. In Troeltsch's words:

> If we wish to determine their relative value, it is not the religion alone we must compare, but always only the civilization of which the religion in each case constitutes a part incapable of severance from the rest. But who will presume to make a final pronouncement here? Only God himself . . . can do that.[27]

Troeltsch was the first modern Christian theologian to introduce an explicitly pluralistic understanding of the religious Ways of humanity. Every religious Way possesses its own unique validity and truth for its adherents. None possess absolute validity, including the Christian Way. Thus, dialogical encounter with non-Christians becomes a methodologically absolute means for deepening Christian faith and practice.

The major assumptions governing Cobb's encounter with non-Christian religious Ways push Troeltsch's conclusions to the furthest boundaries of what Tillich called the Christian "theological circle." In fact, if he were to push further, Cobb would find himself in danger of "passing over" beyond the Christian circle of faith altogether, possibly "returning" not as a Christian theologian but as a philosopher of religion strongly interested in Christian beliefs.

Each of the living religious Ways of humanity, Cobb believes, expresses valid, and different, authentically real human encounters with the Sacred. No particular religious Way—or specific version of a religious Way—can justifiably claim superiority over another Way. It is, he says, especially idolatrous for Christians to do so. In other words, as I have noted elsewhere, Cobb's application of the theology-of-religions model to interreligious dialogue entails explicit rejection of Catholic and Protestant versions of no-salvation-outside-the-Christian Way.[28]

Given this rejection, Cobb thinks the Christian goal of interreligious dialogue should be: (1) the mutual "creative transformation" of the Christian Way and the religious Way with which Christians are in dialogue; and (2) going "beyond dialogue." Since Cobb's concept of creative transformation is his application of Whitehead's notion of creativity, and since his christology identifies Christ with the Logos as the primary example of creative transformation, a brief account of the meaning of "creativity" is in order.

Whitehead wrote of creativity as categorically ultimate. In his words:

> Creativity is the universal of universals characterizing ultimate matters of fact. It is that ultimate principle by which the many, which are the universe disjunctively, become the one actual occasion, which is the universe conjunctively. It lies in the nature of things that the many enter into complex unity.[29]

Because creativity is part of the categorical scheme through which Whitehead interpreted Einstein's theories of general and special relativity, creativity possesses no independent existence apart from actual things and events. It is found only in concrete instances of the "many becoming one and increased by one."[30] In this sense creativity is very similar to the Buddhist teaching of "dependent co-origination" (*pratītya-samutpāda*).

Approached through Whitehead's category of creativity, interreligious dialogue becomes a critical process in which we "pass over" to religious Ways other than our own, appropriate what we can, and "return" to our own religious Way. In the process, our faith is tested, stretched, and transformed by what we have, and have not, appropriated from our dialogical partner. It is this process that Cobb calls mutual creative transformation.

As a Christian theologian, Cobb devotes his writings to the creative transformation of the Christian Way. Whether creative transformation results for non-Christians through dialogue with the Christian Way is up to non-Christians to determine for themselves.[31] But Cobb's conception of God is a good illustration of the process of creative transformation at work in his theology through his dialogue with the Buddhist Way.

Even before his systematic encounter with the Buddhist Way, Cobb's reformulation of traditional Christian conceptions of God inspired by Whitehead's category of creativity led him to a dynamic notion of God largely absent from traditional Christian self-understanding. In place of a substantial, static, unchanging divine entity underlying, while transcending, the flux of the temporal process, Cobb views God as a formative element—indeed the chief example—of this flux. Following Whitehead's lead, but not uncritically, Cobb speaks of an eternal "primordial nature" of God, or God as God is in God's own self-nature, and of a changing "consequent nature" of God—God as God affects and is affected by the multiplicity of past, present, and future things and events at every moment of space-time. The primordial nature of God is an abstraction from the actual process of what God is in God's processive consequent nature. Both "natures" are interdependent or "polar," and mutually constitute what God "is" in God's own experience of the universe—and in the universe's experience of God.

Because of the parallels Cobb believes exist between Whitehead's notion of God and the Buddhist doctrine of dependent co-origination, dialogue with the Buddhist Way plays an usually important role in his reinterpretation of traditional Christian thought. That is, dialogue with the Buddhist Way has led him to reflect on how adequately he and other process theologians have understood the nonsubstantial character of God in relation to Christian experience. Here Cobb's theology has appropriated much from Mahayana Buddhist teaching.

For example, the Mahayana Buddhist doctrine of "emptying" (*śūnyatā*) plays a pivotal role in Cobb's thought about God. The question is, What does Buddhist philosophy mean when it teaches that an event, for example, a moment of human experience, is "empty"? According to Cobb, who interprets this idea quite accurately,[32] it means, first of all, that the experience is empty of substance. The separate moments of a person's experience are not unified by an enduring self or "I" remaining self-identical through time. There is no "subject," even in a single moment, to which the experience "belongs." Second, the experience lacks all possession because whatever constitutes it does not belong to it. The particular elements of the experience, in Buddhist language, its *dharmas*, are a momentary coming together of what is other than the experience. Third, the experience possesses no form that it imposes on its constituting elements. That is, it is empty of form because the form of an experience results from what constitutes it. Finally, the experience is empty of permanent being (*svabhāva*, "own-being"). The constituting elements of an experience are not the "being" of that experience. Instead, the constituting elements of an experience become the new experience, or better, this becoming is the experience. Consequently, Mahayana philosophy concludes, there is no being, there are "no things." There is only "emptiness."

Cobb perceives remarkable affinities between Whitehead's account of the consequent nature of God and the Buddhist notion of Emptying. Since the consequent nature of God (God in relation to the temporal process in its entirety) is God's aim to bring to fulfillment the concrete realization of all possibilities in their proper season for each thing and event at every moment of space-time, God imposes no prior principle of selection. Or, as formulated by Whitehead, "the consequent nature of God is composed of a multiplicity of elements with individual self-realization. It is just as much a multiplicity as it is a unity; it is just as much an immediate fact as it is an unresting advance beyond itself."[33] Or, as Cobb interprets Whitehead on this point, "God is 'empty' of 'self' insofar as 'self' is understood as an essence that can be preserved only by excluding 'other' things, or at least not allowing them to be received as they are."[34]

Conceiving God in this way—in dialogue with the Buddhist Way guided by Whiteheadian process categories as a bridge opening up Buddhist experience for Christians—is an example of what Cobb means by the process of creative transformation of the Christian Way. Indeed, he argues, far from being foreign to Christian experience, the process of creative transformation is a means of confirming Christian experience. And while most ideas of God cannot be included in Buddhist faith, practice, and worldview, Cobb thinks a Whiteheadian notion of God may not be foreign to Buddhist religious experience. Therefore, Buddhist appropriation of a process understanding of God might lead to the Buddhist Way's creative transformation as well. But the specific direction and outcome of this dialogical process cannot be foretold in advance. In all probability, the result will be not some final synthesis of Buddhist and Christian thought but the emergence of new processes of creative transformation within both the Buddhist and Christian Ways. That is, the process of interreligious dialogue should lead "beyond dialogue." Two assumptions govern this idea.

First, Cobb does not think Christians can or should condemn any of the major religious Ways of humanity. He regards every religious Way as a bearer of truth and wisdom. He also recognizes that the truths they bear are, in many instances, quite different from the truth and wisdom born by the Christian Way. Therefore, the point of Buddhist–Christian dialogue, or Christian dialogue with any other religious Way, is to share differing apprehensions of truth.

Second, Cobb believes that while Christians should recognize truths discovered by non-Christians through their special meditative techniques or their unique historical experiences, the systems of thought that center on these different truths also conflict with the systems of thought Christians bring to the dialogue. "But it is my deepest conviction," he writes,

> that no truth contradicts any other truth. In this respect I am, I suppose, a rationalist, and I do not see how a Christian can be anything else. It is the truths of other traditions that I want to appropriate, and it is the truth of Christianity I want to share. But a new truth cannot be simply added to a collection of accepted doctrines. The appropriation of any new truth requires the re-thinking of everything. That is why I speak of transformation.[35]

Thus Buddhists and Christians in dialogue encounter truth from one another. But the goal should be to pass "beyond dialogue" creatively transformed by what they have learned. Or, as Cobb poetically states it, in dialogue and beyond dialogue, a Christian can become a Buddhist while remaining Christian too. The same possibilities exist for Buddhists as well.

Malcolm David Eckel has accurately noted that Cobb's theology of religions presupposes "mutual fulfillment" as the reason for engaging in interreligious dialogue. This is clear not only in Cobb's *Beyond Dialogue*. The formal features of what he means by "mutual fulfillment" are stated even more clearly by Cobb in an earlier article entitled "Buddhist Emptiness and the Christian God."[36]

In this article Cobb argues that there are two principles of ultimacy at issue in Buddhist and Christian traditions: an "ontological ultimate," which might be called "ultimate reality," and "the principle of rightness," which might be called "the ultimate good." In Christian tradition, Cobb thinks, both these principles are identified with God. But he also argues that the Mahayana Buddhist understanding of the ontological ultimate is not only compatible with the Christian idea of God; it is in some ways preferable. The principle of rightness, however, has no parallel in Mahayana Buddhist tradition. Therefore, while Buddhist philosophers might be able to teach Christians a great deal about the nature of ultimate reality, when it comes to discerning the ethical purpose of human existence, Buddhists must reach outside their own tradition for something their tradition lacks. Thus, as dialogue with Buddhist ideas of ultimate reality can transform Christian ideas of God, so Buddhist dialogue with Christians can transform Buddhist ethics. In this way, dialogue leads to the mutual transformation of both traditions.[37]

Still, for all Cobb's openness to non-Christian traditions, his theology of religions remains as thoroughly inclusive as Küng's because of his identification of Christ as God's Logos immanent in all things as their "initial subjective aim, that is, their fundamental impulse toward actualization,[38] that simultaneously lures all things to achieve their "creative transformation."[39] God's Logos as the principle of creative transformation in all things and events is for Christians most completely encountered in the historical Jesus. So what Christians experience in the incarnation of the Logos in the historical Jesus is also what non-Christians encounter in their religious Ways even if they do not name it Christ or apprehend what Christians in faith apprehend working in the historical Jesus. Thus, the truths of non-Christian religious Ways are included in and deepened by Christian experience of the only historical incarnation of God's Logos in Jesus as the Christ.[40]

The Primordial Model

What I have called the "primordial model" of interreligious dialogue has existed in some form in Western and Eastern cultures since ancient times. The two most widely known contemporary Western and Eastern examples of this model are Aldous Huxley's "perennial philosophy" and the Indian sage Sri Ramakrishna's teaching that "all paths lead to the same summit."[41]

As a contemporary model of interreligious dialogue, the primordial model is exemplified primarily in the work of a few historians of religions. The research of these scholars has led them beyond the theological circles of their particular religious traditions to more globally inclusive views of religious faith and practice. So that I can specify the principal structure of the primordial model, I shall (1) briefly outline the defining elements of Huxley's perennial philosophy as background for (2) clarifying how the primordial model is theoretically operative in the work of Huston Smith. This approach, it must be born in mind, assumes that among contemporary historians of religions, Smith most clearly and coherently applies the primordial model in his work. Indeed, the primordial model is the theoretical foundation of everything he has published during the last fifteen years.[42]

Aldous Huxley is most remembered for his claim that there exists a "highest factor" common to all religious Ways that underlies, while transcending, the specific differences between these Ways. The teachings of the great mystics of the major religious traditions unanimously point to this "highest factor," and it is the content of this unanimity that Huxley calls "the perennial philosophy." In words brimming with Vedantist and theosophical assumptions, he defines the major propositions of the perennial philosophy as:

That there is a Godhead or Ground, which is the unmanifested principle of all manifestation.

That the ground is transcendent and immanent.

That it is possible for human beings to love, know, and, from virtually, to become actually identified with the Ground.

That to achieve this unitive knowledge, to realize this supreme identity, is the final end and purpose of human existence.

That there is a Law or Dharma, which must be obeyed, a Tao or Way, which must be followed, if men are to achieve their final end.

That the more there is of I, me, mine, the less there is of the Ground, and that consequently the Tao is a Way of humanity and compassion, the Dharma or Law of mortification and self transcending awareness.[43]

For those of us who are not mystics, the only means of apprehending this Ground is to study the teachings of the great Western and Eastern mystics. What we learn from them is that the "basic reality" common to every religious Way is more inclusive than the collective wisdom of any particular religious Way. Therefore, it is better to follow the great mystics because their teachings about this basic reality are common, if not identical.

According to Huxley, then, the differences between the religious Ways of humanity are imposed by the theologians of these Ways. But these differences reflect limited cultural and historical factors, and therefore not only cannot reveal the common Ground of all religious Ways, but also hinder human apprehension of this Ground. In other words, being an orthodox Christian or Buddhist cuts Christians and Buddhists off from the Sacred reality for which they search.

Far better, Huxley believes, to trust the mystics of each religious Way. Their experiences and teachings point to commonly shared truths about the Sacred. Whatever doctrinal differences occur between various mystics Huxley explains as unimportant because they originate from limiting historical and cultural factors. It is these "common truths" shared by "all great mystics" that Huxley calls the "perennial philosophy."

The Vedantist and theosophical assumptions of this view are clear:[44] (1) there is a perennial philosophy, a "highest factor" common to all religious Ways; and (2) the experience and teachings of the mystics point to this common factor—that reality is one, duality is false, and God is nonpersonal.[45] It is also subject to the criticism that it is debilitatingly ahistorical, ignorant of the specific teachings and practices of the religious Ways of humanity, uncritical in its assumptions about the nature of religious experience and mysticism, and, consequently, is based on a false understanding of religious faith and practice. More important for purposes of this essay, Huxley's concept of the perennial philosophy is thoroughly nondialogical. It represents, in fact, a subtle form of religious imperialism. After all, it is easy to apprehend the "common factor" underlying all religious diversity when this factor is so uncritically projected on the "data" to begin with. There seems to be little respect for, or understanding of, religious diversity in Huxley's version of the perennial philosophy.

The question is, Can these criticisms of the perennial philosophy be overcome? Probably not in the form they assume in Huxley's thought. But Huston Smith believes that the perennial model does not require the uncritical ahistoricism of Huxley's approach. It is to Smith's thought in this regard that we now turn.

The most convenient means of describing the primordial model—which Smith prefers to call "the primordial tradition"—is his recent treatment of Steven Katz's assertion that there is no perennial philosophy.[46] Katz's critique of the perennial philosophy is especially powerful and rests on a single epistemological assumption: "There are NO pure (i.e., unmediated) experiences."[47] By this, Katz means that neither mystical experience nor ordinary forms of experience give justification for believing they are unmediated. All experience is processed, organized, and made available through extremely complex epistemologically and socially conditioned ways.

If Katz's assumptions are valid, perennial philosophy is an illusion for two reasons: (1) his assumption rules out the possibility of cross-cultural experiences, because all experience is contextual; and (2) his assumption renders cross-cultural typologies suspect, since these too are culture-bound to specific historical contexts.

However, Smith believes that Katz's argument against perennial philosophy contains a fundamental error. The claim of perennial philosophy—or "the primordial tradition"—is not that mystical experiences are cross-culturally identical. Its claims do not appeal to experience at all, except trivially in the sense that everything we are aware of is an experience of some sort. None of the "perennialists" mentioned by Katz—Frithjof Schuon and Aldous Huxley—undertook a phenomenology of mystical states. Smith reads this fact to mean that the "perennial philosophy" or the "primordial tradition" does not rest on mystical phenomena. "Logically," he says, "it doesn't even presuppose its existence at all."[48] Rather than mystical experience, the core of primordial tradition is philosophical doctrine.

These doctrines derive, according to Smith, from "metaphysical intuitions, and to discern their truth as metaphysical axioms one need not have a "mystical experience." He argues:

> The legitimacy of a metaphysical truth, evident to the intellect, does not depend on *samadhi* or gifts of "infused grace." Nowhere does the *Brahma*

Sūtra, e.g., appeal to mystical experience to support its metaphysical claims and arguments. The drift is opposite. Ontological discernments are enlisted to elucidate or validate the yogas and the experiences they deliver.[49]

Katz's second charge against perennial philosophy is directed against cross-cultural typologies, which he thinks are "reductive and inflexible, forming multifarious and extremely variegated forms of mystical experience into improper interpretive categories which lose sight of the fundamentally important differences between the data studied."[50]

But are typologies necessarily reductionist and inflexible? Is Huxley's perennial philosophy, or Smith's primordial tradition, inflexibly reductionist? Smith's answer is no, and to support this answer he outlines what he calls a "primordial typology."[51] Since his primordial typology is a typology, it is capable of several interpretations, themes, and variations other than his. For this reason, his "primordial typology" reveals the structure of what I call the primordial model of interreligious dialogue.

First, the perennial philosophy, or the primordial tradition, is a philosophy, not a sociology or an anthropology arrived at through empirical methodologies. In common with all philosophies, it is ultimately arrived at through deductive methods rather than inductive methods. Also, as a species of philosophy, it is not concerned with particulars such as "what happened in Berkeley; in the end it is concerned with the whole of things."[52] The fact that there is diversity in religious faith and practice, that is, is not only important—"what happened in Berkeley." This diversity is providential because it points to underlying realities and unities. But diversity is not ultimate—city life in Berkeley, California, is certainly different from city life in Yelm, Washington. But both are instances of urban life. Or, in Smith's analogy, "Red is not green, but the differences pale before the fact that both are light."[53]

Accordingly, the primordial typology stresses unity within diversity, unity so metaphysically necessary that apart from it, diversity could not even exist. It is diversity that points to this underlying unity, as pieces of a jigsaw puzzle fit together to form the whole picture.

Viewed from this perspective, what is "perennial," meaning "no matter what, when, or where," about the primordial typology is: (1) "God" or "Godhead" or "Absolute" or "the Sacred"—whichever one prefers—is the ultimate reality to which each religious Way points; (2) human beings possess the capacity to ascertain truth about this Sacred reality; (3) the most important of these truths is the Sacred's ultimacy in comparison with the world finitude; (4) the Sacred, however it is named, is beyond all names and predicates; it is ineffable and yet can be symbolically pointed to in names and predicates; and (5) the *neti-neti* ("not this, not that") nature of the Sacred is the only point, finally, where the primordial model sees the various religious Ways of humanity converging indistinguishably.

Concluding Observations

The question to be asked at this juncture is, What does the religious story of humanity look like according to the theology of religions and the primordial models? When compared, some interesting contrasts and parallels emerge.

Humanity's religious story, when viewed from a theology-of-religions model, is foremost a story of diversity, pluralism, and relativity. In Christian language, God may not have been without witnesses; but like witnesses reporting a common experience in a court of law, there are profound experiential differences and ideological disagreements about the nature of the reality experienced.

Second, the diversity of the religious Ways of humanity can be comprehended only from the perspective of one's own "circle of faith," be this Buddhist, Christian, or Muslim. We can, and should, "pass over" to other circles of faith, apprehend what we can, and "return" to our original circle of faith renewed and enriched.

Third, religious diversity can never be overcome because of the cultural, historical, and linguistic factors conditioning and limiting human understanding. At this point, the theology-of-religions model agrees with Stephen Katz. Perhaps "all paths lead to the same summit," but we can never know it because we can only, in the words of George Santayana, "be religious in particular, never in general." Some paths may be easier than others, more fully developed, more direct as a route to the Sacred. Some paths may be dead ends.

Fourth, the diversity of humanity's religious story must be interpreted through a theoretical framework capable of treating the teachings and practices of all religious Ways as hypotheses requiring testing and confirmation of their validity; not every religious hypothesis is of equal value and validity. For Christians, this theoretical framework will be guided by Christian theological norms and experience; for Buddhists, it will be guided by Buddhist norms and experience.

Finally, the most that can be hoped for through interreligious dialogue is passing beyond dialogue and creatively transforming our own faith within the context of our own theological circle. The diversity of humanity's religious story cannot, in the end, be fully integrated. The Sacred, however it is named, can in the end be apprehended only from the perspective provided by our own circle of faith.

Humanity's religious story looks quite different when viewed through a primordial model of interreligious dialogue. Most obviously, it is a religious story stressing unity amidst diversity. From this perspective, it is inconceivable that the Sacred has not allowed benevolence and grace to flow to every human being at all times and in all places. Christians might call this "revelation"; if so, it must be impartial, which is to say, equal. The Sacred does not play favorites; all paths do lead to the same summit; they need not be interpreted as forms of Advaita Vedanta; and it does not ultimately matter which path one takes so long as it is followed truly and authentically.

Further, this is precisely why religious diversity is important. Neither the equality nor the universality of truth requires that the religious Ways of humanity be identical. Rather, diversity is to be celebrated, for it is diversity that "fleshes out" the Sacred by apprehending it from different angles. Religious diversity supplements our view of the Sacred without compromising the fact that each religious Way preserves, in its own right, adequate "truth sufficient for salvation"—an obviously important theological justification for the practice of interreligious dialogue.

Finally, the primordial picture of humanity's religious story comes very close to Whitehead's version of God, albeit interpreted in a somewhat different way than contemporary Christian process theology. There is a Sacred reality that is an absolute reality. It is also infinite. As infinite, it transcends everything else—everything else being finite and relative. But the way the Sacred transcends the finite and the relative is by the process of integrating the relative into itself so completely that even the absolute/relative distinction is finally annulled. Or, paraphrasing Nagarjuna's words, "form is emptiness, emptiness is form" because "*nirvāṇa* equals *saṃsāra*."

That the theology-of-religions model shares much in common with the primordial model is obvious. Both models are cognizant of the problem of the relativity of belief and seek means to overcome this relativity. The theology-of-religions model does so by the process of returning to one's original religious standpoint after "passing over" into the faith of another human being. Cobb refers to this movement as passing "beyond dialogue." The primordial model, however, seeks to overcome the relativity of belief by focusing on the structural elements it perceives to be common to lived religious experience in spite of the limiting conditions imposed by cultural and historical contexts. It asserts that these common elements are found in the teachings of the great mystics of each tradition, whose teachings point to a Sacred reality that transcends cultural, traditional, and historical limitations. It is also evident that both models presuppose that all religious Ways embody truth about the Sacred, however it is named, and that this truth demands empathetic understanding and appropriation. Consequently, both models recognize the goal of interreligious dialogue to be the "creative transformation" of human beings and communities.

But "creative transformation" possesses different meanings for each model. I have already alluded to one of these differences. According to the theology-of-religions model, we can rarely pass completely beyond the "homeland" of our inherited circle of faith. Indeed, this is explicitly not the goal of interreligious dialogue from a theology-of-religions point of view. The governing intention of dialogue from this perspective is temporarily passing over from and returning to our own religious Way, enriched by what we have learned and appropriated. As Cobb would say, the goal of dialogue is to go beyond dialogue, into the depths of our own faith and practice while allowing persons dwelling in other circles of faith the same privilege and responsibility.

From the primordial perspective, however, we can never go beyond dialogue. Nor should we try. The diversities of the religious Ways of humanity are pointers to a Sacred reality that transcends while simultaneously unifying all diversity of faith and practice. While it is true that much religious faith and belief—in every religious Way—is often superstitious, uncritical, irrational, and even dangerous, as the terrible events surrounding the People's Church in Jonestown in 1978 illustrate—the Sacred cannot be limited, or once and for all defined, by any particular religious Way's encounter or teachings. Viewed primordially, we are always in dialogue—in the odyssey of passing over and returning, not to a "creatively transformed" inherited historical circle of faith, but to a primordial point of view that might include our original circle of faith but also a lot more. The dialogue never ceases, and for this reason the primordial model paints a radically different picture of humanity's religious story from that of the theology-of-religions model.

But the way I have set up and compared the structural elements of the theology-of-religions and the primordial models of interreligious dialogue surely generates another question: Are both models equally conducive to interreligious dialogue? Or, stated differently, Which model, from my viewpoint, provides the most adequate means for confronting the issues of modern religious and secular pluralism? I have hidden my preference up to this point; now I must step out of the methodology of history of religions, make a philosophical-theological judgment, reveal my preference, and justify it.

Obviously, the most important advantage of a theology-of-religions model is that it inhibits theological and ideological imperialism. It opens Christians—or Buddhists or Muslims—to the experience and claims of religious Ways other than their own. In the process, Christian experience is stretched, tested, and informed by human encounter with the Sacred that has taken place beyond the boundaries of the Christian Way. Then the lesson can be learned: one need not devalue the religious faith and practice of non-Christians in order to establish the superiority of the Christian Way.

So from a theology-of-religions perspective, one need not think of the religious Ways of humanity as competitors. For just as we can recognize another human being's experience of love because of our own experience of this reality, so it is possible to recognize the validity of the faith and practice of another human being because of our own faith and practice. Or again in Christian language, "God has not been without witnesses"; if so, we should learn from these witnesses wherever and whenever we can.

But the theology-of-religions model also instructs us to pass "beyond dialogue." There comes a time when Christians—or Buddhists or Muslims—must end dialogue and, in John Dunne's words, "return home." Surely, one can do so without parochialism and theological imperialism. The list or those who have done so in the Christian Way is long and honorable: Ernst Troeltsch, Paul Tillich, Thomas Merton, David Tracy, Langdon Gilkey, and John Cobb, to name a few notable examples.

But if one apprehends reality, "the way things really are," or thinks one does, from the perspective of Whiteheadian process philosophy, then passing beyond dialogue seems both unnecessary and metaphysically impossible. If reality is process, and relativity is a universal fact of experience, than stopping dialogue with another religious Way, going beyond dialogue by returning to our own religious Way—even if that Way is creatively transformed by the dialogue—eventually cuts us off from encounter with the Sacred.

Therefore, the theology-of-religions model is, for all of its strengths, finally a monologue. As a theological concept within process theology, it is also incoherent. Accordingly, I think the primordial model finally offers us the most adequate means for confronting the reality and facts of modern religious and secular pluralism. We are always in dialogue with reality, whatever form reality assumes in our experience, because experience as such, and therefore knowledge—of anything, in a universe governed by universal relativity—must be contextual. Passing beyond dialogue is a metaphysical impossibility. Trying to do so is a delusion.

Notes

1. D. T. Suzuki, *Manual of Zen Buddhism* (New York: Grove Press, 1960), 129.
2. This chapter is a revision of an earlier essay I published entitled "Two Western Models of Interreligious Dialogue," *Journal of Ecumenical Studies* 26 (Winter 1989): 8–28.

3. This image is found in the *Avamtamsaka-sūtra* (Japanese, *Kegon-kyō;* Chinese, *Hua-yen ch'eng*), or "Flower Wreath Discourse." For an interesting discussion of the cosmology symbolized by Indra's net, see Francis H. Cook, "The Jewel Net of Indra," in *Nature in Asian Traditions of Thought*, ed. J. Baird Callicott and Roger T. Ames (Albany: State University of New York Press, 1989), 213–29.

4. See my essay "Interfaith Dialogue as a Source of Buddhist-Christian Creative Transformation," in *Buddhist-Christian Dialogue: Mutual Renewal and Transformation*, ed. Paul O. Ingram and Frederick J. Streng (Honolulu: University of Hawaii Press, 1986), 77–96; and Peter L. Berger, *The Heretical Imperative* (Garden City, N.Y.: Doubleday, 1979), chap. 1, for a description of the modern context of contemporary religious and secular pluralism.

5. John S. Dunne, *The Way of All the Earth* (South Bend, Ind.: University of Notre Dame Press, 1978), preface, chap. 1.

6. Donald K. Swearer, *Dialogue: The Key to Understanding Other Religions* (Philadelphia: Westminster Press, 1977), 40–50.

7. Wolfhart Pannenberg, *Theology and the Philosophy of Science* (Philadelphia: Westminster Press, 1976), 315.

8. Ibid. (emphasis added).

9. Adolf Harnack, *Die Aufgabe der theologischen Fakultäten und die Allgemeine Religionsgeschichte* (1901, 9 ff., cited in Pannenberg, *Theology and the Philosophy of Science*, 360–61.

10. Pannenberg, *Theology and the Philosophy of Science*, 361.

11. From this point on, I shall employ the term "history of religions" to refer to the term *Religionswissenschaft*.

12. Pannenberg, *Theology and the Philosophy of Science*, 361 (emphasis added).

13. Ibid., 361–62.

14. Ibid, 263.

15. Ibid.

16. Ibid., 365.

17. Ibid., 366.

18. Ibid., 369–71.

19. Wolfhart Pannenberg, *Jesus—God and Man* (Philadelphia: Westminster Press, 1968), 205.

20. See Karl Rahner, *Theological Investigations*, vol. 5 (Baltimore: Helicon Press, 1966), 131, and related essays in vols. 6, 9, 12, and 14 of *Theological Investigations*.

21. See Hans Küng, *On Being a Christian* (New York: Pocket Books, 1978), 89–116; idem, *Christianity and the World Religions* (New York: Doubleday, 1896), xiii–xix.

22. Ibid., 91.

23. John Hick, *God and the Universe of Faiths* (New York: Macmillan, 1973), chaps. 9–10. See also idem, *An Interpretation of Religion* (New Haven: Yale University Press, 1989), chap. 14.

24. See my book *The Modern Buddhist-Christian Dialogue* (Lewiston, N.Y.: Edwin Mellen Press, 1989), 49-51.

25. Cobb acknowledges the influence of Pannenberg's concept of theology of religions in his interpretation of religious pluralism and interreligious dialogue in *Beyond Dialogue* (Philadelphia: Fortress Press, 1982), 33-35. He also thinks, however, that Pannenberg arrives at his understanding of religion through a generalizing of Western religions that may not be applicable to Eastern religious experience. Further, Cobb thinks Pannenberg's notion of science might also be too Western and therefore inadequate to the task of understanding Eastern religious Ways. See Cobb's review of *Theology and the Philosophy of Science* in *Religious Studies Review* 3, no. 4 (October 1977): 213-15.

26. Ernst Troeltsch, "The Place of Christianity Among the World Religions," in *Christianity and Other Religions*, ed. John Hick and Brian Hebblethwaite (Philadelphia: Fortress Press, 1982), 11-31. Jürgen Moltmann's understanding of modern religious pluralism also expresses trends originating in this essay and has also influenced Cobb's thought in this regard; see Moltmann, *The Church and the Power of the Spirit: A Contribution to Messianic Ecclesiology* (New York: Harper & Row, 1975), 151-60.

27. Troeltsch, "Place of Christianity," 26.

28. Ingram, *Modern Buddhist-Christian Dialogue*, 52-63.

29. Alfred North Whitehead, *Process and Reality* (New York: Macmillan, 1967), 31.

30. Ibid.

31. John B. Cobb, Jr., "Buddhist Emptiness and the Christian God," *Journal of the American Academy of Religion* 45 (1977): 11-25.

32. Ibid.

33. Whitehead, *Process and Reality*, 53.

34. John B. Cobb, Jr., and David Ray Griffin, *Process Theology: An Introductory Exposition* (Philadelphia: Westminster Press, 1976), 142.

35. John B. Cobb, Jr., "Response to Wiebe," *Buddhist-Christian Studies* 5 (1985): 151-52.

36. See Malcolm David Eckel, "Perspectives on the Buddhist-Christian Dialogue," in *The Christ and the Bodhisattva*, ed. Donald S. Lopez and Steven C. Rockefeller (Albany: State University of New York Press, 1987), 52-55.

37. There is, in fact, a group of Buddhist philosophers who argue that Buddhist tradition needs to be completed through dialogical appropriation of the social-ethical elements of Christian tradition. Yet these same philosophers also argue that Christianity needs to be fulfilled by appropriating the mystical traditions of Mahayana Buddhism, particularly those Mahayana traditions rooted in the notion of Emptiness originating in the thought of the Buddhist logician Nagarjuna. The leading Buddhist philosopher of this group with whom Cobb still remains in dialogue is Masao Abe. See "God, Emptiness, and the True Self," in *The Buddha Eye: An Anthology of the Kyoto School* (New York: Crossroad, 1982), 68.

38. John B. Cobb, Jr., *Christ in a Pluralistic Age* (Philadelphia: Westminster Press, 1975), 76.

39. Ibid., 106–8.

40. Ibid., 176–89.

41. Indeed, Huxley's concept of perennial philosophy presupposes the Advaita Vedantist teaching that all paths lead to the same summit. See Aldous Huxley, *The Perennial Philosophy* (New York: Harper & Row, 1945); and Swami Nikhilananda, *The Gospel of Sri Ramakrishna* (New York: Harper & Row, 1952).

42. The fullest theoretical formulation of the primordial model in Smith's work is his *Forgotten Truth: The Primordial Tradition* (New York: Harper & Row, 1976).

43. Aldous Huxley, *Time Must Have a Stop*, chap. 20, quoted by Charles M. Holmes, *Aldous Huxley and the Way to Reality* (Bloomington, Ind.: Indiana University Press, 1970), 141.

44. Huxley was a member of the Vedanta Center of Los Angeles and attempted to establish a community called Trabuco College in Trabuco Canyon in southeast Los Angeles County in the early 1940s. Founding members of Trabuco College included Gerald Heard, Christopher Isherwood, and John van Drutten. Huxley's aim was to create a community based on the perennial philosophy so that it could spread throughout the world. See Holmes, *Aldous Huxley*, 139–40.

45. Ibid., 141.

46. Huston Smith, "Is There a Perennial Philosophy?" *Journal of the American Academy of Religion* 55 (1987): 553–66. Smith notes that he prefers the term "primordial" to "perennial" because the latter refers only to time, while the former includes space. The object of Smith's criticism is Steven T. Katz, "Language, Epistemology, and Mysticism," in *Mysticism and Philosophical Analysis*, ed. Steven T. Katz (New York: Oxford University Press, 1978).

47. Katz, "Language, Philosophy, and Mysticism," 24–26.

48. Smith, "Is There a Perennial Philosophy?" 554.

49. Ibid.

50. Katz, "Language, Philosophy, and Mysticism," quoted by Smith, "Is There a Perennial Philosophy?" 557.

51. Smith, "Is There a Perennial Philosophy?" 557–656.

52. Ibid., 561.

53. Ibid.

見
跡二

2

Seeing the Traces

ONCE WHEN THE GREAT GOD ŚIVA SPORTED WITH HIS EQUALLY GREAT CONSORT, the goddess Pārvartī, she covered Śiva's eyes with her hands. Suddenly, the whole universe was plunged into darkness, for when Śiva's eyes are closed the universe is like a black hole with no light anywhere—except for the hidden fire in Śiva's third eye that always threatens the destruction of worlds. Hindu deities are all-seeing and are said never to close their eyes. From the near dis-

A modified version of this chapter was published under the title "Seeing Traces of the Ox: Scripture and Interreligious Dialogue," *Buddhist-Christian Studies* 13 (1993): 87–101.

aster of Śiva's and Pārvartī's play, it is a good thing they do not; the well-being of the world is dependent on the open eyes of the gods.[1]

This chapter takes its first clue from the importance of "seeing" in the Hindu religious Way, but it is not about how Hindu gods "see" or how Hindus "see" God. The clue is this: it is not only the gods who must keep their eyes open; so must we, in order to make contact with them and our deepest selves, and in the process reap their blessings and secrets. Keeping our eyes open is called *darśan*, and this chapter is about how to keep our eyes open to the reality of religious pluralism so that we might reap new possibilities for creative transformation.

But this chapter is also about how scripture both hinders and enhances "seeing." How does scripture–any scripture–help us see or hinder us from seeing? Is there some unity, mostly glimpsed darkly through our scriptural glasses, over and beyond what any scripture or tradition leads us to expect to see?

Here my second clue is from the accompanying poem of the second of the Ten Ox-Herding Pictures:

> By the stream and under the trees, scattered are the traces of the
> lost;
> The sweet-scented grasses are growing thick–did he find the Way?
> However remote, over the hills and far away the beast may wander,
> His nose reaches the heavens and none can conceal it.[2]

It is with the aid of the scriptures and the study of teachings that we begin to see the traces of the ox of religious pluralism. That is, we "see the traces" of the truth of a religious Way's faith and practice–ours or someone else's–lurking behind scripture and teachings. Or, to paraphrase Master Hakuin, scripture helps us to comprehend the objective world of the senses as a reflection of the Sacred and our deepest selves.[3]

Yet at this stage we are unable to distinguish truth from falsehood, what is good from what is not, for our minds remain locked on words *about* the Sacred rather than on the Sacred as such. In Master Hakuin's words, we "have not entered the gate of enlightenment"; we have only noticed its provisional scriptural traces. Still, it's a start.

My questions, then, are these: Are modern persons who live their faith and practice within the boundaries of a scriptural tradition bound to the either/or of inclusive/exclusive interpretations of religious Ways other than their own? Must scripture–any scripture–necessarily mean that (1) religious faith and practice outside our own scriptural tradition are either inferior or downright erroneous (exclusivism); or (2) that any truths in religious Ways other than our own only partially reflect sacred realities most fully revealed by our particular scriptural tradition (inclusivism)? The thesis of chapter 3 is that neither scriptural exclusivism nor scriptural inclusivism is an adequate response to the rich diversity of humanity's collective experience of the Sacred. There is another option, which I call "primordial theology." Accordingly, this chapter will both describe and defend a "primordial" understanding of scripture as the most viable means of "seeing the traces" of the Sacred camouflaged by the religious pluralism of our age. But first some preliminary observations about "seeing" and "scripture."

On Seeing (Darśan)

Conscious experience of anything is very much a now-you-see-it-now-you-don't affair. A fish flashes in the creek that runs in front of my house, then before my eyes dissolves in water like salt. I have seen elk and mountain lions ascend bodily into the heavens, and great blue herons and bald eagles fade into leaves. These events stunned me into stillness and concentration; they say of experience that most of what exists nature conceals with stunning nonchalance, so that when we do see, vision seems like a deliberate gift—like the revelation of a dancer who, for my eyes only, flings away the seventh veil. Nature conceals as well as reveals.

This does not mean that seeing is merely sense imprinting of data on a *tabula rasa*, passive brain. Even at the level of physiology, seeing is an interpretative act—dare I say, a "hermeneutical act." For human beings, seeing is also largely a matter of verbalization. Most of the time we need words to call attention to what passes before our eyes, or we simply will not see it. We must have the words for it, say them, think them, describe what we are seeing as we see it, or chances are we will not see.

Of course, some things are hard *not* to see, and words seem beside the point: exploding volcanoes, storms, a beautiful spring day, the great blue heron gliding ghostly silent under the bridge that passes over the creek in front of my house before disappearing into early morning fog, or what Elijah is reported to have seen and heard while hiding for his life in a cave on Mount Horeb. But most of the time, if we want to notice anything, we have to maintain a running verbal description of the present. Otherwise, we never know what's happening. Annie Dillard aptly describes this most ordinary kind of seeing—of which academic seeing is one example: we are like blind men at a ball game; we need a radio.[4]

When we see this way—which is most of the time—we analyze, describe, theorize, sort, categorize, argue, debate, file, probe, and grapple with the world, sometimes as seriously as Jacob wrestled with his angel. Then understanding what is seen becomes a function of questions asked, contexts embodied, methodologies followed, presuppositions consciously and unconsciously held.

But there is another kind of seeing, one that mystics regard as primary. This form of seeing is also an interpretation of what is seen, but it is different from ordinary seeing because it requires letting go of the instruments of see- ing—our theories, assumptions, theologies, our selves and our purposes. Dil- lard characterizes the difference between ordinary seeing and this second way of seeing as the difference between walking with and without a camera.[5] When we walk with a camera, we walk from shot to shot, reading the light on a cal- ibrated meter. When we walk without a camera, our own shutter opens, and "the moment's light prints on our own silver gut." When we see this way, we are transfixed and emptied, and we become scrupulous observers.

To the person who sees this way, in what the Lakota shaman Black Elk described as seeing "in a sacred manner,"[6] it is less like seeing than like being seen for the first time, as if knocked breathless by a powerful glance. It is the seeing of nondual unity underlying diversity, apart from which there is no diversity, before unity is split into diversity by the verbalizations of the first kind of seeing.

Mystics of all religious Ways have seen in this "sacred manner."[7] But they also interpreted the meaning of mystical seeing—before and after the experi- ence of non-duality—verbally, according to the traditions that trained them. Mystical seeing and ordinary seeing are interdependent, and saints and monas- tics of every order East and West dedicated themselves to joining them together.

It is a lifetime struggle marking the literature of the world's spiritual geniuses. What this literature shows is that there are no hard and fast rules. They discovered that the mind's muddy river carries along with it a ceaseless flow of ordinary trivial seeing, that it cannot be dammed, and that trying to is a waste of effort that can lead to insanity. They discovered instead that we must allow the muddy river to flow unchecked in the channels of conscious- ness so that once in a while, we can raise our sights above trivia, look along it as we flow with it, mildly and with detachment, while gazing beyond it "to the realm where events act and react interdependently without utterance."[8]

But our first hints of this nonverbal unity originate in ordinary verbal seeing. The trick is learning how to let go of the verbal clues so we can see over the channels bordering consciousness. Here, for those religious Ways that ground their teachings and practices in a scriptural tradition, scripture itself may point us beyond verbal seeing "to the realm where events act and react interdependently without utterance." Explaining this assertion requires clarification of the interrelation between scripture and tradition.

On Scripture and Tradition

Seen from the ordinary perspective of the comparative study of religions, "scripture" generically refers to an anthology of oral and written traditions that (1) express and transmit spoken and written sounds and words as sacred power; (2) engender meanings, values, ideals, cohesiveness, and self-identity of a community through standards of behavior normative for individuals; (3) orient and relate a community toward a reality seen as sacred and transcendent; and (4) depict a path and exhort persons to follow it to establish interrelationships with a sacred reality.[9]

Scripture fascinates because of its relation with tradition: it is a nondual, heads-and-tails, chicken-or-egg affair in which scripture defines tradition as much as tradition defines the scripture that engenders it. The evidence abounds. Catholic tradition defined originally disparate pieces of Christian writing into a sacred canon that simultaneously created Christian tradition and *praxis*—a process never officially ratified by any church council.[10] Jewish scripture is broad and includes the oral traditions which Jews think underlie it; it is not limited to biblical writings and is seen as constantly developing. What Jews count as scripture defies categorization; it is neither exclusively legalistic nor narrative, neither history nor poetry. Certain sacred writings are recognized by all Jews; others are sectarian and their authority is limited to a specific group, their sanctity possibly temporary. So Jews do not so much "read" Torah or Talmud as "learn" it, and learning requires not only study of biblical texts but also detailed study of the traditional commentators whose views determined what scripture is.[11] Finally, Buddhist tradition maintains similar attitudes toward its scripture. Buddhist texts have been objects of intense veneration and study; life and limb have been sacrificed to ensure their preservation and correct understanding. Yet Buddhist tradition also asserts that its sacred texts have, in and of themselves, no inherent value; their worth depends entirely on what is done with them.[12]

In short, no scripture defines itself as "scripture" apart from tradition. The single exception might appear to be the *Qurʾān*. Islamic tradition is unique among the world's scriptural religious Ways in that its Book is the only one that explicitly defines itself as "scripture." As the second *sura* declares, "This is the Book; in it is guidance sure, without doubt, to those who fear God."[13] But even in Islam, scripture does not interpret itself, for the *Qurʾān* is "recited" and lived according to the "tradition" (*sunna*) and "custom" (*ḥadith*) of the Prophet in the practice of "surrendering" (*ʿislām*) to God.[14]

The universal interdependency of scripture and tradition has startling implications, not the least of which is that scripture—any scripture—is capable of a diversity of interpretations, depending on the questions asked. There are, and have always been, more ways than one to skin *any* scripture's meaning. This fact alone may make a collection of paradigmatic stories, legends, myths, injunctions, and historical narratives "scripture." All scriptures mirror the universals of human experience: life and death, joy and sorrow, creativity and tragedy, hope and fear, peace and violence, the sacred and profane, within specific historical and cultural contexts. When tradition inflexibly dogmatizes scripture into only one appropriate contextual interpretation of the Sacred and our relation to it, scripture's inherent flexibility vanishes along with its ability to function as "scripture." At worst, it becomes irrelevant to the historical complexities of human existence, particularly in an age of religious pluralism. At best, it becomes an object of merely academic curiosity.[15]

Seeing the nondual interrelation between scripture and tradition does not mean that all interpretations are equally valid or of equal worth. Faith and experience guided by intelligence and reason must guide hermeneutical *praxis*. Still, while scriptures are capable of not only exclusive and inclusive reading, there are also more primordial possibilities generated by questions inherent in our postmodern collective experience of contemporary religious pluralism.

For Christians, the test case for the validity of my thesis is the New Testament. For Buddhists, of course, my thesis's validity must be tested by the Buddhist canon and for Muslims, by the *Qurʾān*. Since I must write with a numerically Western Christian audience in mind, what follows will focus on New Testament scriptural interpretation.

Primordial Seeing in the New Testament

Traditional Protestant, Orthodox, and Catholic versions of the Christian Way allow revelation, not salvation, outside Jesus as the Christ. That is, the historical Christian claim is that Christ is ontologically necessary for salvation. But this claim poses a serious dilemma: How can insistence on the ontological necessity of Christ be reconciled with Christian insistence on the universal love of God that Christ reveals? Can God's universal love and desire to save all persons be so exclusively tied to one vehicle?

Some contemporary theologians suggest rather strained inclusive ways out of this exclusive dilemma: emphasizing God's "mystery" and suggesting that at the end of history all human beings will know Christ and have a chance for salvation;[16] asserting Roman Catholic notions of "anonymous Christianity"[17] and "ordinary" and "extraordinary" means of salvation;[18] dialogically "passing over" to non-Christian religious Ways and "returning" to the Christian Way;[19] or going "beyond dialogue" after dialogical encounter with non-Christians.[20] Each of these inclusive types of Christian theology of religions asserts that "salvation" may occur outside the Christian fold because non-Christians are included in the saving grace that comes from God only through Christ—however mysterious, anonymous, extraordinary, or dialogically beyond the presence of such grace might be.

The difficulty with Christian inclusivism is its empirically unjustifiable claim that what is true in other religious Ways mirrors what Christians experience through faith in Christ. This may seem tolerant, but in the end inclusive theologies of religion turn out to be intolerant Christian versions of Hindu Advaita (Nondual) Vedanta teaching that "all paths lead to the same summit" *if* they look like Upanishadic Hinduism. When everything is said and done, Christ is the "way, the truth, and the life," and thereby the only way to salvation—even for non-Christians who do not know or have explicit faith in Christ.

Specifically, Christian exclusivism and inclusivism presuppose the ontological necessity of Christ for salvation, and theologians of both types point to the New Testament as their scriptural witness. But in the context of modern religious pluralism, is it an abuse of language to read the entire New Testament as a "one and only" assertion that faith in Jesus as the Christ is a post-Easter ontological requirement for salvation? Clearly, the vast majority of Christian exegesis asserts just this. But in the New Testament itself, only passages such as Acts 4:12 or John 1:14 and 14:6 explicitly assert the ontological necessity of faith in Jesus as the Christ for salvation. Accordingly, most of the material in the New Testament is open to noncanonical, primordial exegesis.

For example, the famous last judgment scene in Matthew 25:31-46[21] numbers among participants in the Kingdom of God those who have loved their neighbor without knowing anything about Jesus.[22]

> When the Son of man comes in his glory, and all the angels with him, then he will sit on his glorious throne. Before him will be gathered all the nations, and he will separate them one from another as a shepherd separates sheep from goats, and he will place the sheep at his right hand and the goats at his left. Then the King will say to those at this right hand, "Come, O blessed of my father, inherit the kingdom prepared for you from the foundation of the world; for I was hungry and you gave me food, I was thirsty and you gave me drink, I was a stranger and you welcomed me, I was naked and you clothed me, I was sick and you visited me, I was in prison and you visited me. Then the righteous will answer him, "Lord, when did we see you hungry and feed you, or thirsty and give you drink? And when did we see you a stranger and welcome you, or naked and clothe you? And

when did we see you sick or in prison and visit you? And the King will answer them, "Truly I say to you, as you did it to one of the least of these, my brethren, you did it to me." Then he will say to those at his left hand, "Depart from me, you cursed, into eternal fire prepared for the devil and his angels; for I was hungry and you gave me no food, I was thirsty and you gave me no drink. . . . Then they will also answer, "Lord, when did we see you hungry or thirsty or a stranger or naked or sick or in prison, and did not minister to you?" Then he will answer them, "Truly I say to you, as you did it not to one of the least of these, you did it not to me." And they will go away into eternal punishment, but the righteous into eternal life.

This passage has an odd ring to it. Matthew's theology always identifies Jesus with the Son of Man.[23] However, the last judgment depicted in these verses reads like the theology of Q—which explicitly does *not* call Jesus the Son of Man, probably because Q is more conservative redactionally than Matthew and only implies that Jesus is the Son of Man.[24] But Matthew 25:31-46 is not a Q passage because it is not paralleled in Luke. Why does Matthew's gospel assert a Q-like theocentrism, when Matthew's primary theological vision is christocentric?

The question, if not a solution, becomes clearer when the theocentric universalism of Matthew's last judgment scene is compared with one of those rare Q sayings found in Mark 8:38 that warns that the Son of Man will be ashamed of those who are ashamed of the Son of Man's words, and such persons will be judged by God accordingly. This passage portrays Jesus not as the Son of Man but as a prophetic announcer of what the Son of Man will do. Nor does Luke's version (9:26) or Matthew's version (16:27-28). However, there is also a Q saying redacted by Matthew in 10:32 that *does* explicitly identify Jesus as the Son of Man, while its Lukan parallel (12:8-9) does not—possibly because Luke's theology is anti-eschatological and focuses the reader's attention on God, not on Jesus as the Son of Man. In other words, this is one of those points where the writer of Luke's Gospel appropriated a Q-saying to express his or her particular theocentric understanding of God's action in the historical Jesus.[25]

These comparisons are evidence that at the redactional level, Matthew's Gospel explicitly identifies Jesus with the Son of Man and thereby asserts that, post-Easter, faith in Jesus is ontologically necessary for entry into the Kingdom of God. This is not Q's explicit understanding of Jesus, but Matthew reads his theology into the Q saying preserved in 10:32. This is what makes the last judgment scene in 25:31-46 so striking: it is not paralleled in Mark or Luke; its source is not Q, yet it expresses Q's non-christology.

There seems to be no agreement among New Testament exegetes about how to explain the theological inconsistency between the theocentrism of

Matthew's last judgment scene and the christocentrism of the vast majority of the material in Matthew's Gospel. But one point can be made: mixed within Matthew's usual assertion of faith in Jesus as an ontological requirement for salvation—whatever "salvation" can mean—there also exists scriptural support for the primordial view that salvation has occurred, and does occur, apart from faith in Jesus as the Christ. Reading Matthew's last judgment scene as an explicit requirement of faith in Jesus for entry into the Kingdom of God is an abuse of this particular text.

Similar scriptural ambiguity about the ontological necessity of Jesus as the Christ for salvation seems also to occur in Paul's description of how God has made saving truth universally plain to humanity prior to Jesus, and how humanity generally has failed to respond to it (Romans 1:18–23). There has, in other words, always been what later Christian tradition called "general revelation" apart from Christ.

Undoubtedly, this text indicates also that *some* persons who *did* respond to general revelation *were* saved apart from Christ. At least Paul thought "Abraham's faith" apart from Christ saved him and faithful Jews thereafter who followed Torah, as well as Gentiles who responded to God apart from Torah or Christ.

Like most of the elements of Paul's thought, however, issues get rather complicated. For example, most New Testament scholars interpret this passage within the context of Paul's law–gospel dialectic. Thus, according to Günther Bornkamm, God gives "law" to all human beings at all times, for Judaism in the form of Torah and for Gentiles as "natural revelation." "Law" is what we can naturally know of God apart from Christ; therefore pre-Jesus or post-Jesus persons "apart from Christ" are without excuse for rebelling against God's demands. They "know" God but have not responded. But post-Jesus, "law," in the sense both of Torah and of "natural revelation" can now only be understood through gospel: now no one can fulfill the demands of the law apart from faith in God's grace through Jesus' resurrection.[26]

But are matters this simple? Should Romans 1:18–23 be read as christocentric post-Jesus reflection on the possibility of salvation apart from Christ? Paul's theology is, to be sure, thoroughly christocentric. However, a more theocentric reading of this passage is possible in the context of another passage from Romans where Paul was reflecting on the same issue (2:12–16):

> All who have sinned without the law will also perish without the law, and all who have sinned under the law will be judged by the law. For it is not the hearers of the law who are righteous before God, but doers of the law who will be justified. When Gentiles who have not the law do by nature what the law requires, they are a law to themselves, even though they do

not have the law. They show that what the law requires is written on their hearts, while their conscience also bears witness and their conflicting thoughts accuse or perhaps excuse them on that day when, according to my gospel, God judges the secrets of men by Christ Jesus.

Paul's theological vision—in these two passages—seems more inclusive and theocentric than historically allowed by traditional Christian exegesis. Some Gentiles have "done by nature" what God's law requires. They are saved apart from Christ, as will be attested *by* Christ when God "judges the secrets of men." In other words, it is an abuse of these two texts to say that Paul believed that "natural revelation" never worked or was not working in his own day apart from Christ—even if Paul intended 2:16 to express a christocentric view of the human-Gentile condition.

This idea is carried on in Acts 14:15–18. One day in the city of Lystra, the author reports, Paul in the company of Barnabas cured a crippled person. The "crowds" who witnessed this miracle were justifiably impressed and, not unreasonably confused, cheered in Lycaonian, "The gods have come down to us in the likeness of men." Barnabas they called Zeus, and Paul, because he did the talking and healing, they called Hermes.

But before the Lycaonians could offer sacrifice, Paul instructed, "We also are men, of like nature with you, and bring you good news. . . ." The good news, of course, is that salvation is now available to them through faith in Christ. But Paul also expanded on this good news: even though Christ is the way to salvation now, God has never been without witnesses, for "he did good" and gave them "from heaven rains and fruitful seasons."

Traditional Christian exegesis of this passage does not go much beyond Rudolf Bultmann's characterization. Luke places this speech in Paul's mouth to represent Luke's theology that God is one and exercises creative power on the world's behalf, and has always done so—even before Jesus. But after Jesus' death, God's saving power is completed in him. Accordingly, now persons should respond to Jesus, and renounce other avenues to God. That is, *after* the resurrection, Christ is ontologically required for salvation. There is no other way.[27]

However, this passage has no explicit christological conclusion. Undoubtedly, the author of Luke-Acts thought that faith in Christ was ontologically required for salvation. It was this faith that motivated the author to write his or her "history." Still, this passage leaves the issue quite open and functions as a "preview of the Gentile *kerygma* that Luke reports Paul preached in Areopognus."[28] According to this passage—a call to monotheism—God has always revealed saving truth to all nations; all human beings have encountered God, even though most have been, and still are, ignorant of this.

It is an abuse of this text, as well as Acts 14:15–18, to deny that some people, perhaps many people, responded to this universal revelation and were, and are, "saved" apart from Christ. While the author of Luke-Acts certainly thought this highly improbable post-Christ, this passage does not lock us into his post-Christ christocentrism.

On Seeing Scripture Primordially

Like our experience of nature, scriptural seeing is pretty much a now-you-see-it-now-you-don't affair. An insight flashes through a text, then dissolves into intellectual and emotional fog. I have read Lord Krishna's instruction to Arjuna in the *Bhagavad-gītā* about the many incarnations of Brahman into an infinite variety of sacred forms, and this has helped me see the possibilities of God's incarnation in Christ. I have read Buddhist Pure Land texts through Shinran's eyes and have seen with him the "other-powered" grace of Amida Buddha's compassion, and this has helped me see the grace of God that Augustine, Aquinas, and Luther saw in Paul's writings when they thought and wrote about faith. I have read how Moses stood alone on a mountain and saw the back side of God passing in review, and that has let me see how the One God recited by Muhammad in the *Qurʾān* can be closer to a person than a jugular vein.

These experiences have stunned me to silence, for scripture points to— never surrounds—the Sacred. They indicate that no scripture tells the whole story, only traces of it; that any scripture can help us see other traces of the Sacred in other scriptures—if approached with sensitive and critical openness. They say of the Sacred that it conceals with eye-catching nonchalance, so that when we do see its traces lurking in scripture, our vision seems like a deliberate gift. Scriptures conceal as well as reveal, but much depends on questions asked and the assumptions through which scriptures are seen.

As there is more than one way to skin a scripture, there is more than one way to skin postmodern experience of pluralism. But at least three interdependent factors of this experience provide questions that scripture must address if we are to see the Sacred's traces through it. These questions are not new with our time and experience, but our time and experience have raised them to a level of cross-cultural urgency that no religious Way can ignore.

First, postmodern historical consciousness compels us to awareness of the historical-cultural limitation of all knowledge and religious faith, and the difficulty, if not the impossibility, of judging the claims of others on the basis of our own claims. It may even be impossible to judge between competing claims about one's own scripture. Looking for traces of the Sacred in our—or anyone else's—scripture must start with the fact of historical-cultural relativity.

I am certainly not the only one to notice this. Recently, Gordon Kaufman proposed the recognition of the historical relativity of all truth claims and religious forms, as well as the abandonment of all traditional one-way-only claims to be the "highest" form of truth, as a condition for interreligious dialogue.[29] John Hick continues to note how postmodern historical consciousness does not provide "facts" or "empirical data" that lead to the conclusion that any particular religious Way has contributed more good or less evil than others. Seen in this way, the world's religious Ways are on a par with one another.[30] Even as traditional and cautious a Christian theologian as Langdon Gilkey no longer claims finality for the Christian Way, even though this recognition can lead to "dangerous debilitating relativity." The question is how to avoid this pitfall. Gilkey's advice is to attribute validity to religious Ways other than our own, incorporate whatever insights one can into one's own faith and practice, while recognizing the utter relativity of the referent of religious faith.[31]

Second, historical consciousness points to something every theological-philosophical tradition tacitly assumes and every "mystical" tradition explicitly asserts: the object to which religious experience points is finally, when everything is said and done, infinite Mystery beyond every particular form and exceeding every particular grasp of it. In premodern cultures, traditional claims of superiority might have made sense. But in the context of postmodern experience, the infinity and ineffability of the Sacred *demand* religious pluralism and forbid any one religious Way from having the only or final say.

Wilfred Cantwell Smith continues to focus on the notion of "idolatry" to make this point: religious imperialism trivializes the Sacred by reducing its "mystery" to limited forms too easily managed and handled by politically and dogmatically correct doctrines that better serve the needs of religious institutions than of faithful people.[32] Drawing on their experience of living as Christians within the religious plurality that characterizes Indian culture—where Brahman has been, and continues to be, encountered in an infinite variety of limited forms—Raimundo Pannikar and Stanley Samartha appropriate Hindu mystical experience to lay theological foundations for Smith's warning against idolatry.[33]

Third, the difficult economic and political realities generated by postmodern existence demand that every traditional religious claim of superiority—Christian, Islamic, Buddhist—be replaced by mutual openness guided by a collective quest for the "liberation" of all human beings as well as of nature. Writing as feminist Christians encountering religious pluralism, Rosemary Ruether and Marjorie Suchocki call for a "liberation theology of religions." In their view, holding the Christian Way as the norm of religious experience is similar to sexist attempts to render male experience the universal norm for humanity. Both lead to "outrageously absurd chauvinism," useful to those exercising political power, but oppressive to the majority who do not.[34] The liberation of human beings from oppression—including religious oppression—like the liberation of nature,[35] demands primordial reading of every scriptural tradition.

What are the principles of primordial hermeneutics? What guides primordial reading of scripture—any scripture—so we can see the traces of the Sacred sequestered within its language? How do we know that what we think we see in scripture—ours or someone else's—is actually there to be seen? It comes down to epistemology; any serious interest in anything leads to epistemology. The moment we undertake the least mental task, if we so much as try to classify an insect or split an electron or interpret a scripture, we end up, as Dillard puts it, "agog in the lap of Kant."[36]

The problem is language. Language barely accounts for things and events, much less the flux and mystery of personal experience. If it did, poets and theologians—or historians of religions who take mysticism seriously—could get on with their trade with the aplomb of pipe layers. But poets and artists and a few theologians know differently; language itself is a process of selection and abstraction from unknowable flux to a world that shades into gradations too fine for words. Or, as Kant stated it more precisely, no language ever signifies "things as they are" because, from electrons to the Sacred, no one *knows* things as they are. All language can do, and therefore all any scripture can do, is an air-tight job of signifying a writer's and a reader's *perceptions* of things as they are. There are no epistemological guarantees connecting any linguistically constructed object with any linguistically constructing subject.

But language need not know the world perfectly to communicate perceptions adequately. Historical consciousness may relativize experience and knowledge; it may be that we can at best obtain only probable knowledge, but that in itself is no mean feat. Human beings have come a long way on probable knowledge seen darkly through symbolic glasses. For symbols have a remarkable cognitive property: there is no absolute boundary, and probably no final ontological difference, between symbol and the reality it comes to mean.[37] Any symbolic object—say an art object or a myth or a collection of sacred narratives—is simultaneously an agent and an object of cognition, each a lens focused on itself.

If "things as they are" cannot be absolutely known or stated, Pontius

Pilate's question is very much to the point: What is truth? To which we might add post-Kant, What is knowledge? If symbols help us jump the bounds of the approximately known to blurry feints at the unknown, can they really add to knowledge or understanding?

I think they can; even though we may never exhaust or precisely locate what symbols specify, we nevertheless may approximate. Every form of knowledge is partial and approximate. If we know electrons and trees and great blue herons less than perfectly, and call it good enough, we might as well understand realities like love, death, freedom, or the Sacred imperfectly and call that good enough too. In other words, primordial hermeneutics embraces historical consciousness and the relativity of knowledge and belief at the heart of modern pluralism—as a lover embraces her beloved. Apart from their experience of loving, lovers have no cognitive certainties or guarantees; still, there are immense possibilities for passionate adventure and new discoveries, and lovers find that good enough.

Finally, the hermeneutical circle of primordial scriptural exegesis closes on something close to what John Hick calls "the pluralistic hypothesis": the religious Ways of humanity are different ways of experiencing, conceiving, and living in relation to an ultimate Sacred reality that transcends our collective visions of it.[38] Indeed, this is the theoretical framework through which I interpreted Matthew 25:31-46; Romans 1:18-23; 2:12-16; Acts 14:15-18; and Luke 17:22-32. Here salvation is not tied ontologically to whatever God incarnated in the historical Jesus.

Seeing religious pluralism from this theoretical perspective allows us to see traces of the Sacred not seeable through the lenses of exclusive or inclusive readings of scripture. It also sharpens our awareness of the historical contexts of all scriptural visions: even as the focus of the majority of the world's scriptural texts might be exclusive, these same texts can also help us see primordial traces of a Sacred reality that unifies the plurality of its expressions in human experience. Finally, the pluralistic hypothesis teaches us that being a Christian, Buddhist, Hindu, or Native American need not require denying the "saving" validity of the Sacred encountered in religious Ways other than our own.

How can the traces of the Sacred's unity I think I see lurking behind the lenses of scriptural traditions be imagined? It will require a great deal of highly speculative imagination. But the safety valve of all speculation is what fiction writers have always known: "What if?" and "It might be so." So long as "What if?" and "It might be so" remain as variables deeply understood, speculation does not easily become dogma, but remains the fluid, creative thing it is and guarantees its efficacy. Imagining what if and how it might be so are the themes of the next chapter, "Seeing the Ox."

Notes

1. Diana L. Eck, *Darśan: Seeing the Divine Image in India* (Chambersburg, Penn.: Anima Books, 1981), 1.
2. D. T. Suzuki, *Manual of Zen Buddhism* (New York: Grove Press, 1960), 130.
3. Ibid.
4. Annie Dillard, *Pilgrim at Tinker Creek* (New York: Harper & Row, 1974), 31.
5. Ibid.
6. See Black Elk's account of his great vision in John G. Neihardt, *Black Elk Speaks* (New York: Washington Square Press, 1932), 17–39.
7. I acknowledge that there is some debate over this question. For example, Steven Katz argues against Huston Smith that there is no reason to assume that non-duality is the core of all mystical experience. See Katz, "Is There a Primordial Philosophy?" *Journal of the American Academy of Religion* 55 (1987): 22–28. In my opinion, neither textual nor historical evidence supports Katz's assertions, even though I agree with him that there are "no unmediated experiences," including mystical experiences of non-duality. I also think, along with William James, that mystics interpret the experience of non-duality according to the theological-philosophical traditions that trained them, and thereby draw different theological conclusions. See William James, *The Varieties of Religious Experience* (London: Longmans, Green, & Company, 1912), 53–77.
8. Dillard, *Pilgrim at Tinker Creek*, 33.
9. In formulating this generic view of scripture, I have followed hints gleaned from Frederick M. Denny and Rodney L. Taylor, eds., *The Holy Book in Comparative Perspective* (Columbia: University of South Carolina Press, 1985); and Wilfred Cantwell Smith, *What Is Scripture? A Comparative Approach* (Minneapolis: Fortress Press, 1993).
10. For an excellent summation of the formation of the New Testament canon, see Harry Y. Gamble, "Christianity: Scripture and Canon," in *The Holy Book in Comparative Perspective*, 36–62.
11. See Jonathan Rosenbaum, "Judaism: Torah and Tradition," in *The Holy Book in Comparative Perspective*, 10–35; and Smith, *What Is Scripture?* chap. 5.
12. See Reginald A. Ray, "Buddhism: Sacred Text Written and Realized," in *The Holy Book in Comparative Perspective*, 148–80; and Smith, *What Is Scripture?* chap. 7.
13. *The Holy Qurʾān*, trans. A. Yusuf Ali (Brentwood, Md.: Anima Corporation, 1983), 17; and Smith, *What is Scripture?* chap. 4.
14. See Wilfred Cantwell Smith, *The Meaning and End of Religion* (Minneapolis: Fortress Press, 1991), 80–118; and Fazlur Rahman, *Islam* (Chicago: University of Chicago Press, 1966), chaps. 2–3.

15. This is abundantly clear in the West. Scripture, both Hebrew Bible and New Testament, has been so encrusted with institutional dogmatisms that serve the needs of institutions rather than persons that most Westerners find scripture irrelevant and without authority. Indeed, the irrelevance and non-authority of all scriptures is one of the defining characteristics of postmodern pluralism.

16. Wolfhart Pannenberg, "Religious Pluralism and Conflicting Truth Claims," in *Christian Uniqueness Reconsidered,* ed. Gaven D'Costa (Maryknoll, N.Y.: Orbis Books, 1990), 99–104.

17. Karl Rahner, *Theological Investigations,* vol. 5 (Baltimore: Helicon Press, 1966), 131.

18. Hans Küng, *On Being a Christian* (New York: Pocket Books, 1978), 89–116.

19. John Dunne, *The Way of All the Earth* (South Bend, Ind.: University of Notre Dame Press, 1978), 3–26.

20. John B. Cobb, Jr., *Beyond Dialogue* (Philadelphia: Fortress Press, 1982).

21. At one time, Paul F. Knitter read this, and other New Testament passages, to mean that Christ is not an ontological necessity for the salvation of non-Christians as part of his argument that traditional christocentric theology should be replaced by theocentric theology. See *No Other Name? A Critical Survey of Christian Attitudes Toward the World Religions* (Maryknoll, N.Y.: Orbis Books, 1989), chap. 9. Also see idem, "Towards a Liberation Theology of Religion," in *The Myth of Christian Uniqueness: Towards a Pluralistic Theology of Religions,* ed. John Hick and Paul F. Knitter (Maryknoll, N.Y.: Orbis Books, 1989), 178–200.

22. I have received very special help in the exegesis of the New Testament passages cited in this chapter from my colleague and friend Douglas E. Oakman. His scholarly expertise in New Testament textual exegesis has served me and his students at Pacific Lutheran University well indeed. While I am grateful to him, I take full responsibility for conclusions drawn in an area of scholarship in which I am far from expert.

23. Ivan Hevener, *Q: The Sayings of Jesus* (Collegeville, Minn.: Liturgical Press, 1987), 16–50. Also see Burton L. Mack, *The Lost Gospel of Q: The Book of Christian Origins* (San Francisco: HarperSanFrancisco, 1993), 183–85.

24. Mack, *The Lost Gospel of Q,* 202–5; Rudolf Bultmann, *Theology of the New Testament,* vol. 1 (New York: Charles Scribner's Sons, 1959), 68 ff.; *The New Jerome Biblical Commentary,* ed. Raymond E. Brown et al. (Englewood Cliffs, N.J.: Prentice Hall, 1990), 756 ff.; and Günther Bornkamm, *Jesus of Nazareth* (New York: Harper & Row, 1960), 228–31.

25. Mack, *Lost Gospel of Q,* 186–88, 227–28.

26. See Günther Bornkamm, *Paul* (New York: Harper & Row, 1969), 120–22; Herman Ridderbos, *Paul: An Outline of His Theology* (Grand Rapids, Mich.: William B. Eerdmans, 1975), 135–39; and Ernst Käsemann, *Perspectives on Paul* (Philadelphia: Fortress Press, 1971), 24–25.

27. Bultmann, *Theology of the New Testament,* 1:68 ff.

28. See *New Jerome Biblical Commentary,* 750.

29. Gordon D. Kaufman, "Religious Diversity, Historical Consciousness, and Christian Theology," in *Myth of Christian Uniqueness*, 3–15.

30. John Hick, "The Non-Absoluteness of Christianity," in *Myth of Christian Uniqueness*, 16–36.

31. Langdon Gilkey, "Plurality and Its Theological Implications," in *Myth of Christian Uniqueness*, 37–50.

32. Wilfred Cantwell Smith, "Participation: The Changing Christian Role in Other Cultures," *Religion and Society* 18, no. 1 (1979): 56–73; idem, *Towards A World Theology* (Philadelphia: Westminster Press, 1981), chap. 8; idem, "Idolatry in Comparative Perspective," in *Myth of Christian Uniqueness*, 53–68.

33. See Raimundo Pannikar, *The Unknown Christ of Hinduism* (Maryknoll, N.Y: Orbis Books, 1981); idem, "The Jordan, The Tiber, and the Ganges," in *Myth of Christian Uniqueness*, 89–116; and Stanley J. Samartha, "The Cross and the Rainbow," in *Myth of Christian Uniqueness*, 69–88.

34. See Marjorie Hewitt Suchocki, "In Search of Justice: Religious Pluralism from a Feminist Perspective," in *Myth of Christian Uniqueness*, 149–62; and Rosemary Radford Ruether, "Feminism and Jewish-Christian Dialogue," in *Myth of Christian Uniqueness*, 137–48.

35. Paul O. Ingram, "Nature's Jeweled Net: Kukai's Ecological Buddhism," *The Pacific World* 6 (1990): 50–73.

36. Annie Dillard, *Living Fiction* (New York: Harper & Row, 1982), 53.

37. Compare Paul Tillich, *Dynamics of Faith* (New York: Harper Torchbooks, 1957), 41–54, with Alfred North Whitehead, *Symbolism: Its Meaning and Effect* (New York: Capricorn Books, 1927), *Religion in the Making* (Cleveland and New York: World Publishing Company, 1960), chaps. 2–3, and *Process and Reality* (New York: Macmillan, 1967), 255–79.

38. John Hick, *An Interpretation of Religion* (New Haven: Yale University Press, 1989), 235–36. Hick limits the pluralistic hypothesis to the "great post-axial faiths," by which he means those religious Ways that evolved from pre-axial beginnings in the eighth to sixth centuries B.C.E.: Judaism, Buddhism, Confucianism, Taoism, and later, Christianity and Islam. I see no necessity for excluding Native American and other so-called pre-literate religious traditions from the pluralistic hypothesis.

3
Seeing the Ox

THE THIRD OX-HERDING PICTURE, "SEEING THE OX," DEPICTS THE MAN IN PROCESS of discovering the whereabouts of his ox by the sounds he hears and the shadows he glimpses in the bushes. For the first time, according to the accompanying commentary, he is beginning to "see into the nature of things." His senses are in harmonious order, and in spite of the rigor of the chase, he is attentive and fully present to himself. His senses have been like salt in seawater; when they are properly focused he will discover that the ox is none other than himself, because the ox and the man are nondual. Or, according to the accompanying poem:

On a yonder branch perches a nightingale cheerfully singing;
The sun is warm, and a soothing breeze blows; on the bank the
willows are green;

The ox is there all by himself, nowhere is he to hide himself;
The splendid head decorated with stately horns—what painter can
    produce him?[1]

"Seeing the Ox" is the topic of this chapter. It deals with the meaning of "seeing and with what is "seen." What are seen are images of the Sacred, not the Sacred as such. Accordingly, the thesis of this chapter is that the various religious Ways of humanity are ways of "seeing" the Sacred through the lenses of culturally and historically conditioned symbolic images. Specifically, the issue of this chapter is the nature of the Sacred and its relation to the world as "seen" from the primordial point of view developed in chapter 2. When we search for the ox, for what are we searching? Do we ever see it? If so, what do we see?

On Postmodern Seeing (Darśan)

Annie Dillard has written that our contemporary, postmodern situation is much like that of Perry's and Henderson's after they reached the North Pole in 1909. They contrived an imaginary point on the Arctic Ocean farthest from land in any direction, a navigator's point on a map to console themselves after they had nowhere else special to go. They called it the "pole of relative inaccessibility."[2] There is also a pole of relative inaccessibility on the Antarctic continent, that point of land farthest from saltwater in any direction.

If the historical evidence of humanity's religious experience is credible, the Sacred is the pole of relative inaccessibility located in metaphysics. For one of the few things everyone who has seen the ox's traces knows is that the Sacred is relatively inaccessible. It is that point farthest from every known point, symbol, teaching, and expectation in all directions, which means it is the pole of most trouble. I also take it as given—on the basis of humanity's religious history—that it is the pole of great price.

But in these postmodern times, it is not evident that humanity's religious experience is credible evidence for the existence of a sacred reality. Those who accredit such evidence are likely to be a cognitive minority. Experience of the Sacred is not so evident, for example, as it was to Native American people. Like primal people everywhere, they saw the Sacred in multiple forms in nature and felt connected to themselves, the environment, and the Great Spirit—an unsuitable English translation, but there is none better for the ox's traces many Native Americans still see. Today Western culture has silenced nature. The Chinese used to say that the universe of the ten thousand things flows ceaselessly from and returns to the Tao, the Way—their word for the relatively inaccessible Sacred. Today, except for a few poets and mystics East and West, each of the ten thousand things manifests precisely nothing. According to the ancient Israelites, God used to rage about frequenting sacred groves. I wish I could find one. Postmodernity has pushed the Sacred's point of relative inaccessibility farther out from the pole of contemporary experience, a situation in the Western world created partly by the biblical tradition itself. Or, as Martin Buber observed, the crisis of "primitive" peoples comes with the discovery of that which is fundamentally not-holy, the a-sacramental, which has no "hour."[3]

We are no longer "primitive" now; but we are the cumulative tradition of "primitive" humanity's crisis, and the whole world seems not-holy. Secularism has drained light from the sacred groves and the high places and from along the banks of streams. There is only silence, because we can now live wherever and however we wish. The ancient Israelites knew this. They believed they could ask the Sacred, at a time when it was absolutely accessible, for anything. It would always grant their wish.

Once in a wilderness a collection of nomadic Hebrew tribes did just that. They heard the Sacred's speech and found it too loud. They were at Sinai and witnessed darkness as thick as smoke where God was:

> Moses brought the people out from the camp to meet God, and they took their stand at the foot of the mountain. Mount Sinai was all smoking because the Lord had come down upon it in fire; the smoke went up like the smoke of a kiln; all the people were terrified and the sound of a trumpet grew louder and louder. Whenever Moses spoke, God answered him in a peal of thunder. (Exodus 19:17–19, *New English Bible*)

It scared them senseless, and they asked Moses to beg God, please, never to speak directly to them again: "Speak to us yourself . . . and we will listen; but if God speaks to us, we will die" (20:19). And God, pitying and understanding their lack of courage, agreed not to speak to the people anymore. "Say to them," he ordered Moses, 'Get into your tents again.'"

It is difficult to undo our own damage and ask that which we have asked to leave to come back. It is hard to desecrate a grove or a forest or a people and change our minds. Today all holy mountains are keeping mum. The burning bush has been doused and cannot be rekindled. We light matches in vain under every green tree. All we get are forest fires. But the wind used to cry, and hills and mountains used to shout the Sacred's presence. It used to flow in great rivers. It even used to fill the dwellings of human beings. But in our times, sacred speech, which ancient Brahmins in India saw as the goddess Vac, has all but perished from the lifeless things of the earth, and living things say very little to very few.

And yet we still hunger for the Sacred. What, after all, have we been doing since human beings first painted animals on the walls of caves in France? What are we doing now, but trying to call the Sacred—the Pole of Relative Inaccessibility—back to the mountains, forests, rivers, and the dwellings of human beings? Or, failing that, trying to raise a peep out of anything that is not us? What is the final difference between a cathedral and a physics lab, a prayer in a monastery and a radio astronomer's search for life in other galaxies?

Are not these searchers saying, "Hello?" Some of us spy on whales or on interstellar objects; others bump, grind, and smash protons in particle accelerators; others search for the relatively Inaccessible Sacred Ox until they are blue in the face through humanity's traditional religious Ways. A few of us spy through the scholarly lenses of history of religions. However we search, we do so because no one wants to be alone. Since the religious Ways of humanity have always focused on the search for a Sacred reality that is, according to them all, relatively inaccessible to every searcher, what are we apt to see when we make dialogue with these Ways the locus of our particular search for the ox? If we see the Sacred, what do we see? What does the ox look like? Two contemporary guides—a historian of religions and a philosopher of religion—suggest exciting theoretical possibilities: Wilfred Cantwell Smith and John Hick.

Wilfred Cantwell Smith
Cumulative Tradition and Faith

More than any other historian of religions, Wilfred Cantwell Smith is responsible for changes in the ways a new generation of scholars now thinks about religious experience. Seen through pre-Cantwell Smith eyes, there exist a number of long-lived historical religious entities, for example, Christianity, Hinduism, Buddhism, or Islam. Each of these religious entities is wrapped in the institutionalized framework of its own beliefs and practices that divide it from other religious entities and from the secular world. Thus, Christianity, Hinduism, Buddhism, and Islam are contrasting socioreligious entities bearing distinctive creeds and practices; most religious persons are members of one or another of these mutually exclusive religious entities.

Seeing the religious life of humanity as organized into a number of communities based on rival sets of religious beliefs creates certain kinds of questions about religion. The beliefs of religious persons are beliefs about God or Allah or Brahman or the Dharma or the Tao—depending on the religion—that define a way of salvation or liberation and are accordingly a matter of life and death. Looking at the plurality of religions through these lenses, then, we see competing claims to possess saving truth. Each religious community believes its own gospel to be true and other gospels to be false, insofar as they differ from it. So the only proper question posed by the existence of religious pluralism is, Which religious entity is true?

In practice, those who raise this question are normally convinced that theirs is the true religion. For them, the primary task is to demonstrate the spiritual-theological superiority of their own religion and the consequent moral superiority of the community that institutionally embodies it. Mutual criticism of religions and derogatory assessment of one by another have been important parts of demonstrating the superiority of one religion against all others.

Cantwell Smith's work demonstrates alternative possibilities, even for those committed to a particular Way.[4] First, he shows how the presently dominant concept of "religion" in popular usage and scholarly discourse has a history that can be traced back to the European Renaissance. At that time, different streams of religious life were reified in Western thought into solid structures called "Christianity," "Judaism," or "Islam." Having reified religious experience in this way, Western scholars exported the notion of "religion" to the rest of the world, causing non-Christians to think of themselves as Hindus, Buddhists, Confucians, or Muslims against all others.

Cantwell Smith suggests an alternative view of religious pluralism: something of vital religious importance takes different forms within the historical contexts of each religious Way. This "something vital" he calls "faith," which, he argues, is quite different from "belief."[5]

Generically, "faith" refers to both an outlook on life and the quality of life that religious persons express through the practice of whatever explicit beliefs they follow. That is, faith is experienced by religious persons everywhere as an intention to "trust," to bet one's life on, to set one's heart on; in faith, one assents to truth—to reality as it is, not as one wants it to be. Religious persons are always persons of faith, no matter what specific religious labels they wear.

From a global perspective, therefore, faith is not the same as "belief." According to Cantwell Smith, historical evidence suggests that there has been less diversity in the *forms* in which human beings have experienced something called "faith" than in the ways human beings have propositionally articulated the *meaning* of faith through systems of "belief." He writes:

> Beliefs have changed, and will go on changing; but that, it emerges, is not and has hardly ever been the point at issue. Various beliefs may have conduced to faith, but they have not constituted it. Also vice versa: beliefs have at times remained relatively constant, while faith has varied. Two persons may have believed much the same thing, but the faith of one has been

strong and good, been even beautiful, warm, humble, loving, joyous, while the faith of the other may have been minor, inept, awry. Beliefs may have conduced to faith, but they have not engendered it.[6]

This conclusion hangs on the fact that the meaning of the English word "belief" has changed. "Belief" now denotes the assertion of propositional conclusions, the truth of which remains uncertain for lack of conclusive evidence. Thus, "belief" in contemporary scholarly and popular parlance normally denotes the propositional assertions of ideas that are at best opinions, at worst falsehoods, as illustrated in *The Random House Dictionary*: "belief" is an "opinion" or "conviction," as in "the belief that the world is flat."

Accordingly, "belief" now denotes "the opposite of knowledge." To believe anything involves uncertainty, lack of knowledge, while in normal contemporary usage "to know" means "not to believe." For example, "I *know* my Redeemer lives" is not the same as "I *believe* my Redeemer lives." Contemporary persons do not "know" the Sacred exists, and only a few "believe" in its existence in spite of evidence to the contrary. Nowadays, even believers in the existence of a relatively inaccessible Sacred reality some call God, and others Dharma, the Tao, or Brahman normally equate their faith with belief in an unprovable opinion.

Much of what Smith means by these conclusions derives from his understanding of the nature of religion: he is famous for rejecting "religion" as an abstract noun meant to define what religious people do when they practice religion. He writes:

> My suggestion is that the word, and the concept, should be dropped . . . that it is misleading to retain them. I suggest that the term "religion" is confusing, unnecessary, and distorting. . . . I have become strongly convinced that the vitality of personal faith, on the one hand, and, on the other hand (quite separately), progress in understanding—even at the academic level—of the traditions of other people throughout history and throughout the world, are both seriously blocked by our attempt to conceptualize what is involved in each case in terms of (a) religion.[7]

He notes, for example, that until the seventeenth century, religious people lived religiously without benefit of a noun called "religion" that defined how they lived.[8] Accordingly, the history of the word "religion" is a "process of reification" that so abstracts the experience of faith from the lives of concrete living persons, that the term falsifies the experience it supposedly defines. One piece of evidence Cantwell Smith cites in support of this conclusion is the fact that, at present, no single definition of "religion" has been accepted by the majority of scholars in the field of religious studies.[9]

As there is no such entity as "religion"—there exists only the faith of religious persons lived through the contexts of their historical circumstances—there are likewise no such entities as Christianity, Buddhism, Islam, or Hinduism. There exist only Christian, Buddhist, Muslim, or Hindu persons who live more or less faithfully within the historical contexts of Christian, Buddhist, Muslim, or Hindu "cumulative traditions."

In its generic sense, then, "religious experience"—not "religion"—comprises two components: cumulative tradition and personal faith. Cumulative tradition is relatively easy to identify: it refers to externally observable forms of religious behavior—rituals, doctrines, theological systems, myths, and practices, undertaken by religious persons in their search for the Sacred.[10] Historians of religions study cumulative traditions in comparison, not "religion." That is, cumulative tradition designates both what religious persons practice to make faithful contact with the Sacred and what they practice as a result of this contact—how they see the ox's pole of relative inaccessibility. Thus, there is Buddhist cumulative tradition—observable religious practices that distinguish the Buddhist Way from other religious Ways, for example, Islamic, Jewish, Christian, or Hindu cumulative traditions.

If we take seriously Smith's suggestion that the noun "religion" be dropped from our vocabulary, if religious experience is trusting assent to the Sacred as encountered in the historical-cultural contexts of particular cumulative traditions, how should we describe the "object of faith" upon which religious persons bet their lives? How do we describe the relatively inaccessible ox religious people trust? Do all cumulative traditions, in their own particular ways, point to the same ox? What do historians of religions, theologians, sociologists, poets, and fiction writers write about when reflecting on the object of religious faith?

Cantwell Smith's answer is that at the stage of our present knowledge, we cannot know. What we can know is that "faith" is always experienced and conditioned by the historical condition of our specific cumulative traditions. Therefore, it is illegitimate for any particular cumulative tradition to claim absolute truth about the relatively inaccessible Sacred. All such claims—Christian, Islamic, Hindu, or Buddhist—are morally, historically, and theologically wrong. For Christians, this means traditional modes of theological reflection must give way to new forms of thought and practice that permit experiencing the relatively inaccessible sacred reality Christians experience as God incarnated in the historical Jesus as salvifically active in non-Christian Ways. Furthermore, this entails affirming religious pluralism as the only morally acceptable and theologically adequate response to a religiously plural world.[11]

Of course what we believe *about* the object of faith, the content of our specific cumulative traditions, is supremely important. Christians "bet their lives on" God incarnated in the life, death, and resurrection of the historical Jesus of Nazareth. Buddhists bet their lives on what the historical Buddha discovered on the night of his enlightenment twenty-five hundred years ago.[12] Christian faith and Buddhist faith are not conceptually the same; but both Christians and Buddhists experience faith, which they express through the systems of beliefs and practices constituting their respective cumulative traditions. But no cumulative tradition has cornered the market on the relatively inaccessible ox; each needs to encounter the other and imaginatively stretch and test and expand its experience of faith.

John Hick: The Pluralistic Hypothesis

John Hick philosophically sharpens the theological implications of Cantwell Smith's conclusions.[13] The simple fact of pluralism, he notes, in itself raises no religious problems. "It is only when we add what can be called the basic religious conviction that a problem is generated."[14]

By "basic religious conviction" Hick means the conviction that our religious experience and beliefs are not illusions, that they refer to a transcendent Sacred reality—which I have described as "relatively inaccessible." Or, restated, the basic religious conviction—historically embodied in what Cantwell Smith called cumulative tradition—is not illusory or self-deceiving. Whether this conviction is justifiable is the central issue of philosophy of religion. But all religious persons claim that their beliefs and practices truly refer to a transcendent sacred reality.

Most often, according to Hick, the basic religious conviction carries an additional claim: one's particular Way is the most valid response to the Sacred because it alone expresses true beliefs and is the only way to "salvation." The philosophical and theological issues of religious pluralism originate from this claim of final validity. Can the claims of the variety of gospels that compose humanity's religious Ways all be true? If not, is only one gospel fully true, or are all gospels false? How can we verify our answers to such questions?

For Hick, one thing seems clear enough. The basic religious conviction need not imply that religious experience is straightforwardly vertical or that religious beliefs are straightforwardly true or false. Human nature and historical circumstance also make contributions to our religious awareness and produce wide ranges of corresponding perceptions in our human consciousness of the Sacred. Some of these are undoubtedly distortions. Nevertheless, Hick thinks the historical evidence cited by scholars like Wilfred Cantwell Smith,

Huston Smith, and others safely allows us to assume that each religious Way represents a wide range of responses to the Sacred. Many, perhaps most, of these responses may very well be inadequate, but none is reducible to simple illusion.[15]

Hick applies this conclusion to the entire range of humanity's religious experience.[16] He writes:

> I cannot . . . as a Christian, solve the problem of religious pluralism by holding that my own religion is a response to the divine reality but that all others are merely human projections. I cannot say, with Karl Barth, that "the Christian Religion is true, because it has pleased God, who alone can be the judge in this matter, to affirm it to be the true religion," so that "it alone has the commission and the authority to be a missionary religion, i.e., to confront the world of religions as the one true religion with absolute self-confidence to invite and challenge it to abandon its ways and start on the Christian way" (*Church Dogmatics*, 1/2, pp. 350, 351). Such sublime bigotry could only be possible for one who has no real interest in or awareness of the wider religious life of mankind.[17]

According to Hick, "the wider religious life of mankind" occurs within the limits imposed by finite historical existence and may be divided roughly into two polar types of religious experience, each comprising a multiplicity of themes and variations. Perhaps most common is the experience of the Sacred as personal presence and will, experienced in what Martin Buber called an I–Thou encounter. This type of religious experience is at the heart of theistic faith and practice, in Eastern as well as Western traditions.

The second type Hick calls nature or cosmic mysticism, in which the universe is experienced as the expression of one Sacred reality, as illustrated by these lines from the *Tao Te Ching* (Classic on the way and its power):

> There was something formless yet complete,
> That existed before Heaven and Earth;
> Without sound, without substance.
> Dependent on nothing, unchanging,
> All pervading, unfailing.
> One may think of it as the mother of all things under heaven.
> Its true name we do not know;
> "Way" is the name we give it.[18]

In this form of religious experience, the Sacred is encountered neither as personal nor as impersonal, but as nonpersonal, more than personal or impersonal, altogether transcending all such dualities.

Now religious experience of any type is the historically and culturally conditioned experience of finite creatures. This is true even of unitive mystical experience, because this type of religious experience is mediated through specific historical and cultural variables. Yet if we assume, as all religious Ways do, that the Sacred is absolute and relatively inaccessible to history and culture, then it must be concluded that any religious Way's experiences and beliefs include partial and limited experiences of the Sacred. No finite experience could ever encompass the Sacred's full, primordial reality. Religious experience and the meanings articulated in the religious Ways of humanity refer primarily to states of human consciousnesses, to images that point toward that which we can never fully experience. In short, all forms of religious experience imagine the ox through personal or nonpersonal images, symbols, and analogies that point our attention to a primordial Sacred Mystery that transcends its symbolic images and analogical pointers. No one has seen the ox completely; we see only its symbolic traces.

It is this reading of the history of religions that leads Hick to posit the "pluralistic hypothesis." Since (1) the basic assumption of humanity's religious Ways is the existence of an absolutely unlimited sacred reality that may not be identified or equated without remainder with anything we can experience or define, then (2) all religious Ways constitute "different ways of experiencing, conceiving, and living in relation to an ultimate divine reality which transcends all our visions of it."[19] Accordingly, different forms of religious experience—different teachings, practices, and images—are not necessarily contradictory or competitive in the sense that the validity of one entails the nonvalidity of all others. Each religious Way embodies real encounters with the relatively inaccessible Sacred in the special position of its own historical-cultural perspective. Therefore, it is best to regard each as relatively true, never absolutely true.

The pluralistic hypothesis is a hypothesis, not a theory. It is something to be thought about and tested, a "what if" possibility to be explored in a fashion similar to the way fiction writers explore scene and character development in novels and short stories to catch different nuances of reality. Or, in the words of Ghandi and Einstein, the pluralistic hypothesis is a "thought experiment." What if the pluralistic hypothesis is more than hypothesis? What if the pluralistic hypothesis is an accurate theoretical portrayal of humanity's religious situation?

How this question is answered depends on our epistemological assumptions. Hick's distinctive answer is thoroughly grounded in the epistemology of Immanuel Kant. He deeply appreciates Kant's view that we are necessarily aware of the world in which we dwell through certain forms and categories structurally inherent in the human mind. It was this insight that enabled the modern world to recognize the mind's own positive contribution to the character of its perceived environment. Yet while in some respects Hick's pluralistic hypothesis is Kantian, in other respects it is un-Kantian. Therefore, it will be useful at this point to describe the analogies of his hypothesis with the Kantian model of perception developed in the *Critique of Pure Reason*.[20]

The strand of Kantian epistemology Hick appropriates is Kant's distinction between phenomenon and noumenon,

> but transposed from the problem of sense perception to that of awareness of God. In using something analogous to Kant's phenomenon/noumenon distinction, I am not opting for any view of the place of this distinction in the *Critique of Pure Reason*. I am, rather, taking a structural model from his system and using it in a sphere—the epistemology of religion— . . . . It should also be stressed that Kant himself would not have sanctioned the idea that we in any way *experience* God, even as a divine phenomenon in distinction from divine noumenon.[21]

In other words, while for Kant God is never experienced, but postulated, for Hick God *is* experienced in ways analogous to that in which, according to Kant, we experience the world—"by informational input from external reality being interpreted by the mind in terms of its own categorical system and thus coming to consciousness as meaningful phenomenal experience."[22]

This means that human mind is so constituted that we experience the relatively inaccessible Sacred, not as an abstractly general idea but through categorically specific and relatively concrete images. Abstract concepts of the Sacred, for example, the concept of the "uncreated creator of the universe," are conceptualized and experienced through a range of historical-cultural images similar to what Joseph Campbell called "masks of eternity."[23] Therefore, "if we ask what functions in a role analogous to that of time in the schematization of the Kantian categories," the answer, Hick suggests, "is the continuum of historical factors which have produced our different religious cultures."[24] Here his philosophy of religious pluralism intertwines with the historical analysis of Wilfred Cantwell Smith: variations of culture and history make humanity's collective experience of the Sacred concrete through specific images. We see darkly through the collective lenses of these mask-like traces of the relatively inaccessible Sacred and catch relatively incomplete glimpses. There is no other way to see it, and no one knows the whole story. Still, all of us some of the time, and some of us all of the time, can see sufficiently through the Sacred's masks if we look hard enough—and do not confuse the partial truth seen in each mask with the whole Sacred reality that wears it.

Masking the Sacred

According to Cantwell Smith's historical analysis and Hick's pluralistic hypothesis, we can only know enough of the relatively inaccessible Sacred to make contact with it by any means ready at hand: worship, meditation, ethical self-discipline, philosophical-theological reflection, art, music, any *praxis* we can think of. For there is an anomalous specificity to our experience in space-time, a scandal of historical and cultural particularity by which the Sacred burgeons up or showers down in the shabbiest of occasions and leaves our dealings with it in the hands of myopic and clumsy amateurs. This is what we are and ever were; the Sacred *kann nicht anders* ("cannot be other"). Experience of the Sacred in time is history; in space it is shocking mystery.

An ancient Indian text, *The Bhagavad-gītā*,[25] or "Song of the Blessed One," records just how shocking this mystery can be. The warrior-hero Arjuna and his friend and charioteer, Sri Krishna, survey a battlefield just before the final conflict of a civil war. More than the usual political and economic issues about which men wage wars are at stake. The highest stakes of all are to be decided by this conflict—the survival of the universe itself.

But as he surveys the arrayed armies on the field of battle, just before giving the signal to begin the fight, Arjuna, "the conqueror of sloth," the commander of the army that *has* to be victorious to prevent the universe from regressing to chaos, suddenly and inexplicably loses heart. "O Krishna," he confesses:

> at the sight of these my kinsmen, assembled here eager to give battle, my limbs fail and my mouth is parched. My body is shaken and my hair stands on end. The bow Gandava slips from my hand and my skin is on fire. I cannot hold myself steady; my mind seems to whirl. . . . I see omens of evil. Nor do I perceive, O Krishna, any good in slaughtering my own people in battle. I desire neither victory nor empire nor even any pleasure. (*Gītā* 1:28–31)

Arjuna's dilemma is every person's dilemma, for we must fight an identical civil war—an internal spiritual war of contradictory forces of our own making, which we must survive if we are to win self-fulfillment—even if we are not warriors like Arjuna. For he has suddenly, without advanced warning, confronted the ambiguities and contradictory impulses that have created his life, and feels caught in circumstances beyond his control, even as they are of his own making. So what he is used to doing suddenly seems impossible and without meaning. Confronted with this, his impulse is flight from what he must do, even if he does not understand why, to think it over. Arjuna, the warrior, wants to be a pacifist, but for the wrong reasons.

In such a crisis of spirit, it is a good thing to have a friend like Krishna, who, along with Rāma, is one of the two primary incarnations of the god Vishnu, the Preserver. Krishna's task is to convince his friend Arjuna that he must fight the war of contradictions, the civil war, that lies ahead, and that he must be victorious by resolving his life's contradictions, not running from them, because no one can run away from this fight. We *are* our contradictions. They are us, and we can never run from ourselves. So the question is not *whether* Arjuna—or we—will fight the emotional and religious turmoil that turns our lives into a battleground of opposite forces, but *how* we will fight this battle from which no one can run.

The key is finding our *svadharma*, our "self nature," who we really are as opposed to what we delude ourselves into thinking we are, then find that method for battle that fits our nature and enter the path that leads to final self-realization. Krishna teaches that there are three such methods, suitable to three general personality types: Karma Yoga, the way of non-attachment to the fruits of action, for those of an activist nature such as Arjuna; Jñana Yoga the way of knowledge and wisdom gained through meditation, for those of rationalist-contemplative bent; and Bhakti Yoga, the way of devotion to a Lord (*īshvara*), for the majority of human beings, whose natures are such that their primary mode of confronting the world is through emotional inter-action with it.[26]

Bhakti Yoga centers on devotional religious practice and reflects the pre-dominant form of religious experience. According to Krishna, the heart of Bhakti Yoga is the many incarnations of Brahman, the Sanskrit word for the relatively inaccessible Sacred. As Krishna explains:

> Wherever there is a decline of Dharma, O Burner of Worlds, and a rise of Adharma, I incarnate Myself.
>
> For the protection of the good, for the destruction of the wicked, and for the establishment of Dharma, I am born in every age. (*Gīta* 4:7-8)

In other words, there have been many incarnations, *avatārana* ("descents") of the Sacred in an infinite variety of forms in the processes of historical space-time. Thus, Krishna, an *avatār* of Vishnu, himself an *avatār* of Brahman, "descends" into history always and everywhere when there is a decline of Dharma (proper social behavior, virtuous behavior, the proper way of things that corresponds to Truth) in response to humanity's needs. But the infinite incarnations of Brahman are, in the words of the *Chāndogya Upani-shad*, "like dew drops on the lotus leaf, touching it but not clinging to it," because it is by the power of *māyā* ("delusion") that Brahman masks the Sacred's infinitude with self-limiting finite forms to which human beings can relate in terms of their own specific natures and needs.

Of course, upon hearing this Arjuna is as confused as my students who read this part of the *Gītā* for the first time. So Arjuna asks Krishna for clarification by requesting a visual demonstration: he asks Krishna to "show" his *māyā* by removing the limited Krishna-mask that is only a trace of Brahman in order to see the whole Sacred reality. And of course Krishna tries to talk Arjuna out of his request. Finite beings, he says, can only relate to finite bits and pieces of Brahman's reality. Still, Arjuna persists, like an overeager novice impatient to grow into knowledge without the work and discipline of his own search, and begs to be shown Brahman "without attributes" (*nirguṇa brahman*). Krishna relents and removes his form, and Arjuna is overwhelmed and confesses:

> In thy body, O Lord, I behold all the gods and diverse hosts of beings—the Lord Brahma, seated on the lotus, and all the rishis and celestial serpents. I behold thee with myriads of arms and bellies, with myriads of faces and eyes, but I see not thy end nor thy beginning, O Lord of the Universe, O Universal Form. (*Gītā* 17:16–17)

The lesson is hard, and in fear and trembling, Arjuna begs the relatively inaccessible Brahman to assume once more the mask of his friend Krishna.

From the *Gītā's* standpoint, a once-and-for-all incarnation of the Sacred in the rough-and-tumble of historical space-time makes no sense and has no value. Rather, the infinite incarnations of Brahman are an ever-continuing process *not* dependent on a single localizable event in history—another way of saying the relatively inaccessible Sacred becomes relatively accessible to human experience in history through a multitude of limited, finite "traces" of the Sacred's reality.

However, the *Gītā* adds a final twist: that incarnation of Brahman worshiped by any particular person is dependent on that person's "self-nature" (*svadharma*). As Krishna instructs Arjuna:

> Whatever may be the form a devotee seeks to worship with faith—in that form alone I make his faith unwavering. Possessed of the faith, he worships that form and from it attains his desires, which are in reality granted by Me alone. (*Gītā* 7:21–23)

Thus, the gods human beings worship are "masks" that express our own natures: the desires, needs, fears, hopes, joys, knowledge, ignorance that are in each of us, that we project, as Sigmund Freud believed, onto external reality. But unlike Freud, the *Gītā* teaches that the forms of the Sacred we create are, by the power of Brahman's *māyā*, *given* reality. In other words, we create our own *avatārs*, which the relatively inaccessible Sacred accommodates exactly to our minds. These may be deities of the most ancient Vedic orthodoxy (Indra, Agni, Varuṇa) or of later Hindu piety (Śiva, Brahmā, Vishnu, or Kālī); they may be the numerous Bodhisattvas of Buddhist teaching; they may be the ancestor spirits of Native American tradition; it may be God incarnated in the life, death, and resurrection of Jesus of Nazareth. Casting a spell of *māyā*, the Sacred allows each seeker a relationship with it that reflects each individual's needs.

Indeed, this is a doctrine of grace, but grace with a warning:

> But finite is the result gained by these men of small minds. Those who worship the deities go to the deities; those who worship Me come to me. (*Gīta* 7:23)

A single incarnation of the Sacred is a trace, a mask, that imposes limits on the Sacred's reality. We do not see the Sacred; we see its historical and cultural traces. But through the traces, we can perceive its relative inaccessibility under the conditions of space-time. All traces of the Sacred—its *avatār*s or incarnations—say more about us than they do about the Sacred. Still, they link us to it, but only when we refuse to reduce its relative inaccessibility to a single relatively accessible mask.

Has Anyone Seen the Ox?

Cantwell Smith's focus on the historical-cultural relativity of all religious ideas and practices, Hick's pluralistic hypothesis, and the *Bhagavad-gīta*'s theology of many incarnations teach us three lessons. First, the Sacred is the real *par excellence*, at one and the same time power, efficiency, and source of the living and nonliving forces that travel this universe at every moment of space-time. The religious desire to live with the Sacred is also the desire to live in accord with objective reality, not to be paralyzed by endless and purely objective experiences but to live in a world that is real, efficient, and not illusory.

The second lesson is captured in the Hindu tantric saying, *nadevo devam arcayet*, "by none but a god shall a god be worshiped." The deity we worship is a function of our state of mind. This means that it is also a product of our particular history and culture. Inevitably, any image of the Sacred will be a local ethnic idea, a historically conditioned mask, a metaphor, therefore, and thus to be recognized as transparent to transcendence.

But do we ever see the Sacred as such? The answer to this question is the third lesson. We do not see the Sacred, for it is transcendent, beyond the ox-like traces of its names and forms, yet sensed through its numerous names and forms. Thus the Sacred's relative inaccessibility becomes relatively accessible through its traces. We sense the Sacred, but never directly, for it exceeds all limitations, through mask-like symbols.

Of course, in one sense, all knowledge *is* symbolic, and to go deeply into any field—physics, say, or art or history of religions—is to learn faith in its symbols. At first we notice that these tools and objects of thought are symbols; we translate them, as we go, into our own familiar symbols and metaphors. Later, we learn faith and release them. We learn to let them relate on their own terms, hydron to hydron, paint to surface, religious mask to religious mask—and only them do we begin to make progress. In this sense, faith is the requisite of knowledge.

However, symbols not only refer; they act. There is no such thing as *mere* symbol. Whenever we climb to higher levels of abstraction—as I have climbed in this chapter—symbols are all there are. They are at once our only tools of knowledge and that knowledge's only object. It is no leap to say that space-time is itself a symbol. And if the material world is a symbol, it is the symbol of mind, or of God, which is more or less meaningless, as we choose. But it is never *mere*, because in the last analysis, symbols do not stand for things; they manifest them, in their historical fullness. We begin by using symbols, and end by contemplating them.

Moreover, even though every expression and symbolic form of the relatively inaccessible Sacred is relative, it is not necessary that we conclude that all expressions are true or equally valid. If this were so, there would be no reason to write the sort of book I am writing that criticizes both exclusive and inclusive theologies as conceptual errors. Nor would there be a basis for negative criticism of distorted forms of religious faith and practice masked in such guises as racism, or employed to justify oppression of the poor, oppression of women, or political oppression. The point is that some ideas, some symbols, some practices may be closer approximations of the Sacred than others; these are found in all religious Ways. Some may be downright illusions; these too are found in all religious Ways. But issues of truth cannot be decided in advance merely by declaring normative theological judgments about truth or falsehood from the point of view of one's own religious standpoint. No one can occupy the absolute standpoint such absolute judgments demand. Far better to acknowledge that all knowledge is partial and incomplete and, on the basis of this acknowledgment, engage in dialogue with religious perspectives other than our own to avoid both the distortions of our own traditions and the distortions of others.

Likewise, the symbols of the Sacred—every one of humanity's historical images and masks—do not stand for the Sacred; they manifest the Sacred's relative inaccessibility in its historical fullness encountered in the lives of human beings. So it has always been, for how else could the Sacred be experienced except within the cultural strands of human history? Some of these strands have given rise to personal images of the Sacred, each formed in interaction with a particular community or religious Way. But the Sacred is also experienced nonpersonally, both in the negative sense that personality is a function of limited personal interaction and cannot be literally attributed to Sacred, and in the positive sense that the Sacred is validly experienced in nonpersonal as well as personal ways. How to enter into dialogical encounter with each form of humanity's experience with the Sacred is the topic of the next chapter, "Catching the Ox."

Notes

1. D. T. Suzuki, *Manual of Zen Buddhism* (New York: Grove Press, 1960), 130.
2. I have appropriated this metaphor from Annie Dillard's essay "An Expedition to the Pole," in *Teaching a Stone to Talk* (New York: Harper & Row, 1982), 18–19, hopefully in ways I like to think she would approve.
3. Martin Buber, *I and Thou* (New York: Charles Scribner's Sons, 1958), 23.
4. Much of what follows is based on Wilfred Cantwell Smith, *The Meaning and End of Religion* (New York: Macmillan, 1963), chaps. 1–2. Also see his slightly earlier book *The Faith of Other Men* (New York: New American Library, 1963), 105–28.
5. See Wilfred Cantwell Smith, *Faith and Belief* (Princeton: Princeton University Press, 1979), 3–19; idem, *Belief in History* (Charlottesville: University of Virginia Press, 1977), chap. 1.
6. Smith, *Faith and Belief*, viii.
7. Ibid., 50.
8. Ibid., 15–44.
9. Ibid., 44–48.
10. Ibid., 154–57.
11. One of Smith's earliest statements in this regard is chap. 1 of *The Meaning and End of Religion*, and the conclusions of this chapter run throughout his published writings. Also see *Towards a World Theology* (Philadelphia: Westminster Press, 1981) for the most fully developed expression of his pluralistic "theology of world religions," which he would substitute for traditional Christian claims for truth.
12. See my comparison of Buddhist and Christian experience of faith in *The Modern Buddhist-Christian Dialogue* (Lewiston, N.Y.: Edwin Mellen Press, 1988), chap. 4.
13. See John Hick, "A Philosophy of Religious Pluralism," in *Problems of Religious Pluralism*, ed. John Hick (New York: St. Martin's Press, 1985), 28–45. This essay was originally published in *The World's Religious Traditions: Essays in Honor of Wilfred Cantwell Smith*, ed. Frank Whaling (Edinburgh: T. and T. Clark, 1984).

14. John Hick, *God Has Many Names* (Philadelphia: Westminster Press, 1982), 88.

15. This idea is most fully developed by Hick in *An Interpretation of Religion* (New Haven: Yale University Press, 1989), chaps. 10–11.

16. Hick excludes "pre-axial age" religious experience from this analysis, e.g., primal traditions such as Native American, Australian aboriginal, or Shinto. His focus is on the historic "post-axial age" faiths, e.g., Christianity, Buddhism, Islam, Judaism, Hinduism, Confucianism, and Taoism. See *Interpretation of Religion*, 21–33.

17. Hick, *God Has Many Names*, 90.

18. *The Way and Its Power*, trans. Arthur Waley (New York: Grove Press, 1958), 174.

19. Hick, *Interpretation of Religion*, 237.

20. See ibid., 241–49, and Hick, *God Has Many Names*, 103–7.

21. Hick, *God Has Many Names*, 104.

22. Ibid., 105.

23. See Joseph Campbell and Bill Moyers, *Joseph Campbell: The Power of Myth* (New York: Doubleday, 1988), 207–331, and the video entitled *The Masks of Eternity* in the Time-Life video series "Joseph Campbell and the Power of Myth."

24. Hick, *An Interpretation of Religion*, 237.

25. The complete title of the *Bhagavad-gita* is *Śrimad-bhagavad-gita Upanishad*, or "Teachings Given in the Song of the Sublime Exalted One." While, technically speaking, the *Gita* is regarded by Hindus not as "scripture" (*śruti*, "that which is heard") but as "tradition" (*smṛti*, "that which is remembered"), Hindus generally revere this text more than any other. The *Gita* is eighteen chapters of poetic dialogue found in an epic poem called the *Mahabharata*. The main interlocutors of the dialogue are the warrior Arjuna, the "conqueror of sloth," and his friend, Sri Krishna—one of two primary incarnations of the deity Vishnu, the Preserver. My analysis addresses only the *Gita's* theology of incarnation. For a recent translation of entire text, see *The Bhagavad Gita in the Mahābhārata: A Bilingual Edition*, ed. and trans. J. A. B. van Buitenen (Chicago: University of Chicago Press, 1981). Also see Eliot Deutsch, *The Bhagavad Gita* (Lanham, Md.: University Press of America, 1968). All quotations from the *Gita* I have cited are from Swami Nikhilananda's translation, *The Bhagavad-gita* (New York: Ramakrishna-Vivekananda Center, 1944).

26. For a good introductory description of these three yogas and the personality types for which they are best suited, see Huston Smith, *The Religions of the World* (New York: Harper-Collins, 1991), 20–41.

得牛 四

4
Catching the Ox

"CATCHING THE OX," THE FOURTH OX-HERDING PICTURE, REQUIRES THAT ITS traces be seen. Yet once the traces are seen, catching what we see becomes very difficult, especially for writers trying to catch the ox with words. Like the man in the fourth picture, seeing without knowing what he sees, we have the ox in our hands, though not without hard struggle. It constantly yearns for sweet-scented fields and fights for unrestricted freedom. Its wild nature refuses domestication. To paraphrase this picture's commentary, if the man wishes to be in complete harmony with his ox, he must use the whip freely.[1] Or, as the poem says:

> With the energy of his whole being, the man has at last taken hold of
>   the Ox;

But how wild its will, how ungovernable its power;
At times it struts up a plateau,
When lo! It is lost again in a misty unpenetrable mountain pass.[2]

This chapter is concerned with how human beings have everywhere, in all times and places, tried to capture the relatively inaccessible Sacred they have seen through its mythological, scriptural, and doctrinal traces. The specific issue of this chapter is the relation between personal and nonpersonal experiences and symbols of the Sacred, and it draws heavily upon John Hick's "pluralistic hypothesis" and Wilfred Cantwell Smith's analysis of faith. My thesis is that both personal and nonpersonal experience and symbols reflect one Sacred reality from limited cultural and historical perspectives.

Of all persons who seek to catch the ox, writers must seem the strangest. We lust after the perfect word, the glorious phrase that will somehow make the exquisite avalanche of what we see sayable. We live in mental and emotional barrios where any idea may turn to honest labor, if it gets the right incentive—a little wine, a light flogging, a delicate seduction, a kick in the behind. It is a great deal of trouble because writers, like all living beings, must live in their senses.

The problem is, there is a point of ecstasy beyond which the senses cannot lead us. Ecstasy means being flung out of our usual selves. But that is still to feel the commotion inside, which is why writers and artists are pulled into mysticism. Whatever else mysticism does, it transcends the here-and-now for truths unexplainable in the straightjacket of language. But even this transcendence registers on the senses, too, as a rush of fire in the belly, a quivering in the chest, a quiet fossil-like surrender in the bones.

We can see anything from a new perspective, but it is still an experience of vision. Computers now help us interpret some of life's complicated processes, which we previously used our senses to see. Astronomers are more likely to look at their telescope's monitors than to consider the stars with their naked eyes. But we continue to use our senses to interpret the work of computers, to see the monitors, and to judge and analyze. Never will we leave the mansions of our perceptions.

If we are in a rut, it is an exquisite one. Like prisoners in a cell, we grip our ribs from within, rattle them, and beg for release. Especially when language filters our perceptions of the relatively inaccessible ox's sensory traces. There are always questions. According to the Bible, God once instructed Moses to burn sweet incense to God's liking. Does God have nostrils? Can, or does, God really prefer one smell of this earth to another? The processes of decay complete a cycle necessary for growth. Carrion—the stale honey-sweet odor of death—is stench to our nostrils but smells delicious to animals who rely on it for food. What those same animals excrete will make soil rich and crops abundant. There is no need for divine election; perception is itself a form of grace. We catch the ox with our senses and lasso it with words, knowing the rope will eventually break, for the Sacred is beyond words, yet always there, stalking us.

So, like the stealth of autumn, the Sacred is apt to catch us when we are not looking. Was that a goldfinch perching in the early September woods surrounding my house? A robin or a maple closing up shop for the winter? Keen-eyed as cougars, we stand still and squint hard for signs of movement while early morning frost sits heavy on the leaves and turns barbed wire into a string of stars. The Sacred is a force and, like others, can be resisted. Even if we do not want to catch the ox, it is there backtracking us all the same. It is as if the relatively inaccessible Sacred is saying, "I am here, but not as you have known me or want to know me. Do you see this look of silence, and of loneliness unendurable? It too has always been mine, and now it shall be yours."

Historically, the relatively inaccessible ox's traces have been sensed and caught in personal and nonpersonal masks. In spite of numerous differences between their cumulative traditions, the personal deities of theistic religious Ways and the nonpersonal Sacred reality of nontheistic religious Ways have this in common: they have effected the transformation of human lives from self-centeredness to centeredness in the deity worshiped or in the Sacred reality nonpersonally apprehended in the zero-point of meditative awareness called *samādhi* or *satori*. This transformed state is one of freedom from narrow self-focused egoism, a consequent realization of inner peacefulness and integration with the universe, coupled with awareness in love and compassion of the oneness of humanity with life in all forms.

Accordingly, if I have read the historical evidence of humanity's religious experience adequately, devout Jews or Christians or Muslims or theistic Hindus or Pure Land Buddhists throwing themselves in faith into reliance on the Lord, the Bhagavan, the Highest Person, the all-compassionate Amida Buddha, all undergo in varying degrees this salvific transformation. Likewise, single-minded Advaitic Hindus, Theravada or Zen Buddhists, or Taoists seriously practicing a path of meditation that leads to the dissolution of the metaphysical boundaries between self and other, self and world, self and the Sacred also undergo in varying degrees the same liberating transformation. Such similar processes of self-transformation suggest that theistic and nontheistic masks of the ox reflect different modes of catching the relatively inaccessible Sacred. The deities the majority of human beings revere are personalized masks through which the ox is partly caught by the theistic religious Ways of humanity. Likewise, the nonpersonal traces of the Sacred caught by the disciples of nontheistic religious Ways are no less real.

Catching the Ox Personally

How are the multitudes of religious awareness formed? According to John Hick's pluralistic hypothesis "they are formed by the presence of a divine reality, this presence coming to consciousness in terms of different sets of religious concepts and structures of religious meaning that operate within different religious traditions of the world."[3] The vast majority of human beings have come to consciousness of the relatively inaccessible Sacred through a range of specific deities. Such religious experience is primary not only in the numerical sense that most human beings who have experienced the Sacred and captured the ox have done so through the masks of various gods. Judging from the Paleolithic cave paintings of the Grotto of Lascaux in France, experience of the Sacred as a personal deity or set of deities with whom one is in relationship represents also the most archaic expression of religious experience.

However, no one has ever encountered deity "in general" or, for that matter, the nonpersonal relatively inaccessible Sacred "in general." We never experience anything "in general" but only "in particular,"[4] always wrapped in specific masks. For as there are different concrete ways of being human and of participating in history, so it is that within the contexts of these different historical-cultural ways the presence of the Sacred is experienced differently.

Christians capture the relatively inaccessible Sacred ox through stories of the life, death, and resurrection of the historical Jesus of Nazareth confessed to be the Christ. Christians bet their lives on these stories about the historical beginning of a new salvific relationship between themselves and God the Father and the Father's continuing work in the world through the Holy Spirit. Similarly, Jews bet their lives on the gift of Yahweh's Torah ("Instructions") and the resulting covenant established between the people of Israel and their Lord through Moses on Mount Sinai. Muslims surrender their wills (ʿislām) to Allah, "the God," as "recited" by the Prophet Muhammad in the Qurʾān, "the Book wherein there is no doubt," wherein God recorded the "straight way" of humanity's most complete religion. In Indian devotional religious faith and practice (bhakti), the Sacred is experienced as Śiva, Kālī, Vishnu, Paramatma, Krishna, Rāma, Durgā—in as many forms of Brahman as you please. Even Mahayana Buddhists, perhaps the majority, encounter the Dharma beyond name and form masked by a multiplicity of Bodhisattvas. Native Americans, like primal people past and present, encounter the Sacred masked by wind, animals, mountains, lakes, rivers, sun, moon, stars, and the natural forces of growth and decay.

Still, there is something nonpersonal about these masks of the Sacred. It is not just that the gods often interrelate with nature and human beings non-personally—Jesus noticed that like God's rain, God's love for creation is disinterested and falls on the just and the unjust equally, so don't take it personally. The "masks of God" also reveal that the relatively inaccessible ox is infinitely beyond the scope of our understanding and our abilities to capture it through any mask. For masks are symbolic pointers without which we cannot get very far; but the pointers should not be confused with the sacred reality to which they point. Or, restated from a different angle, the "masks of God" are metaphors; it is difficult to get very far without our metaphors, but they hinder our seeing when we get stuck on them. Getting stuck on our metaphors is idolatry and constitutes the error of all religious fundamentalisms. This error too is an ancient perception found in every religious Way. According to the *Rig Veda*:

> They call It Indra, Mitra, Varuna and Agni
> And also heavenly, beautiful Garutman:
> The Real is One, though sages name it variously. (I:164:46)[5]

Even so, personal masks of the Sacred are evident even in so stridently a nontheistic tradition as Theravada Buddhism. For example, in the account of Gautama the Buddha's death recorded in the *Dīgha-nikāya* (Collection of long discourses), it is said that "the gods of the ten world systems assembled together to behold the Tathāgata ('the Thus-Come One')" (*Dīgha-nikāya* II:253)[6] because they "often assembled there that they might visit the Exalted One and the band of brethren."[7] Furthermore, the Indian creator deity, Brahma, plays a vital part in the inauguration of the Buddhist Way.

According to the story, when Gautama achieved the meditative wisdom that transformed him from an unenlightened seeker into an awakened Buddha, he thought the truth he discovered might be too lofty and difficult for humankind to grasp. But Mahā Brahmā, Great Brahma, the supreme creator intervened on humanity's behalf:

> And the Great Brahmā, brethren, draping his outer robe over one shoulder and stooping his right knee to the ground raised his joined hands toward Vipassi the Exalted One, the Arahant, the Buddha Supreme and said: "Lord, may the Exalted One preach the Truth! May the Welcome One preach the Truth! There are beings whose eyes are hardly dimmed by dust, they are perishing from not hearing the Truth; they will come to be knowers of the Truth. (*Dīgha-nikāya* II:37)[8]

So the Buddha felt compassion and set the Wheel of Dharma spinning for the salvation of the world.

While no doubt Theravada ("elder's school") Buddhist tradition is not atheistic in the sense of denying the existence of gods, it is thoroughly nontheistic in its denial that the gods are helpful in our quest for liberation. For the deities are temporal beings still locked within the finite process of space-time that the Buddha transcended. They are, in Kant's language, divine phenomena rather than the Sacred noumenon itself.[9] Yet the need to experience the Dharma in personal form played an important role in Buddhist history, particularly in the evolution of the Mahayana Buddhist Way.

Mahayana ("great vehicle") faith and practice emerged during the latter years of the last century B.C.E. and the beginning of the first century C.E., primarily as a result of interaction with the classical movements of Hindu devotionalism that swept through northern India during this time. There occurred a fairly rapid elevation of the person of the Buddha from the greatest of human teachers to a transcendent being of universal power and significance, allied with a multiplicity of "saviors" called *bodhisattvas,* Buddhas-in-the-making whose "being is enlightenment," and who help us wake up to the Dharma.

A number of Mahayana texts even refer to a "cosmic Buddha." For example, the *Lotus Sutra* describes the Buddha as *devatideva,* "supreme god of gods."[10] Other Buddhist tantric texts posit a universal Buddha called Mahavairocana ("Great Sun") as the absolute ultimate reality of which all other Buddhas are limited expressions.[11] Finally, the *trikāya,* or "three body," teaching of Mahayana tradition notes that historical Buddhas such as Gautama constitute a "historical body" (*nirmānakāya*). There are also incarnations of nonhistorical Buddhas who dwell in their own Buddha Land, enjoying their "body of bliss" (*sambhogakāya*). But these two forms of enlightened existence are partial manifestations of the supreme ultimate reality called the *dharmakāya,* or "body of enlightenment," which is, being formless and transcending all things and events in space-time, that to which all particular Buddhas awake at the moment of enlightenment.[12]

But perhaps the best known example of Mahayana Buddhist attempts to personalize the nonpersonal relatively inaccessible Sacred is the practice of Bodhisattva veneration. Bodhisattvas, "Buddhas-to-be," personify enlightened compassion. Instead of entering fully into the enlightened state called *nirvāna,* thereby becoming "extinct" in the phenomenal world of space-time, they elect to remain "this side of *nirvāna"* to lead every sentient being from suffering. As compassionate forms of the Dharma, they are objects of worship and devotion.

Similar developments occurred in Chinese religious history. According to traditions that predate both the *Tao Te Ching* (Classic on the way and its power) and the teachings of Kung Fu Tzu (Confucius), all things and events in the universe originate in, mirror and are mirrored by, and return to the Tao's (the "Way's") balancing act between opposite polar forces called *yin* and *yang*. Thus the Tao is the ultimate reality "in, with, and under," to use Martin Luther's words, all things and events in nature—including the deities. It is beyond form, beyond definition, for "the Way that can be told of is not an Unvarying Way" and "Those who know do not speak; those who speak do not know."[13] Deities do not transcend the natural forces of *yin* and *yang*, but like all things, reflect these forces.

Yet the Chinese people primarily experienced the Tao through a number of ancestor and community deities (*shen*), in spite of the pervasive reverence for the nonpersonal philosophy of the *Tao Te Ching* and the mysticism of Chuang Tzu (between 399 and 295 B.C.E.) and the established Confucian tradition originating with Confucius and continuing through a lineage of teachers from Mencius (371-289? B.C.E.) to Chu Hsi (1130-1200 C.E.).

However, it is in the Western monotheistic religious Ways—Judaism, Christianity, and Islam—that the nonpersonal relatively inaccessible Sacred is most radically encountered as a divine person, *personae* in Greek, beyond imagination, the absolute creator and lord of the universe "He" creates. God is infinite, beyond definition, yet religiously experienced through personal attributes that correspond to our experience of other human beings, yet remaining beyond the limitations of our finitude. However, the language of infinity does not arise from religious experience itself, although it is present in much of the ritual language that has evolved in the great monotheisms. That is, concepts of infinity originate in Jewish, Christian, and Islamic theological reflection, not in the religious experience of practicing Jews, Christians, or Muslims.

In classical Christian theology, for example, God is discussed largely in terms of possessing a series of infinite attributes: infinite goodness and love, infinite wisdom and justice, omnipotence and omniscience, eternity. God is described in this language as good, loving, wise, just, powerful, and all-knowing—and as an added metastatement—possessing these qualities infinitely. God's self-existence is also a kind of infinity—infinite uncaused existence.

However, the infinite attributes imputed to God by Christian, Jewish, and Muslim theology do not reflect the religious experience of human beings. As finite observers, we can never directly experience, observe, or verify infinite dimensions of an infinite reality. Consequently, while it *is* given in religious *experience* that God is good, loving, powerful, and just, it cannot be given in human experience that God has these personal qualities to an infinite extent.

Such judgments are secondary-level doctrinal abstractions drawn from religious experience.

So the Sacred's personal qualities—goodness, for example—can only be affirmed on the basis of a believer's experience of God's grace. There appears to be no other way to verify it. As one of the Psalms says: "O taste and see that the Lord is good! Happy is the man who takes refuge in him!" (Psalm 34:8). But we cannot "taste and see" that the Lord is infinitely good, even though it may be true that what we experience is goodness beyond the boundaries of normal experience. The further conviction that this goodness is infinite is an abstract conclusion drawn from theological reflection on this experience.

What I am suggesting is that in the first-order experience of religious persons, the relatively inaccessible Sacred is not apprehended as an infinite being having unlimited personal attributes; it is "seen" under concrete images ranging in magnitude from limited to indefinitely great. This can be illustrated by example from the Hebrew Bible, where God is described as a warrior-king for his people: "The Lord is a man of war" (Psalm 15:3). God is also described as speaking (Genesis 1:3), as hearing (Exodus 16:12), as laughing (Psalm 2:4) and as having eyes (Amos 9:4), hands (Psalms 139:5), arms (Isaiah 22:14) and feet (Nahum 1:3) which he rests on a footstool (Isaiah 66:1). God comes down from heaven (Genesis 11:17) and cools off from the heat of the day by walking in the Garden of Eden (Genesis 3:8). God grows jealous, angry, and weeps. God changes his mind. On rare occasions, God is even seen by human beings.

Of course, the meaning of "personal," and of a whole family of related English words—"person," "personality," "personhood," "personalize"—ultimately derives from observing the same basic facts of human existence. We grow and interact with other human beings, each of us undergoing our own stream of experience and reacting in our own way, partly because of our genetic ground plan, partly because of participation in the cultural life of a society of human beings, each of us aware of our individual self-identity through time. This is why, according to John Hick,

> . . . the Real *an sich* cannot be said to be personal. For this would presuppose that the Real is eternally in relation to other persons. Whilst this is of course conceivable, it constitutes pure *ad hoc* speculation rather than the most economical interpretation of the available data. For these include the facts (a) that the only persons whom we know, namely humans, have existed (in their present form, *homo sapiens*) for about fifty-thousand years, and therefore cannot provide an eternal dialogue-partner for the Real, and (b) that among humans the Real is experienced in non-personal as well as in personal ways. We may reasonably conclude, then, that the Real is personal not *an sich* but in interaction with human (and/or other finite) persons.[14]

In other words, personality is not an eternally unchanging essence but an ever-changing series of relationships constituted by the ways human beings experience other human beings and the world, and are experienced by other human beings as they act upon us and as we act upon them. Somewhere in the process, selfhood and personality emerge, covered by a range of overlapping public *personae* that we wear as we interact with the relationships constantly forming us.

Originally, a *persona* was a mask Roman actors wore as they played different roles. But unlike the masks of classical Roman theater, our *personae* are not simply external coverings we put on or take off relative to a particular group or social role we must play; we *are* the *persona* we become within those relationships. Accordingly, my students' images of me—part of my *persona* in relation to them—*are* me, insofar as I am part of a university community conjointly formed with them. For a *persona* is a social reality living in the conscious experience, memories, and ongoing interactions of a community.[15]

The fact that we are *personae* within different social contexts provides an analogy for imagining the plurality of the Sacred's *personae* that have evolved within different religious Ways. If the relatively inaccessible Sacred is always present to human beings wherever they live, the gods of theistic forms of religious experience are *personae* of the Sacred experienced in different streams of humanity's religious history.

This analogy, however, is only partial. Different *personae* worn by the same human self are particular and finite collections of relationships in constant transition. But the multiple *personae* of the Sacred do not mask a greater self-entity than all human selves, but an ultimate reality that transcends human conceptuality and the range of personal and nonpersonal masks through which we relate to it. Even so, as John Hick notes,[16] and as the *Bhagavad-gīta* teaches, experience of the Sacred as personal expresses the way deities are formed in interrelation with their worshipers. For deities are idealized projections of the character and needs of their worshipers *and* manifestations of the Sacred. Personal masks of the Sacred capture the ox at the interface between the relatively inaccessible Sacred and human creativity and need. Thus, it is as true to say, in the image of Genesis, that humanity is made in the image of God, as it is to say that we make God in our image. This is not idolatry. Like new particles created from the explosion of protons meeting head-on near the speed of light in a particle accelerator, masks of the Sacred are the end result of the relatively inaccessible Sacred colliding head-on with human imagination: in Christian language, where revelation meets human seeking.

Hindu theistic tradition, as illustrated by the *Bhagavad-gīta*'s theology of

Brahman's incarnation in a multitude of *avatār*-forms is echoed in the theistic traditions of the West as well. Every quality we attribute to God—in fact all theological conclusions, wrote Thomas Aquinas (1225-1274), are analogues drawn from human relationships with one another and with the world.[17] The Muslim Sufi master and contemporary of Aquinas, Ibn al ʿArabi (1165-1240) wrote something similar about the relation between the personalized attributes we ascribe to the Sacred and the Sacred's unlimited reality.

> God is absolute or restricted as He pleases; and the God of religious beliefs is subject to limitations, for He is the God contained in the heart of His servant. But the absolute God is not contained in anything.[18]

ʿArabi also wrote about how the relatively inaccessible revealer of the *Qurʾān* meets us where we are, in the analogues of our knowing:

> The Essence, as being beyond all these relationships, is not a divinity . . . it is we who make Him a divinity by being that through which He knows Himself as Divine. Thus, He is not known [as "Allah"] until we are known.[19]

Finally, Ibn al ʿArabi, even more than Aquinas, was fully aware of the primordial implications of this idea.

> In general, most men have . . . an individual concept of their Lord, which they ascribe to Him and in which they seek Him. So long as the Reality is presented to them, according to it they recognize Him and affirm Him, whereas if presented in any other form, they deny Him, flee from Him and treat Him improperly, while at the same time imagining that they are acting toward Him fittingly. One who believes [in the ordinary way] believes only in the deity he has created in himself, since a deity in "beliefs" is a [mental] construction.[20]

Catching the Ox Nonpersonally

Most religious persons try to catch their ox by means of various *personae* which are normally regarded within the faith-worlds that engender them as absolute ultimate reality. I have drawn two opposite conclusions: (1) the *personae* upon which human beings bet their lives in faithful trust are limited glimpses of the relatively inaccessible Sacred; they are different forms of the same ox; and (2) since all personified masks of the Sacred point beyond their limited *personae* to a Sacred reality reducible to no form, nonpersonal experience of the Sacred most closely approximates what the ox's reality is. This does not mean that all religious ways have conceptually identical teachings. Obviously, this is not true and never has been. The modes of experience by which the Sacred manifests itself to human consciousness are shaped by the conceptual frameworks and religious practices of particular cumulative traditions.

These two conclusions reflect my reading of the *Bhagavad-gīta,* but more ancient Indian texts make similar claims. "Thou art formless," declares the *Yogava'sistha,* "thy only form is our knowledge of thee" (1:28).[21] According to the *Chāndogya Upanishad,* Brahman, "Sacred Power," is "One without a second" (VI.2:3);[22] mistaking our sensual experience of multiple things, persons, and events as the full truth about the way things really are is a cosmic delusion (*māyā*) grounded in "ignorance" (*avidyā*) about the one reality that unifies all things and events at every moment of space-time. Caught in self-created delusion (*māyā*), we think of ourselves as separate egos, cut off from other things, events, and persons—from nature itself. Believing we are separate selves, we become selfish—toward everything; and we do not see the "One without a second" that unifies the real pluralities of the universe.

It is the delusion of individual identity—absolutizing our experience of particularity as final truth—that separates us from the universal Brahman incarnated as the "Self" (*ātman*) of each individual thing and event—deities, human beings, sentient life, and nonsentient entities. Of course there is separateness and particularity: male and female, left and right, pleasure and pain, light and dark, black and white, up and down, sacred and profane. But what is masculinity without femininity and vice versa? Is there left without right, pleasure without pain? It is darkness that defines light, pitch that creates harmony. There is no black without white, up without down, sacred apart from profane. For Brahman is the inner reality, the Self, unifying all particulars in this universe, as the unity of "heads" and "tails" in an American coin is what unites the Euclidean surfaces of its two sides. Ignorance (*avidyā*) and delusion (*māyā*) misinterpret our individual experiences of separate individuality for the absolute truth. In other words, Brahman equals Atman, Sacred Power equals the inner Self of everything, because Brahman

> . . . is the Ear of the ear, the Mind of the mind, the Speech of speech, the Life of life, and the Eye of the eye. . . . That which cannot be expressed by speech, but by which speech is expressed—That alone know as Brahman, and not that which people here worship. That which cannot be apprehended by the mind, but by which, they say, the mind is apprehended—That alone know as Brahman, and not that which people here worship. That which cannot be perceived by the eye, but by which the eye is perceived—that alone know as Brahman, and not that which people here worship. That which cannot be heard by the ear, but by which the hearing is perceived—That alone know as Brahman, and not that which people here worship. (*Kena Upanishad* 1:2–8)[23]

Or in a simile often used by Śaṅkara (788–820?), the "founder" of Advaita ("nondual") Vedanta, the relatively inaccessible Brahman is like space enclosed in a jar: it appears to have a separate shape and identity from space in other jars or space occupied by all jars. Break the jar, and what remains is what was always there—limitless space.[24] Likewise, the enclosing wall of *avidyā*—ignorance of the nondual relation between our deepest Selves (*atman*) and Brahman—is dissolved at the moment of *mokṣa*, the "liberating release" from egoism that keeps us bound to the wheel of life and death that occurs at the moment we see (*darśan*) our Self as Brahman.

Similar liberation occurs through the practice of Buddhist meditation. Buddhist faith and practice begin with human experience of "the three marks of existence": old age, disease, and death. Thus, "all life is *duḥkha*, or "suffering" or "unsatisfactoriness." This does not mean that every moment of human experience is *only* pain and anguish; but it does mean that all human experience is subject to *duḥkha*. Pain, disease, decay, hardship, frustrated desire, and involvement in the sorrows of others come to us all, while death gives our lives terminal closure.

The Buddhist point is not that *duḥkha* simply exists; it has a cause, and once the cause is identified, it can be overcome. The cause of *duḥkha* is thirst (*tṛṣta*) and desire (*taṇhā*) for permanent existence in a universe constituted by an ever-changing network of interdependent, "co-originating" impermanent events (*pratītya-samutpāda*, "dependent co-origination"). Things and events come to be and cease to be in an interdependent way, with no thing that endures. We grasp at permanence: permanent life, permanent pleasure, permanent well-being, like someone grasping water in a closed fist. We never succeed, because permanence is not there to be grasped.

We will continue to suffer so long as we misinterpret the world as an object separate from ourselves, as pleasurable or painful, to be grasped or avoided accordingly in our search for permanent self-existence. The liberation the Buddha proclaimed from this self-induced suffering is *nibbāna* (Sanskrit, *nirvāṇa*), the goal and cumulative experience of the practice of meditation.

Most often, Theravada Buddhist doctrine describes *nibbāna* as the "extinction" of greed, hatred, and the delusion that we are permanent selves. Other descriptions stress *nibbāna* as the extinction of the root causes of suffering: thirst (*tṛṣta*), desire (*taṇhā*), and ignorance (*avidyā*). Still again, *nibbāna* is described as the absence of the ignorant delusion that we are separate individual substantial selves. In other words, "*nibbāna* is the consummation of the *anattā* ["non-self"] doctrine."[25]

It seems, then, that the experience of *nibbāna* involves a progressive realization of the emptiness of independent selfhood engendered in our lives through meditative experience of the *Dhamma* (Sanskrit *Dharma*), the Buddhist word for the relatively inaccessible Sacred. Such an experience, while indescribable, is knowable. It is also very pleasant, moving, indeed blissful and joyous to the person who experiences it. It not only transforms unenlightened seekers into Buddhas; it remains knowable after death as *khandha-parinibbāna*, "the full extinction of the elements of existence."

Kandha-parinibbāna is not often discussed in Buddhist literature.[26] It is, however, the causal effect of another form of enlightenment called *kilesa-parinibbāna*, "the full extinction of defilements." This form of enlightenment involves the extinction of greed, hatred, desire, and all other delusions binding us to the realm of suffering existence while we are alive. *Khandha-parinibbāna* is the completion of "the full extinction of defilements" that occurs after the death of a Buddha.

Consequently, *nibbāna* "extinguishes" anything that hinders whatever is supremely valuable, good, and real. For those who attain this state, enlightenment turns out to be an absolutely positive experience of the relatively inaccessible Sacred called the Dhamma–Dharma in Mahayana Buddhist tradition. Its achievement is, in the fullest English meaning of the word, "salvation." For as the Buddha himself is reported to have declared:

> Verily, there is an Unborn, Unoriginated, Uncreated, Unformed. If there were not this Unborn, Unoriginated, Uncreated, Unformed, escape from the world of the born, the originated, the created, the formed, would not be possible. (*Udana* VIII, 3)[27]

Mahayana Buddhist practice and teaching expand and deepen Theravada conceptions of *nibbāna*. To what Theravada Buddhists call the "three marks of existence"—suffering, impermanence, and nonself—Mahayana Buddhists add a fourth mark, "emptiness" (*śūnyatā*). In Theravada teaching, "emptiness" designates the impossibility of being a substantially independent self-entity. Mahayana teaching expands this idea by categorically denying the possibility of substantial self-identity through time within *any* of the "elements of existence" (*dharmas*) constituting existence at every moment of space-time.[28]

The source of the Mahayana concept of "emptiness" was the discovery that *samsāra*, the phenomenal world we experience through the senses, and *nirvāna* are nondual. That is, as experienced from the self-enclosed point of view of our ego, the universe and the world we perceive are an endless round of anxiety-ridden, living-and-dying, sentient beings. But to the egoless consciousness of a mind liberated by the attainment of enlightenment, the ordinary world is seen as no different from *nirvāna*. That is, enlightenment transforms the self *along with* the world. The Chinese Ch'an (Japanese, Zen) teacher Hsüeh-yen Tsu-ch'in (d. 1287) described his experience of the non-duality of *saṃsāra* and *nirvāṇa* this way:

> The experience was beyond description and altogether incommunicable, for there was nothing in the world to which it could be compared. . . . As I looked around and up and down, the whole universe with its multitudinous sense-objects now appeared quite different; what was loathsome before, together with ignorance and passions, was now seen to be nothing else but the outflow of my own inmost nature which in itself remained bright, true, and transparent. This state of consciousness lasted for more than half a month.[29]

Enlightenment is the experience of *śūnyatā*, inadequately translated as "Emptiness," "Void," or "Formlessness." Reality, "the way things really are," the relatively inaccessible Sacred, *is śūnyatā*, Emptiness. But the question is, "Empty of what?" The answer to this question is not easily seen through the standard English translations, for "emptiness" is simultaneously "fullness," if Hsüeh-yen Tsu-ch'in's account of his experience is credible. "Emptiness" is also "fullness," because when we are empty of discriminating self-contained egoism, the world we experience is "emptied" of everything our thoughts have projected upon it; it is experienced just as it is, as we experience ourselves just as we are in interconnection with the world—full of pure suchness (*tathātā*). The Dharma *is* Emptiness, meaning that the world itself is void of self-centered valuations, distinctions, and perspectives. When we cease distorting our environment by discriminating, comparing, contrasting, and evaluating from our own perspective as if it were the only one possible, we experience "the way things really are," as clear mirrors reflect whatever stands before them as they are, without judgment or evaluation.

This is why the Zen Buddhist philosopher and teacher Masao Abe thinks that "Emptiness" is a misleading translation of *śūnyatā*.

> So I think that "everything is empty" may be more adequately rendered in this way: "Everything is just as it is." A pine tree is a pine tree; a bamboo is a bamboo; a dog is a dog; a cat is a cat; you are you; I am I; she is she. Every-thing is different from everything else. And yet while everything and every-one retain their uniqueness and particularity, they are free from conflict because they have no self-nature. This is the meaning of saying that every-thing is empty.[30]

According to Mahayana Buddhism in general, then, and Zen Buddhism in particular, "everything is just as it is" because *śūnyatā* is immanent in the world's processes. It can be experienced at each moment of existence through a mind purified of egoistic anthropomorphic projections. Thus, seen from an enlightened perspective, the universe is like an ocean of interdependent and interpenetrating change (*pratītya-samutpāda*); nothing exists in and of itself, not even the Sacred. Every thing and event exist only in interdependence with every other thing and event at every moment of space-time. "Nothing exists in and of itself" is *śūnyatā*, "emptiness," or perhaps "emptying." All things are "empty" of independent, substantial "self-nature" (Sanskrit, *svabhāva*) remaining self-identical through time.[31] In this sense, then, Sunyata refers to a relatively inaccessible sacred reality beyond the scope of concepts, knowable only through the masks of its manifestations in the experience of meditation.

Hindu and Buddhist experience are not the only religious Ways that affirm that the relatively inaccessible Sacred transcends every conceptual and institutional attempt to catch its reality. Similar insights are affirmed in Chinese Taoist faith and practice as well as in hard-core theistic traditions such as Judaism, Christianity, and Islam. Furthermore, similar insights occur in "primal" religious ways, from Native American traditions to Australian aboriginal experience of "dream time." Since the cumulative religious traditions of humanity claim, in differing degrees, the possibility of direct intuition of a relatively inaccessible sacred reality transcendent to all claims about it, a few remarks about the nature of this sort of experience, in the West often called "mystical," are necessary.

More on Mystical Seeing

According to all traditions of the Buddhist Way, "enlightenment" is a "way of seeing" the way things really are, as opposed to seeing things as we wish them to be. In such an experience, it is claimed, we realize that all things and events interrelate and interpenetrate, that reality is "nondual," that separate selfhood, particularity, and difference are "secondary truths," nothing more than creative fictions. The enlightened ones know better. They have—through reflection, prayer, and meditation—transcended egoism and the entire conceptual apparatus through which the ego reads reality from its limited perspective. In other words, catching the ox through the experience of enlightenment is a unitive, nonpersonal intuition of ultimate reality, or what I have called the relatively inaccessible Sacred.

This is different from ordinary states of consciousness and seeing in which our egos affirm themselves against a world of objects. Enlightenment, according to twenty-five hundred years of Buddhist testimony, transcends the dualistic structure of ordinary consciousness. Enlightenment destroys the subject–object split of ordinary experience by unifying us with all things and events. In the metaphor I appropriated from Annie Dillard, the relatively inaccessible Sacred and our awareness of it are "nondual."

Buddhists regard the unitive knowledge of enlightenment as real and final, radically different from other forms of knowledge. Like the theological claims of Christianity and Islam to absolute revealed truth, Theravada *nibbāna* or Mahayana *śūnyatā* is placed beyond questioning or criticism. Here lies the hiccup that alerts us to the need for comprehensive theoretical interpretation: certain forms of the Hindu Way make an essentially identical claim.

For example, followers of Advaita Hindu tradition tell us that in our true being, our deepest Self (*ātman*) is one with Brahman. By overcoming egoism in a long process of spiritual growth through many lifetimes, we may achieve *mokṣa*, final "spiritual release" from the cyclic processes of birth and death that pin us like butterflies in a collector's tray to the wheel of Samsaric suffering. *Mokṣa* is unitive knowledge of the eternally transcendent Sacred manifested in one's deepest Self: *satyasya satyam*, "the truth of the truth" (*Brihadaranyaka Upanishad* II:iii:6),[32] in comparison to which ordinary truth claims are dreamlike delusions.

So the relatively inaccessible Sacred caught in the unitive experience of Buddhist enlightenment is completely immanent in the ever-changing forms that constitute this universe. But the unitive experience of the "great identity" in Advaitic Hindu tradition *distinguishes* reality from illusion. Accordingly, we have two conceptually incompatible accounts of experience of the Sacred. Is the Sacred the wondrous interconnectedness of the universe's processes, undistorted by the web of concepts through which we structure the self–other duality? Or is the Sacred the eternally unchanging Brahman with which we are ultimately identical—pure being beyond the process of natural existence, in comparison to which everything else is less than real?

Similar questions occur in other forms of mysticism? For example, is the Sacred as experienced through Christian *personae*, sometimes in unitive mystical experience—as indicated by Meister Eckhart when he wrote, "If I am to know God directly, I must become completely He and He I; so that this He and this I become one I"[33]—really a loving father concerned with even the life of sparrows? Or is the Sacred really "the Merciful, the Compassionate, the All-knowing"—three of the ninety-nine beautiful names for God in the *Qur'ān*, whom the Islamic mystic Al-Hallāj (d. 922) saw when he uttered the words that got him flayed alive for idolatry, *Ana'l-Haqq*, "I am God"?[34] Or is the Sacred really all of these—and more?

Observable conceptual differences between different traditions of nonpersonal encounter of the relatively inaccessible Sacred suggest that mystics do not float free from their cultural and historical conditioning any more than nonmystics. Mystics are embodied minds, rooted in specific times and places. They bring their Christian or Islamic or Buddhist or Hindu or Taoist or

Muslim or Jewish or Sikh expectations with them on the mystical path. And, like all human beings, mystics are guided by their training toward the sorts of experiences their respective traditions have conceptually trained them to expect.[35] This does not mean that mystics are irrational or dwell in illusions because they do not and cannot share identical conceptual interpretations of what they experience. Rather, the differences between mystical reports of unitive experience of the ox are evidence for two opposite conclusions: (1) even in nonpersonal mystical experience, a mystic's mind operates within culturally inherited concepts, so that (2) what mystics experience are conceptually and culturally filtered forms of the Sacred, *not* the Sacred as such. For, as mystics universally testify, the relatively inaccessible Sacred cannot be caught; it catches us—perhaps most often—through culturally relative, historically conditioned, limited *personae* and occasionally through nonpersonal unitive experience. But no experience covers the whole story because, as Moses was given to understand on Mount Sinai, no one can see the Sacred completely and live.

So what is mystical consciousness like? What happens if we find ourselves in union with the Sacred? All mystics seem to agree that the experience, whatever "it" is, *must be* experienced to be known, that words used to interpret the experience are secondary and *do not*, when it comes down to it, fully capture the ox. So, what is the experience of partially catching the ox personally or nonpersonally like?

A few years ago I think I caught a glimpse while hiking alone on the northern coast of the Olympic Peninsula in Washington State. I followed a game trail through opaque, self-concealing forest that broke onto a boulder- and driftwood-covered beach. It was an old trail, mostly taken over by deer on their way to a nearby creek that emptied onto the beach. Old-growth western hemlock, Douglas fir, and red cedar loomed overhead from a floor matted with feathery moss, as if pulled up by invisible wires into the coast fog. In this rain-forest, it is always dark and wet, even in summer.

I walked onto the beach into a setting sun that painted everything in orange acrylic—waves breaking hard on the rocks, forest crowding the beach in an unbroken line running northwest to southeast, fog covering the beach like a shroud, light rain dimpling the creek losing itself in the breakers. Sharp sounds popped across the rocks on my left, and I saw two elk—a bull and a cow—run as if on cue over a tree-lined hill.

My thoughts drifted away from the forest, the earth, the sea, the light, the elk, and focused inside myself. I became sharply conscious of my own breathing—a cool, fresh sensation of energy rushing from the life of the forest into my chest, and then warm, moist air brushing against my face soft as a kiss as I exhaled. And suddenly I knew: every breath I take draws the flesh of the earth and the universe into myself. I breathe in soft, saturated exhalations of red cedar and salmon berry bush, fire weed and wood fern, osprey and black bear, martin and black-tail deer, salmon and raven. I breathe the same particles of air that form songs in the territorial calls of thrushes and give voice to humpback whales, lift the wings of bald eagles, and buzz in the hum of insects. I breathe in the earth, pass it on, share it in equal measure with billions of other living and nonliving things. I drink from the creek, and it becomes me; and like the elk on the hill and the gulls hovering in the westerly wind, I bring the earth inside myself as food.

The croaking of a raven brought me out of myself. I looked around and knew: the earth *is* us, we *are* this earth—looking at itself.

In the last two chapters I focused on how primordial "god talk"—theology—might reflect on the history of humanity's experience of the Sacred. My conclusion is that the varieties of personal and nonpersonal experiences of catching the ox, in spite of conceptual and cultural differences, point to one relatively inaccessible Sacred reality. But religious experience not only relates us to the Sacred; it also yokes us to nature. How we interpret our relation with the Sacred concurrently conditions our interrelation with the natural forces that nourish life. In dialogue with the religious Ways of humanity, is it possible to conceive a primordial theology of nature? This is the topic of the next chapter, "Herding the Ox."

Notes

1. D. T. Suzuki, *Manual of Zen Buddhism* (New York: Grove Press, 1960), 130.
2. Ibid., 131.
3. John Hick, "A Philosophy of Religious Pluralism," in *Problems of Religious Pluralism*, ed. John Hick (New York: St. Martin's Press, 1985), 41.
4. See George Santayana, *Interpretations of Poetry and Religion* (New York: Harper Torchbooks, 1957), 1-24.
5. *The Rig Veda: An Anthology*, trans. Wendy Doniger O'Flaherty (New York: Penguin Books, 1981), 80.
6. *Dialogues of the Buddha (Dīgha and Majjhima Nikāyas)*, vol. 2, trans. C. A. F. Rhys and T. W. Davids (London: Oxford University Press, 1938), 151.
7. Ibid., 253.
8. Ibid., 31.
9. See Lynn A. de Silva, *Buddhism: Beliefs and Practices in Sri Lanka* (Colombo: Wesley Press, 1974), 55.
10. See *Myoho-Renge-Kyo: The Sutra of the Lotus Flower of the Wonderful Law*, trans. Banno Kato, rev. W. E. Soothill and Wilhelm Schiffer (Tokyo: Kosei Publishing Company, 1971) chap. 8.

11. See my essay "Nature's Jeweled Net: Kukai's Ecological Buddhism," *The Pacific World* 6 (Fall 1990): 50–64.

12. See chapter 5 below for more detailed explanation of Mahayana "three-body" buddhology.

13. Chaps. 1 and 56 in *The Way and Its Power: A Study of the Tao Te Ching and Its Place in Chinese Thought*, trans. Arthur Waley (New York: Grove Press, 1958), 141, 210.

14. John Hick, *An Interpretation of Religion* (New Haven: Yale University Press, 1989), 264.

15. Ibid., 265. Although Hick writes from a Kantian perspective, Whiteheadian process philosophy seems to have influenced him at this point. See Alfred North Whitehead, *Process and Reality* (New York: Macmillan, 1967), 50–51, 166–67.

16. Hick, *Interpretation of Religion*, 266.

17. Etienne Gilson, *The Christian Philosophy of St. Thomas Aquinas* (New York: Random House, 1956), 160–61; also see 103–10.

18. Ibn al ʿArabi, *The Bezels of Wisdom*, trans. R. W. J. Austin (New York: Paulist Press, 1980), 137, cited by Hick, *Interpretation of Religion*, 274.

19. Ibid.

20. Ibid.

21. *Srimad-Valmiki-Maharisi-Punith Yogava'sistha*, ed. Vasudeva Laksmana Parriskar (Bombay: Tukaram Javaji, 1978), I:44.

22. *The Upanishads*, trans. Swami Nikhilananda (New York: Harper Torchbooks, 1963), 328.

23. Ibid., 99.

24. See Śaṇkara's *Commentary on the Vedanta Sūtra*, in *A Sourcebook in Indian Philosophy*, ed. Sarvepalli Radhakrishnan and Charles A. Moore (Princeton: Princeton University Press, 1957), 526.

25. Winston L. King, *In Hope of Nibbana* (La Salle, Ill.: Open Court, 1964), 82. Also see King's *Theravada Meditation: The Buddhist Transformation of Yoga* (Garden City, N.Y.: Anchor Books, 1970), 52–59.

26. King, *In Hope of Nibbana*, 83.

27. Quoted by King, *In Hope of Nibbana*, 85.

28. Lewis R. Lancaster, "The *Prajñāpāramitā* Literature," in *Buddhism: A Modern Perspective*, ed. Charles Prebish (University Park: Penn.: Pennsylvania State University Press, 1975), 69–71.

29. Cited in Heinrich Dumoulin, *A History of Zen Buddhism* (Boston: Beacon Press, 1963), 274.

30. Masao Abe, *Zen and Western Thought* (Honolulu: University of Hawaii Press, 1985), 223.

31. See my comparison of Buddhist and Christian concepts of selfhood in *The Modern Buddhist-Christian Dialogue* (Lewiston, N.Y.: Edwin Mellen Press, 1988), 267–305.

32. *The Upanishads*, trans. Nikhilananda, 200.

33. Cited in Evelyn Underhill, *Mysticism* (New York: Meridian Books, 1955), 420.

34. Annemarie Schimmel, *The Mystical Dimensions of Islam* (Chapel Hill: University of North Carolina Press, 1975), 66.

35. Robert M. Gimello, "Mysticism in Its Contents," in *Mysticism and Religious Traditions*, ed. Steven T. Katz (Oxford: Oxford University Press, 1983), 61–68. The classical statement of the connection between mystical training and the meaning according to which mystics conceptualize their unitive experience of the Sacred is William James, *The Varieties of Religious Experience* (New York: Longmans, Green, & Company, 1912), 379–411.

五
牧牛

5

Herding the Ox

HERE IS THE COMMENTARY'S INTERPRETATION OF THE FIFTH OX-HERDING PICTURE, "Herding the Ox:"

> When a thought moves, another follows—an endless train of thoughts is thus awakened. Through enlightenment all this turns into truth; but falsehood asserts itself when confusion prevails. Things oppress us not because of the objective world, but because of a self-deceiving mind. Do not let the nose-string loose, hold it tight, and allow no vacillation.[1]

In other words, the man has begun to discover that self and the natural world are interrelated, but he has not yet experienced their non-duality. So he must hold onto the world—tightly by the ox's nose string—lest his ox trample him and run off. Or, as the poem puts it:

The man must not separate himself from his whip and tether,
Lest the ox wander away into a world of defilements;
When the Ox is properly tended, it will grow pure and docile;
Without a chain, nothing binding, it will by its own free will follow the man.[2]

In this chapter I apply the primordial perspective to the relation between human selfhood and that aspect of the world called "nature." My major assumption is that every thing and event in the universe at every moment of space-time is what it is, and what it can become, because of how things and events in the universe continually undergo mutual interrelationship. The natural sciences, as well as many meditative traditions East and West, seem to confirm this assumption. Yet while the structure of this process can be analyzed from a number of perspectives—my view is mostly informed by Whiteheadian process philosophy—it remains the case that the actual entities that constitute reality *are* processes.

One religious implication of this view, portrayed in the fifth Ox-Herding picture from a Buddhist perspective, is that self and nature are interdependent: how we experience selfhood—"non-selfhood," if one is a Buddhist—is interdependent with how we experience nature, and vice versa. Given the notion of the relatively inaccessible Sacred of chapter 3, this chapter suggests a primordial understanding of the ecological issues engendered by human interaction with nature as the environmental context of our meeting with the Sacred.

This interdependency between our sense of self and our sense of nature became especially clear to me during my last visit to Japan, where I was engaged in sabbatical research on a ninth-century Shingon Buddhist monk named Kūkai. One evening I was invited by three Shingon Buddhist lay scholars to a restaurant outside Osaka that specialized in preparing and serving the deadly toxic fish known as *fugu*. Though it has a certain Russian-roulette quality, eating *fugu* is considered by many Japanese a highly aesthetic experience.

Of course, I declined. My aesthetic tastes run in different directions. Still, the experience of watching my friends eat *fugu* made me wonder about the condition that we, in chauvinistic shorthand, refer to as "human." Beings who will one day vanish from the earth in that ultimate subtraction of sensuality called death, we spend so much of our lives courting it: fomenting wars, watching with sickening horror movies in which maniacs slice and dice their victims, or hurrying to our own deaths in fast cars, smoking cigarettes, drinking alcohol, and practicing other forms of chemically induced suicide. Death obsesses us, as well it might, but our responses are so strange.

This is particularly true of our response to nature. All we have to do is look into a mirror. The face that pins us with its double gaze reveals a frightening secret: we look into a predator's eyes. It's rough out there in nature, whether in the wilds of a rainforest or in an urban jungle, partly because the earth is jammed with devout human predators unlike all others: we not only kill for food, we kill each other along with the natural forces nourishing life on this planet.

We stalk and kill nature even as we know what contemporary ecological research makes plain: that we are enfolded in a living, terrestrial environment in which living and nonliving things are so mutually implicated and interrelated that no distinct line separates life from nonlife.[3] This conclusion is not only a biological claim; it is also a claim about the nature of reality. Of necessity, ecological research alters our understanding of ourselves individually, and of human nature generally. Or at least it ought to. For not only do "ecology and contemporary physics complement one another conceptually and converge toward the same metaphysical notions,"[4] so do contemporary Christian process theology and certain East Asian religious teachings and practices. The question is, How can we, the most efficiently aggressive predators in nature, train ourselves to act according to what this research shows?

It is least of all a matter of technology, mostly a matter of vision, that sense of reality according to which we most appropriately structure our relation to nature. For as Proverbs 29:18 warns, "Where there is no vision, the people perish." My thesis is this: dialogical encounter with East Asian views of nature—here illustrated by Taoist and Mahayana Buddhist traditions—and Western ecological models of reality emerging in the natural sciences and Christian process theology, may energize an already evolving global paradigm through which to rethink and resolve the current ecological crisis.[5] What is at stake is nothing less than the "liberation of life."[6]

But first, some remarks about mainstream Christian teaching about nature. In 1967, Lynn White, Jr.'s controversial essay "The Historical Roots of our Ecological Crisis"[7] started a debate that raged through the 1970s among theologians, philosophers, and scientists. At the time, Christian theologians and scientists and philosophers hostile to Christian tradition read this essay as a wholesale indictment of Christianity as the primary cause of the ecological crisis. The focal point of controversy was White's recommendation for reforming the Christian Way in order lead humanity out of the ecological shadow of death he thought "mainstream Christianity" originally created. Specifically, he recommended that mainstream Christianity endorse a "Franciscan worldview" and "panpsychism" in order to deliberately reconstruct a contemporary Western environmental ethic. He even raised the possibility—and rejected it—of appropriating "Eastern views" upon which to reconstruct an environmental ethic. He wrote:

More science and technology are not going to get us out of the present eco-logical crisis until we find a new religion, or rethink the old one. The beat-niks, who are the revolutionaries of our time, show a sound instinct in their affinity for Zen Buddhism, which conceives of the man-nature relationship as very nearly the mirror of the Christian view. Zen, however, is too deeply conditioned by Asian history as Christianity is by the experience of the West, and I am dubious of its viability among us.[8]

While these sentences seem harmless now, they had a powerful effect on Western intellectuals. White's assertion is an either/or: either "find a new religion" or "rethink the old one." He rejected the first alternative.

Initial reaction to White's essay—mostly by intellectual historians, philos-ophers of science, and process theologians[9]— focused on identifying what exactly the "mainstream Christian worldview" is. Surprisingly, there was little Christian bashing; more surprising, most Christian discussion agreed with White's characterization of Christian tradition. But there was little agreement about how to reconstruct a distinctively Christian view of nature, or indeed, whether it could or should be reconstructed.

Recently, the structure of "mainstream" Christian tradition roughly cari-catured by White was formulated into a typology by J. Baird Callicott and Roger T. Ames:[10] (1) God transcends nature; (2) nature is a creation, an arti-fact, of a divine craftsman-like male creator; (3) human beings are exclusively created in God's image, and therefore essentially segregated from the rest of nature; (4) human beings are given dominion by God over nature; (5) God com-mands humanity to subdue nature and multiply the human species; (6) nature is viewed politically and hierarchically—God over humanity, humanity over nature, male over female—which establishes an exploitive ethical-political peck-ing order and power structure; (7) the image of God-in-humanity is the ground of humanity's *intrinsic* value, but nonhuman entities lack the divine image and are religiously and ethically disenfranchised and possess merely *instru-mental* value for God and human beings; (8) the biblical view of nature's instrumental value is compounded in mainline Christian theology by an Aristotelian-Thomistic teleology that represents nature as a support system for rational human beings.

The upshot of this seems clear. The great monotheistic traditions of the West are the major sources of Western moral and political attitudes. The prob-lem is, the biblical creation myth—as read and applied by mainstream Christ-ian teaching—corresponds to neither scientific description nor human experience. Not only that, its insistence on human domination and subjection of nature has encouraged centuries of destructive exploitation of the envi-ronment. Indeed, if one wants theological license to increase radioactivity without constraint, to consent to the bulldozer mentality of developers, or to encourage unbridled harvest of old-growth forests, historically there has been no better scriptural justification than Genesis 1–2. The mythological injunctions to conquer nature, the enemy of God and humanity, are here.

However, placing the full blame for the environmental crisis on the altar of the Christian Way is far too simplistic. Historically, the biblical creation story was read through the sensitivities of Greco-Roman philosophy; in fact, the legacy of Greco-Roman contributions to the ecological crisis may be more influential than distinctively biblical contributions. Genesis 1–2 is also capable of more organic Christian exegesis.

The first Greek philosophers taught natural philosophy, and many included ecologically adaptable and environmentally useful ideas. But the natural philosophy that has survived from the Greeks to bequeath its imprint on modern Western culture is atomism. Atomism pictures nature as particulate, reductive, material, inert, quantitative, and mechanical. It became institutionalized in early modern science and philosophy with Descartes, and still remains the predominant model of nature assumed by Western technology.

Furthermore, Greek philosophical anthropology also assumed an atomistic worldview, paradigmatically expressed in Plato and given its modern version by Descartes. Human nature is dualistic, composed of body and soul. The body, especially in Descartes' version, is like any other natural entity, exhaustively describable in atomistic-mechanistic language. But the human soul resides temporarily in the body—the ghost in the machine—and is otherworldly in nature and destiny. Thus, human beings are both essentially and morally segregated from God, nature, and each other. Accordingly, the natural environment can and should be engineered to human specifications, no matter what the environmental consequences, without either human responsibility or penalty.

Here we have it in a nutshell. The contemporary ecological crisis represents a failure of prevailing Western ideas and attitudes: a male-dominated culture in which it is believed that reality exists only as human beings perceive it (Berkeley); whose structure is a hierarchy erected to support humanity at its apex (Aristotle, Aquinas, Descartes); to whom God has given exclusive dominance over all life forms and inorganic entities (Genesis 1–2); and in which God had been transformed into humanity's image by modern secularism (Genesis inverted). It seems unlikely that mainstream Christian tradition is capable of resolving the ecological crisis that its reading of Genesis 1–2 through the eyes of Greco-Roman philosophy created.

The Ecological Visions of Taoism and Buddhism

The traditional Western-Christian paradigm of nature is now being challenged by new ecological models and theoretical explanations of the interconnectedness of humanity with nature within the natural sciences.[11] Recent Christian discussion, most notably process theology, also focuses on these same scientific models in recognition of the inadequacies of traditional Christian and secular views of nature.[12] Of course, there are a number of Western versions of this emerging ecological paradigm; no two of them are exactly alike in their technical details or explanatory categories. Even so, it is possible to abstract three principles these paradigms share.

The first principle is holistic unity—nature is an "ecosystem" whose constituent elements exist in constantly changing, interdependent causal relationships. What an entity is, or becomes, is a direct function of how it relates with every entity in the universe at every moment of space-time. Second is the principle of interior life movements—all living entities possess a life force intrinsic to their own natures that is not imposed from other things or by God, but is derived from life itself. Life is an emerging force supporting networks of interrelationship and interdependency ceaselessly occurring in every entity in the universe. Or, to invert traditional Christian images, God does not impose or give life; God is the chief exemplar of life. The third principle—that of organic balance—means that all things and events are interrelated bipolar processes that proceed toward balance and harmony between opposites.

Similar organic principles have been structural elements of the classical Taoist worldview for three thousand years, particularly as exemplified in the *Tao Te Ching*, attributed to Lao Tzu, and the writings of Chuang Tzu.[13] Regarding this strand of Taoist tradition, David L. Hall notes that the most important Taoist concepts relevant to Western development of an altered sensitivity about humanity's interrelation with nature are *tao, te, tzu-jan, wu-chih, wu-wei, and wu-yü.*[14]

In the most ancient text of Taoist tradition, the *Tao Te Ching* (Classic on the way and its power), the *tao*—the ultimate reality that underlies, creates, and glues together all things and events in this universe—is characterized as both namable and nameless.

> The Way that can be told is not the Unvarying Way:
> The names that can be named are not unvarying names.
> It was from the Nameless that Heaven and Earth Sprang;
> The named is but the mother that rears the ten thousand
> creatures, each after its kind.[15]

And as the *Chuang Tzu* describes the Tao:

Tao has reality and evidence but no action or physical form. It may be trans-
mitted but cannot be received. It may be obtained but cannot be seen. It is
based in itself, rooted in itself. Before heaven and earth came into being,
Tao existed by itself for all time. It gave spirits and rulers their spiritual powers. It created heaven and earth. It is above the zenith but it is not high. It
is beneath the nadir but it is not low. It is prior to heaven and earth but it
is not old. It is more ancient than the highest antiquity but is not regarded
as long ago.[16]

That is, the Tao is the total process of becoming, or what Hall calls "Becoming-Itself." Thus,

Nameless and namable *tao* are *That Which*. That which *is* and that which
is not are the polar elements of Becoming-Itself. The fundamental truth of
the *tao* is the proposition: Only becoming (coming into being which illustrates some mixture of being and non-being) is; not-becoming (either being
or non-being abstracted from its polar relationship with its opposite) is
not.[17]

In other words, the Tao is "ultimate reality," not as a single universal
order, but as the totality of all possible orders of things and events that have
occurred, are occurring, or can occur in the universe. Furthermore, because
each existing thing and event in nature is an element of the Tao's totality, each
possesses its own *te*, "power" or "virtue." *Te* denotes the Tao as it exists particularly in individual things and events. Thus, *te* points to a thing's or an
event's intrinsic excellence as an individual form of the Tao, and in this sense
constitutes the "nature" of a thing or event that simultaneously defines both
its actuality (what it is) and its potential (what it can become).

The concepts of *tao* and *te* form a third notion, *tao-te*, which Hall thinks
is best understood as the relation between "field" (*tao*) and "focus" (*te*),[18] a
relationship that may be imagined through the model of the holograph. In a
holographic image, each element contains all other elements and all elements
contain every single element. Thus, every single thing and event in nature—in
accordance with its own individual nature (*te*)—mirrors and reflects the totality of nature (the Tao). Likewise, the totality of all possible things and events
that constitute nature (the Tao) is reflected in the nature of every single
thing's and event's particular nature, that is, its *te*.

Given the *tao-te* structure of nature, the function of the concepts of *wu-
chih*, *wu-wei*, and *wu-yü* can be rather easily grasped. *Wu-chih* or "no-knowledge" is interpreted by Hall as "unprincipled knowing," meaning knowledge
that does not root itself in external principles as determining sources of
nature's order and human conduct.[19] That is, "no-knowledge" involves knowing the *te* of things and events as reflective of the Tao rather than knowing a

thing or event in relation to some abstract philosophical category—for example, as an instance of a "universal" or a member of a class. Or as the *Tao Te Ching* puts it,

> Banish wisdom, discard knowledge,
> And the people will be benefited a hundredfold.
> Banish human kindness, discard morality,
> And the people will be dutiful and compassionate.
> Banish skill, discard profit,
>   thieves and robbers will disappear.[20]

Accordingly, *wu-chih* is knowledge of the *tao-te* relationship of each thing and event in the natural order that engenders an understanding of nature that focuses on the *te* of each thing and event as a particular focus or form of the Tao.

Wu-wei, or "actionless action" or "non-ego-assertive action," is action in accord with and expressive of unprincipled knowing. The essential character of such action is that it is "spontaneous" (*tzu-jan*), meaning that it is not guided by abstract rules or calculating principles.

Finally, *wu-yü* means something like "the absence of desires or attachment to the fruits of action," which Hall characterizes as "objectless desire."[21] It is the defining character of "actionless action." That is, actionless action" (*wu-wei*) is "action without desire or attachment to the fruits of action." Another way of characterizing this concept is "objectless action" in the sense that one may act in accord with the Tao and enjoy and reap enjoyment without demanding that one define, possess, or control the object of one's enjoyment.

The collective environmental and ethical meanings of these terms come together in the concept of *tzu-jan*, meaning something like the "self-creativity" inherent in all things and events in nature as reflective forms of the Tao. Hall regards *tzu-jan* as a Taoist "categorical imperative" with the following ethical implication: "Always act with *tzu-jan*—that is, "Act always in accordance with your *te*" or "nature" as a reflection of the Tao in ways that express *wu-wei* and *wu-yü*.[22]

Clearly, these Taoist conceptions imply an understanding of nature as an "aesthetic order" in which we are enjoined to be "spontaneous" (*tzu-jan*)—that is, to practice "actionless-action" (*wu-wei*) in balanced harmony with the forces of *yin* and *yang* by deferring to the natural and intrinsic excellence (*te*) of every thing and event we encounter in the natural order, coupled with enjoying similar human acts of deference directed toward us by virtue of another's appreciation of our *te*. In this sense, Taoist environmental ethics is really an aesthetic that shuns antecedent principles or abstract norms in a manner similar to the way a creative individual would refuse to depend on past norms for the determination of present actions. Taoist creativity—and Taoist instruction about how we should interact with nature ("actionless action")— engenders the spontaneous (*tzu-jan*) production of novelty.

Above all, there can be, in the Taoist worldview, no rules external to the creative processes of nature themselves. Occasionally, however, human beings can model the spontaneous creative processes constituting nature. Such human beings, sensitive to the environmental forces of nature energized through the bipolar forces of *yin* and *yang*, as these forces are continually coalescing in their own lives, seek to live in balanced harmony with nature rather than in opposition to nature. The lives of such persons, informed by *wu-wei*, are like water.

> Nothing under heaven is softer or more yielding than water; but when it attacks things hard and resistant there is not one of them that can prevail. For they can find no way of altering it. That the yielding conquers the resistant and the soft conquers the hard is a fact known by all men, yet realized by none.[23]

Therefore, the highest good is like water. The goodness of water is that it benefits the ten thousand creatures; yet itself does not scramble, but is content with the places that all humans disdain. It is this that makes water so near to the Way.

> And if men think the ground the best place for building
>   a house upon,
> If among thoughts they value those that are profound,
> If in friendship they value gentleness,
> In words, truth; in government, good order;
> In deeds, effectiveness; in actions, timeliness—
> In each case it is because they prefer what does not
>   lead to strife,
> And therefore does not go amiss.[24]

So, the Taoist sage seeks not to transform the natural order to achieve human ends; the sage *cooperates* with the natural order to achieve nature's ends by living *in accord* with the Tao. In the words of the *Chuang Tzu*:

> Do not be a possessor of fame. Do not be a storehouse of schemes. Do not take over the function of things. Do not be the master of knowledge (to manipulate things). Personally realize the infinite to the highest degree and travel in the realm of which there is no sign. Exercise fully what you have received from Nature without any subjective viewpoint. . . . The mind of the perfect man is like a mirror. It does not lean forward or backward in its

response to things. It responds to things but conceals nothing of its own. Therefore it is able to deal with things without injury to [its reality].[25]

Quite similar organic paradigms underlie traditional Buddhist interaction with nature, particularly in its Mahayana form, although there may not be anything in Buddhist tradition exactly corresponding to the Taoist teaching of *wu-wei*. Yet the most widely known image of this Buddhist organic paradigm, Indra's jeweled net, represents a holographic portrayal of the universe quite similar to the Taoist concept of *tao-te*.

In the heavenly abode of the great Indian god Indra, there is hung a wonderful net that stretches out in all directions. The net's clever weaver has strung a single jewel in each eye, and since the net is infinite in dimension, the jewels are infinite in number. If we look closely at a single jewel, we discover that its polished surface reflects every other jewel. Not only that, each of the jewels reflected in the one we are looking at simultaneously reflects all the other jewels, so that there occurs an infinite reflecting process.

Hua-yen (Japanese, *Kegon*, or "Flower-Wreath") Buddhism is especially fond of this image for the way it characterizes the natural order as an infinitely repeating series of interrelationships simultaneously occurring among all particular entities. It illustrates, in other words, the doctrine of "interdependent co-origination" held by all schools of Buddhism: the relationship between things and events in the universe is one of mutual identity and intercausality.[26]

Francis H. Cook illustrates the notion of mutual identity and mutual intercausality expressed in Indra's jeweled net by ten coins.[27] If we take ten coins as symbolizing the totality of existence at any moment of time and examine the relation between them, then, according to Hua-yen teaching, the first coin will be seen as being identical with the remaining nine. Similarly, the second coin will be experienced as identical with the other nine, and so on throughout the collection of coins. So in spite of the fact that the coins may be different denominations, ages, or metals, they are said to be completely identical because each individual coin manifests a common shared reality called "coinness." According to Hua-yen thought, this is the *static* relationship of the coins—each is experienced as self-identically the same "coin" through time.

Yet if we look at these same ten coins again and examine their *dynamic* relationship, then, according to Hua-yen teaching, they will be experienced as totally interdependent and intercausal. From this perspective, coin 1 can be said to be the cause of the totality of coins that are considered to be dependent on the first coin for their being. That is, the first coin is the support, while the total group of coins is that which is supported. Since this particular totality cannot exist without the support of the first coin, this coin is said to be the sole cause for the totality. However, when we shift attention to the second coin and examine its relationship to the other nine, it can be said that this second coin is also the sole cause of the existence of the totality of the ten coins. Likewise, from the standpoint of *each* of the ten coins, it can be said that that coin is the cause of the whole.

But the causal relationship between the coins is even more fluid than this. While each coin can be said, from its own standpoint, to be the sole cause of the whole, simultaneously the whole acts as cause for the one coin. This is because any single coin in the series of ten can exist and function only within the total environment comprising the ten coins. It can never be a question of the coin existing outside its environment because since the ten coins symbolize the totality of being, a coin outside the context of the ten would be a nonentity. Therefore, each individual coin is at once the cause of the whole and is caused by the whole. In short, the universe is a vast body made up of an infinity of individuals all creating and sustaining each other. The universe is in this way a self-creating, self-maintaining, and self-defining organism. Hua-yen calls this universe the *dharma-dhātu*, which Cook translates as "cosmos" or "universe," with the proviso that it is not the universe as commonly imagined in the West, but rather a universe of organic mutual identity and interdependence.[28]

That Taoist and Buddhist teachings in general and Hua-yen teaching in particular assert an ecological conception of nature quite different from mainstream Christian tradition is quite evident. First, Christian tradition understands and explains the universe in terms of a divine plan with respect to its creation and final end. The Taoist and Buddhist universe is completely non-teleological. For these traditions the universe has neither beginning nor end, no creator, and no purpose. The universe just is, to be taken as given, a marvelous fact that can be understood only in terms of its own inner dynamism.

Second, mainstream Christian teaching and our Greek philosophical heritage have taught the West that nature is a world of limited, external, special relationships. We have family relationships, marital relationships, relationships with a limited number of animal species, and occasional relationships with inanimate objects, most of which are external. But it is hard for us to imagine how anything is internally related to everything. How, for example, are we related to a star in Orion? How are Euro-Americans related to Lakota Native Americans or Alaskan Inuit? How are plants and animals related to us, other than externally as objects for exploitation. How are men related to women, and women to men? In short, Western persons generally find it easier to think of isolated beings and insulated minds than to think of one reality ontologically interconnecting all things and events.

In contrast, the Taoist and Buddhist traditions teach that the universe is a universe of nondual-identity-in-difference, in which there is total interdependence: what affects and effects one item in the cosmos affects and effects every item, whether it is death, ignorance, enlightenment, or sin.

Finally, the mainstream Christian view of the universe is one of rigid hierarchy, in which a male creator-god occupies the top link in the chain of being, human beings next, and nature—animals, plants, rocks—the bottom. Even with the steady erosion of interest in traditional Christianity in the West, where the top link—God—has for many become meaningless, the explicit assumption still exists that male human beings are the measure of all things, that somehow the history of the universe is human history.

In contrast, according to Taoist and Buddhist teachings, the universe has no hierarchies. Nor does it have a center, or if it does, it is everywhere. In short, Taoist and Buddhist conceptions of the universe leave no room for anthropocentric biases endemic to Hebraic and Christian tradition, as well as those modern movements of philosophy having roots in Cartesian affirmation of human consciousness divorced from dead nature.

Concluding Observations

The work of earlier physicists such as Faraday and Maxwell, and later physicists such as Einstein and Bohr, as well as the process philosophy of Alfred North Whitehead, has laid significant groundwork for an entirely new Western ecological paradigm shift that views nature more as an "aesthetic order" than a "logical order." Like Western "new physics" and process thought, Taoist and Mahayana Buddhist worldviews also characterize nature as an "aesthetic order" that cognitively resonates with contemporary Western ecological ideas.

According to Roger Ames, an "aesthetic order" is a paradigm that: (1) proposes plurality as prior to unity and disjunction prior to conjunction, so that all particulars possess real and unique individuality; (2) focuses on the unique perspective of concrete particulars as the source of emergent harmony and unity in all interrelationships; (3) entails movement away from any universal characteristic to concrete particular detail; (4) apprehends movement and change in the natural order as a processive act of "disclosure"—and hence describable in qualitative language; (5) perceives that nothing is predetermined by preassigned principles, so that creativity is apprehended in the natural order, in contrast to being determined by God or chance; and

(6) understands "rightness" to mean the degree to which a thing or event expresses, in its emergence toward novelty as this exists in tension with the unity of nature, an aesthetically pleasing order.[29]

Jay McDaniel and other contemporary process philosophers and theologians emphasize the following features of what Ames calls an aesthetic order.[30] First, present happenings emerge not only out of causative relations with the past but also from creative impulses in the present guided by final causes from the future. This means that nonhuman organisms, like human beings, are partially creative and partially unpredictable in the ways in which they respond to, and integrate, environmental and bodily influences. Second, nonhuman organisms—from living cells to blue whales—possess intrinsic value in and for themselves even as they have instrumental value for others. Third, physical matter itself is more alive than dead in its ultimate depths. Fourth, living wholes, such as the human self or animal psyche, are influenced by, while yet more than, the parts of which they are composed. Fifth, reality itself, while pluralistic in nature, is better characterized as interdependent and interfusing than as dualistic and dichotomized.

In contrast to the aesthetic order implicit in Taoist and Buddhist views of nature and contemporary science and process thought, the "logical order" of mainline Christianity characterized by Ames (1) assumes preassigned patterns of relatedness, a "blueprint" wherein unity is prior to plurality, and plurality is a "fall" from unity; (2) values concrete particularity only to the degree that it mirrors this preassigned pattern of relatedness; (3) reduces particulars to only those aspects needed to illustrate the given pattern, which necessarily entails moving away from concrete particulars toward the universal; (4) interprets nature as a closed system of predetermined specifications, and therefore reducible to quantitative description; (5) characterizes being as necessity, creativity as conformity, and novelty as defect; and (6) views "rightness" as the degree of conformity to preassigned patterns.[31]

The predominant logical order of most Western philosophy and theology and much contemporary science involves one mechanistic perspective or a combination of such perspectives, which characterize most Western worldviews: (1) a pervasive determinism in which present happenings are understood to be entirely fixed by causative relations inherited from the past, (2) a utilitarian perspective in which the value of living things is understood to be purely instrumental rather than intrinsic, (3) a devitalized perspective in which the depths of physical matter are understood to be lifeless and inert rather than lifelike and creative, (4) a reductionistic perspective in which living wholes are understood to be utterly reducible to nonliving parts, and (5) a dualistic perspective in which sharp dichotomies are drawn between spirit and matter, sacred and secular, mind and body, thought and feeling, self and world. In short, at a conceptual level, nature is like a machine.[32]

A number of examples of logical order come to mind: Plato's realm of Ideas, for instance, constitutes a preassigned pattern that charts particular things and events as real or good only to the degree they conform to these preexistent Ideas. But aesthetic orders such those posited by Taoism, Buddhism, or process philosophy are easily distinguishable from a logical order. In all of these, there are no preassigned patterns in things and events in nature. Creativity and order work themselves out through the arrangements and relationships of the particular constituents of the natural order. Nature is a "work of art" in which "rightness" is defined by the comprehension of particular details that constitute it as a work of art.

Of course, the technical details of the "aesthetic order" portrayed by Taoist and Buddhist ecological paradigms and, for example, those of Christian process theology, are not identical. This much, however, should be noted: in spite of important technical differences, two common conceptualities are foundational in the Taoist and Buddhist worldviews and Whiteheadian process theology. The first is that there is continuity within nature. For Taoist, Buddhist, and Whiteheadian thought, nature's continuity extends internal relatedness— a metaphysical relatedness in which individuals and societies are constituted by relationships of interdependence—to organic and inorganic nature. The second shared teaching is that human beings have vital connections with nature, since everything in nature is interconnected. This corresponds to the Taoist notions of *tao-te* and the Hua-yen image of Indra's jeweled net.

Whitehead's definition of "living body" gives some precision to these similarities. The living body, he writes, is "a region of nature which is itself the primary field of expression issuing from each of its parts."[33] This means that those entities that are centers of expression and feeling are alive, and Whitehead clearly applies this description to both animal and vegetable bodies. Further, this same definition of living body is an expansion of his definition of the human and animal body; the distinction between animals and vegetables is not a sharp one.[34]

Whitehead also contended that precise classification of the differences between organic and inorganic nature is not possible; although such classification might be pragmatically useful for scientific investigation, it is dangerous for nature. In *Modes of Thought,* he noted how scientific classifications often obscure the fact that "different modes of natural existence often shade off into each other."[35] The same point was made in *Process and Reality*, where Whitehead noted that there are no distinct boundaries in the continuum of nature, and thus no distinct boundaries between living organisms and inorganic entities; whatever differences there are is a matter of degree. This does not mean that differences are unimportant, for even degrees of difference affirm the continuity of nature.[36]

This point is central to Whiteheadian biologist Charles Birch and process theologian John Cobb's definition of "life." They raise the issue of the boundaries between animate and inanimate in light of the ambiguity of "life" on hypothetical boundaries.[37] Viruses are particularly good examples of entities possessing the properties of life and nonlife. Another example is cellular organelles, which reproduce but are incapable of life independent of the cell that is their environment.

The significance of these examples for the ecological model of life that Birch and Cobb propose is that every entity is internally related to its environment. Human beings are not exceptions to this model, nor in Cobb's opinion is God, who is the chief example of what constitutes life.[38] Taoist and Buddhist views in this regard are very similar: every entity in nature is internally related to every item in its environment. While there is no reality in Taoist and Buddhist thought corresponding to God, it is the internal relationship each thing in the universe has with all things in the universe that constitutes the life of that thing *and* the life of the universe.

As there is continuity between organic and inorganic in Whiteheadian process thought, so too there is continuity between human and nonhuman. Whitehead underscored this continuity by including "higher animals" in his definition of "living person." Both human beings and animals are living persons characterized by a dominant occasion of experience which coordinates and unifies the activities of the plurality of occasions and enduring objects that ceaselessly form persons. Personal order is linear, serial, object-to-subject inheritance of the past in the present. Personal order in human beings and in nature is one component of what Whitehead called "the doctrine of the immanence of the past energizing the present."[39] This linear, one-dimensional character of personal inheritance from the past is called the "vector-structure" of nature. A similar picture of nature evolves in the Taoist notion of *te* and *tsu-jan* and in Hua-yen interpretation of interdependent causation symbolized by Indra's jeweled net.

At this point, the question is, so what? Why is it important for Western organic environmental paradigms to encounter Asian versions of organic views of nature? The answer is, because what people *do* to the natural environment corresponds to what they *think* and *experience* about themselves in relation to the things around them. This may seem obvious to philosophers, scientists, and theologians. But it is not so obvious if we shift attention from theoretical issues to empirical confirmation of our worldviews in actual human practice. Three facts require brief consideration.

First, the brute fact of worldwide environmental degradation seems to imply that what people think *does not* substantially affect what they do and how they live in relation to the environment. Second, in a world shrunken to a global village by communication and transportation technologies, multinational corporations, and nuclear weapons, pointing to Asian views of nature as possible resources for resolving the ecological crisis may not even be an option for many but the most geographically isolated people. As the world now exists, "development" and "progress" mean industrialization; industrialization, even when pursued in a climate of anti-Western ideology, means Westernization nevertheless. Third, technology is neither culture-neutral nor value-neutral. To adopt modern technology is simultaneously to adopt the values in which that technology is immersed, as the industrialization of modern Japan amply demonstrates. Modern technology is embedded in the Bacon-Newton complex of ideas—science as manipulative power over inert lumps of dead matter. Mainline Christianity is the religious foundation of this view.

But as brutish as these facts are, we must also note that the present environmental crisis is also less a unique, unprecedented Western-Christian event than the continuation of events as old as Occidental and Oriental civilization. All life forms, plants as well as animals—and if Whitehead is correct, nonliving entities—modify the environment. Human beings are not exceptions. What is exceptional about the human species is that its stratagem for survival and adaptation—culture—has not only amplified the environmental impact of human beings on nature; it has to a large degree placed us in charge of our own evolution.

Therefore, even at the level of empirical confirmation of scientific theory, it seems evident that "the ruination of the natural world is directly related to the psychological and spiritual health of the human race since our practices follow our perceptions."[40] Culture and worldview, faith and practice, merge in language and indicate perceptions in persons and in societies. When we relate to nature as a "thing" separate from ourselves or as separate from God, we not only engender but also perpetuate the environmental nightmare through which we are now living. The Christian term for this separation of ourselves from nature is "original sin"; the Buddhist word is "desire" (*taṇhā*).

Therefore, quite apart from problems of cultural and theological redirection, our immediate goal should be to preserve whatever biological diversity we can. It is not necessary for the human species to be a blot on the environment or a burden on other life forms. On the contrary, as Taoist and Buddhist views of nature and Whiteheadian process thought confirm, human beings can actually enhance the diversity, integrity, stability, and beauty of life on this planet. An irresponsible, technologically exploitive civilization informed by a scientifically obsolete, rationalist, mechanistic worldview is not the only possibility, provided we give this planet a chance and cease rushing like lemmings toward global destruction.

An Aesthetic Postscript

The environmental destructiveness of Western rationalism's hyper-*yang* view of its own culture and of nature has been to a large extent delayed. But the ecological limits of the earth are now stretched and, in some cases, broken. Dialogue with Asian views of nature, here illustrated by Taoist and Hua-yen Buddhist teachings, can foster the process of Western self-critical "consciousness raising" by providing alternative places to stand and imagine new possibilities. In so doing, we might discern deeper organic strata within our own inherited cultural biases and assumptions, and apprehend that we neither stand against nor dominate nature.

But like any particular dialogue, dialogue between Taoists or Buddhists and Christians about nature has an inner and an outer dimension. Discussion of organic paradigms must not remain at the level of verbal abstraction. Taoists or Buddhists can understand and appreciate the conceptions and technical language of Christian process views; process theologians can understand and appreciate Taoist and Buddhist conceptions of nature. In dialogue, Taoists, Buddhists, and Christians may be conceptually transformed. But this is an outer dialogue. Important as such dialogue is, it is incomplete if divorced from an inner dialogue about how Taoists, Buddhists, and Christians *can personally experience* non-duality between themselves and nature. For to the degree we *experience* the realities to which Taoist, Buddhist, and process Christian concepts of nature point, to that degree are we energized to live in accord with the organic structures of nature that outer dialogue conceptually reveals.

It's like the union of lyrics with music in a great chorale: the "music" of inner dialogue "enfleshes" the abstract lyrics of outer dialogue. What inner dialogue teaches is that we can live any way we want. People take vows of poverty, chastity, and obedience—even of silence—by choice. People destroy the environment—by choice—because they experience it as a machine. Choosing to experience nature organically is to stalk our calling in skilled and supple ways, to locate the most tender live spot in nature we can find and plug into its pulse. This is yielding to nature, not dominating nature.

From a Taoist or Buddhist perspective transformed by encounter with

Christian process thought, outer and inner dialogue means, appropriating Joseph Campbell's words, "following our collective bliss." Would it not be proper, and obedient, and pure, to begin by flowing with nature rather than dominating nature, dangling from it limp wherever nature takes us. Then even death, where we are going no matter what, cannot us part. Seize nature and let it seize us up aloft, until our eyes burn and drop out; let our murky flesh fall off in shreds, and let our bones unhinge and scatter, loosened over fields and woods, lightly, thoughtless, from any height at all, from as high as eagles. Then we discover there was never anything to seize, nothing to grasp all along, because we *are* nature, looking at ourselves.

Or, from a Christian process theological perspective transformed by inner and outer dialogue with Taoism and Buddhism: God does not demand that we give up our personal dignity, that we throw in our lot with random people, that we lose ourselves and turn from all that is not God. For God is the "Life" of nature, *intimior intimo meo*, as Augustine put it—"more intimate than I am to myself." God needs nothing, demands nothing, like the stars. It is life with God that demands these things. Of course, we do not have to stop abusing the environment—not at all. We do not have to stop abusing nature—unless we want to know God. It's like sitting outside on a cold, clear winter's night. We don't have to do so; it may be too cold. If, however, we want to look at the stars, we will find that darkness is necessary. But the stars neither require nor demand it.

Notes

1. D. T. Suzuki, *Manual of Zen Buddhism* (New York: Grove Press, 1960), 131.
2. Ibid.
3. Charles Birch and John B. Cobb, Jr., *The Liberation of Life* (Denton, Tex.: Environmental Ethics Books), chap. 3.
4. J. Baird Callicott, "The Metaphysical Implications of Ecology," in *Nature in Asian Traditions of Thought*, ed. J. Baird Callicott and Roger T. Ames (Albany: State University of New York Press, 1989), 51.
5. I have chosen broad elements of these traditions as a matter of convenience. I could have chosen specific figures or poets like the Japanese Zen Buddhist poet Saigyō or the Soto Zen Master Dogun as dialogical partners with Western secular and Christian models of nature to make the same points in defense of my thesis. But I wanted to focus more broadly on Buddhist and Taoist models of nature and the environment. It would have also been instructive to include Indian philosophy as dialogical partner with Christian views of the natural order. In fact, essays on Saigyō's and Taoist views of nature have already been published by Roger T. Ames, "Putting the Tao Back into Taoism," in *Nature in Asian Tradi-*

tions of Thought, 113–44; and William R. La Fluer, "Saigyō and the Buddhist Value of Nature," ibid., 183–209. For Indian views of nature see Fritjof Capra, *The Tao of Physics: An Exploration of the Parallels Between Modern Physics and Eastern Mysticism* (Boulder, Colo.: Shambala, 1975).

6. See Birch and Cobb, *Liberation of Life*, chaps. 1–2.

7. Lynn White, Jr., "The Historical Roots of Our Ecological Crisis," *Science* 155 (1967): 1203–7.

8. Ibid., 1206–7.

9. See John B. Cobb, Jr., *Is It Too Late? Toward A Theology of Ecology* (Philadelphia: Westminster Press, 1972); and Holmes Rolston III, "Is There an Environmental Ethic?" *Journal of Social, Political, and Legal Philosophy* 85 (1975): 93–109.

10. J. Baird Callicott and Roger T. Ames, "Introduction: The Asian Traditions as a Conceptual Resource for Environmental Philosophy," in *Nature in Asian Traditions of Thought*, 3–4.

11. See E. A. Burtt, *The Metaphysical Foundations of Modern Science* (Garden City, N.Y.: Anchor Books, 1954). Also see Alfred North Whitehead, *The Concept of Nature* (Cambridge: Cambridge University Press, 1971); two recent studies by Kenneth Boulding entitled *The World As a Total System* (Beverly Hills, Calif.: Sage Publications, 1985) and *Ecodynamics* (Beverly Hills, Calif.: Sage Publications, 1981); and Fritjof Capra, *The Turning Point* (New York: Bantam Books, 1982).

12. I have already cited Cobb's *Is It Too Late?* and *Liberation of Life*, ed. Birch and Cobb. Also see Richard H. Oberman, *Evolution and the Christian Doctrine of Creation* (Philadelphia: Westminster Press, 1967), and a series of wonderful essays edited by Ian Barbour, *That Earth Might Be Fair: Reflections on Ethics, Religion, and Ecology* (Englewood Cliffs, N.J.: Prentice Hall, 1972), especially Huston Smith's essay, "Tao Now: An Ecological Testament," 66–69.

13. See *The Way and Its Power: A Study of the Tao Te Ching and Its Place in Chinese Thought*, trans. Arthur Waley (New York: Grove Press, 1958); and David L. Hall, "On Seeking a Change in the Environment," in *Nature in Asian Traditions of Thought*, 99–111.

14. I have followed Hall's suggestions in my organization and use of these concepts ("On Seeking a Change," 108–11).

15. *The Way and Its Power*, trans. Waley, 141.

16. *A Sourcebook in Chinese Philosophy*, ed. and trans. Wing-tzit Chan (Princeton: Princeton University Press, 1963), 194.

17. Hall, "On Seeking a Change," 108.

18. Ibid.

19. Ibid.

20. *The Way and Its Power*, trans. Waley, 166.

21. Hall, "On Seeking a Change," 109.

22. Ibid.

23. *The Way and Its Power*, trans. Waley, 238.

24. Ibid., 151

25. *A Sourcebook in Chinese Philosophy*, ed. Chan, 207.

26. For an interesting discussion of Hua-yen cosmology, see Francis H. Cook, "The Jewel Net of Indra," in *Nature in Asian Traditions of Thought*, 213–29.

27. Ibid., 214.

28. Ibid., 215.

29. Ames, "Putting the Tao Back into Nature," 117.

30. Jay B. McDaniel, *Of God and Pelicans: A Theology of Reverence for Life* (Louisville, Ky.: Westminster/John Knox Press, 1989), 140.

31. Ames, "Putting the Tao Back into Nature," 116.

32. McDaniel, *Of God and Pelicans*, 139.

33. Alfred North Whitehead, *Modes of Thought* (New York: Macmillan, 1938), 31.

34. Ibid., 31–34.

35. Ibid., 25.

36. Alfred North Whitehead, *Process and Reality* (New York: Macmillan, 1978), 109, 179.

37. Birch and Cobb, *Liberation of Life*, 92.

38. Ibid., 176–78, 195–200.

39. Alfred North Whitehead, *Adventures of Ideas* (New York: Macmillan, 1933), 188.

40. Jay C. Rochelle, "Letting Go: Buddhism and Christian Models," *The Eastern Buddhist* (Autumn 1989): 45.

歸騎^六
家牛

6
Coming Home
on the Ox's Back

ACCORDING TO THE POEM OF THE SIXTH OX-HERDING PICTURE:

> Riding on the Ox, the man leisurely winds his way home;
> Enveloped in the evening mist, how tunefully the flute vanishes away!
> Singing a tune, beating time, his heart is filled with joy indescribable!
> Because he is now one with those who know, need it be told?[1]

The man no longer experiences the ox as a reality separate from himself, but as a constituent part of who he is. His internal struggle is over, because he is no longer concerned with winning or losing, with gain or loss. He has learned that his life is not something to grasp, as if he were outside of his life looking in. All along, he has had everything he will ever have because he does not *have* life; he *is* his life as he lives it. So he no longer competes with the ox. Saddling himself on the ox's back, he sings the simple songs of a village dweller as he pays no attention to anything except the journey home.

Yet even as the man's internal struggle with the ox is over, he still faces external dangers that must be met before he can progress further. He has achieved an interior state of intense awareness of non-duality. Such states are blissful, but he must not dwell in their joyful intensity. The bliss of mystical experience often makes interior life stupid, for unresolved issues needing attention are too easily ignored. Egoism and subjectivism too often deafen those who have such experiences to the world around them. Imagination too easily spins out ignorant tales and orthodoxies and too uncritically fancies that the world's winds blow on the self, that leaves fall at the self's feet for a reason, that people are watching. A mind risks real ignorance for the some-times paltry prize of an imagination enriched by mystical experience cut off from the particularities of the world. This is why reason must balance mysti-cal experience of non-duality; the trick of reason is to get the mystic's trans-formed imagination to seize the actual world of particulars, to see it as it is, if only from time to time, as objectively as possible.

I concluded chapter 4 with an account of an experience of nondual unity with nature in order to make a transition to the material of chapter 5. For a brief time, differences between my self and nature melted to zero-point. The experience was as brief as it was beautiful; it integrated me with the world in a way I never dreamed possible, a world of non-duality that momentarily cut off all sense of particularity and separate selfhood and left room for only intense harmony and peace. In nature I perceived the relatively inaccessible ox, or thought I did. Left at the subjectivity of such experience, nature seems only beautiful, safe, peaceful, supportive, and harmoniously nondual.

Reason requires that we correct the subjective one-sidedness of unitive experience and confront as objectively as possible the actual world of partic-ulars. For nature's particulars are also hard. Nature's unity is an impersonal system wherein all life forms feed on other life forms to be alive, wherein human beings are the most efficient killers that have evolved. Indeed, life is as painful, deadly, and impersonally terminal for all living things as it is beauti-ful and nurturing. Both are aspects of our experience of nature. Furthermore, one of the primary characteristics of contemporary human existence is the untold suffering our species imposes on other life forms over and beyond our need for survival.

So while it is true enough that nature is a harmonious system of interrelationships and interdependencies unifying the particulars nurturing all life on this planet, and wherever else life may occur in the universe, nature's harmonies come at a price. It's rough out there. Living things are food for other living things, and there are no exceptions. Or, as Buddhists tell it, life is as sorrowful as it is beautiful; or, in Christian language, life is as fallen into sin as it is good.

It's all very confusing. I alternate between thinking of planet Earth as a home and garden—a sacred place through which I see the ox as it sees me, dear and familiar—and as a hard wilderness of exile in which we are all sojourners, a place of silence and mirages, where even planet Earth itself seems a sojourner in airless space, a wet ball flung by no one across nowhere.

Annie Dillard's characterization of how the forces of evolution operate impersonally, without regard for human purposes and achievements, gives pause for reflection. "It is the best joke there is," she writes,

> . . . . that we are here, and fools—that we are sown into time like so much corn, that we are souls sprinkled at random like salt into time and dissolved here, spread into matter, connected by cells right down to our feet, and those feet are likely to fell us over a tree root or jam us on a stone. The joke part is that we forget it. Give the mind two seconds alone and it thinks it's Pythagoras.[2]

These are enervating thoughts, thoughts of despair if left to themselves. They come at their own time in their own form to all of us, unbidden, when our lives as they unroll become ill, when we lose control of our lives—or the illusion of control. Such thoughts come in that silence Saint John of the Cross knew as "the dark night of the soul," that point in the mystic's life, indeed anyone's life, marked by the perceived absence of the Sacred.

In chapter 5 I argued that relationship, relativity, process, and openness characterize reality. Nature is best portrayed as an "aesthetic order"[3] of considerably more complexity than the "logical order" of nature portrayed through the lenses of traditional Jewish, Christian, and Islamic interpretations of the Genesis creation myth and the mechanistic worldview of Newtonian science. Logical orders presuppose hierarchies of levels of organization from the microworld of subatomic particles to the megaworld of space-time. Theological logical orders stress dualisms in hierarchical relations of superior-inferior value: God/human, male/female, sacred/profane, human/nature, faith/reason, good/evil, my religious community/everyone else's religious community.

Whereas the worldview metaphor that dominates contemporary Western patriarchal culture is the machine, the primary models of the emerging aesthetic worldview are organic. A second conclusion of chapter 5 is that an organic model is a more accurate portrayal of the qualities characterizing life: openness, relationship, interdependence, change, novelty, and mystery. It is obvious how this perspective breaks with the old dualisms of Western culture: spirit/flesh, human/non-human, objective/subjective, reason/passion, supernatural/natural. Organic models refuse to draw hard lines between matter and energy, organic and inorganic, mind and body, human beings and other forms of life, sacred and profane.

Organic models are also ecological models that portray life as an aesthetic order in which all things and events are pictured as united by symbiotic interdependencies that create patterns of internal relationships. Living things do not "enter" into relationship with other entities external to the themselves; living things "find" themselves in interrelationships as the most fundamental givens of existence. It is the process of mutual interrelatedness that constitutes what things are and become, from electrons to mountains, from plants to animals to human beings to the Sacred itself.

However, while I argued in chapter 5 that a new organic paradigm for understanding our relatedness with nature based on process and interdependence should replace traditional interpretations of Genesis as well as the Newtonian mechanistic worldview, I did not spell out the specific character of an organic environmental ethic. This is the goal of this chapter.

Accordingly, the guiding assumption of this chapter is that, appropriating the language of Charles Birch and John B. Cobb, Jr., the business of an environmental ethic is the "liberation of life,"[4] but with a slightly different twist than proposed by Birch and Cobb. The liberation of life would not be an issue had not human beings evolved the way we have. Our species has more freedom than other living things, anti-entropically; we batter a bigger dent in nature's givens, damming rivers, planting plains, drawing in our mind's eye dotted lines between stars. The misuse of our freedom now so oppresses nature that nature's life processes require liberation from us. It is not that humanity now risks killing nature; nature will not die even though death hangs like a shroud over this planet. Life as we know it will die if we do not reverse the environmental damage our freedom causes by exercising this same freedom toward preserving and caring for life in all its forms.

Apart from our species, therefore, life does not require liberation. But since it is our species that has created the forces from which nature needs liberation, it is we who must create the processes that reverse these trends. This presupposition also engenders a second: the liberation of nature from human oppression constitutes the foundation of distinctively human forms of liberation considered in chapters 7 (women's liberation) and 8 (human political, economic, and social liberation).

The Liberation of Life

If reality is best characterized as an aesthetic order by means of organic metaphors stressing interdependence and non-duality, if nature is best seen a "sacred place" where we encounter the ox,[5] by what ethical principles ought we to structure our lives so that we live in accord with nature? Part of the answer to this question requires noting that a primordial environmental ethic is incomplete if it (1) ignores the hard facts of suffering inherent in nature's particularities, and (2) fails to spell out an environmental ethic that balances nature's harmonies with nature's hard facts. That is, we must not explain away or romanticize the harshness of nature's particularities through the wonder of our experience of nature's interdependent harmony. For suffering is not only inherent in the natural processes of life and death; it seems to be a necessary condition for there to be life at all. The pain of being alive and the pain of dying—"natural suffering" and especially the suffering caused by human beings on each other and on the environment—pose special challenges and issues to all human achievement and values.

Still, some of us some of the time experience liberating wholeness and integration, if only for a moment. Furthermore, the content of the liberation we experience depends on the context and circumstances at the time. If we are hungry, liberation means food; if we are abused, it means healing; if we are victims, it means courage; if we are oppressed, it means freedom; if we are ego-centered, it means self-forgetfulness; if we are suffering, it means freedom from suffering.

Such momentary forms of liberation may be transient, but nevertheless they point to something that transcends the particular disintegrations of our lives. They also provide glimpses of the ox and are, in Christian language, "salvific." We cannot meaningfully live, or meaningfully die, without these glimpses. They are, said Peter Berger, tastes of an ultimate, more lasting liberating wholeness—an ultimate peace—for which the hearts of human beings everywhere have yearned.[6]

If such ultimate liberation is not an illusion, it cannot be for humanity alone. Liberation is for all that live and suffer—all life in whatever form that life assumes in a world constituted by mutual entropy as well as interdependent co-origination.[7] But while it is probably impossible to conceive fully the nature of this ultimate liberating wholeness, it is nevertheless occasionally felt as a vague, yet compelling hope in the depth of our experience.

Of course, there are intelligent persons who deny that any sort of ultimate liberation exists. Other persons yearn for liberation at a prereflective, preconscious level while consciously denying its possibility. But if and when we do envision ultimate liberating wholeness, the content of that vision will depend on the religious and cultural traditions that nurture us. A Native American person will imagine liberation one way, a Hindu another, or a Christian theoretical physicist or a secularized biologist another.

Jewish, Christian, and Muslim persons often envision ultimate liberation as a state of affairs called "peace"—*shalom* or *salam* that comes only through relationship with God. This peace is not only between human beings in community but also between people and God, people and the Earth, people and other animals, and between other animals themselves. It is also God's doing, not ours, coming in God's time, not ours, in an unspecified future known only by God. An ancient example of such a vision commonly shared by Judaism, Christianity, and Islam is the prophet Isaiah's. When the Messiah comes, he prophesied,

> The wolf shall live with the sheep,
>   and the leopard lie down with the kid;
> the calf and the young lion shall grow up together,
>   and a little child shall lead them;
> the cow and bear shall be friends,
>   and their young shall lie down together.
> The lion shall eat straw like cattle;
>   the infant shall play over the hole of the cobra.
>   and the young child dance over the viper's nest.
> They shall not hurt or destroy in all my holy mountain;
>   for as the waters fill the sea,
>   so shall the land be filled with the knowledge of the Lord.
>   (Isaiah 11:6-9, *New English Bible*)

For most postmodern persons, it is difficult not to write off Isaiah's vision as unrealistic, even if we yearn for the liberation it pictures. How is it possible to imagine the end of predator–prey relationships, a relationship biologically required for the perpetuation of all species of life, if not for particular members of a species?

That it's rough in nature and chancy for all living things is no surprise in and of itself. But the forms of death and suffering many predators, including human beings, inflict on prey to stay alive seem especially cruel. Every living thing is a survivor, and cruelty seems a mystery and a waste of pain.

But even as we acknowledge this particular brute fact, we bump into another fact not so brutish: the inrush of beauty and power and grace like that blue heron that flashed unexpectedly over the creek in front of my house. Yet all that interested the blue heron was eating the fish in the creek, not revealing the Sacred to a barely awake human being stumbling through wet fog to get his morning paper. It flew away because it experienced me as a predatory threat, and the fish hardly found the experience of being eaten alive of intrinsic value.

The point is that if nature reveals one certainty, it is that extravagant pain and extravagant beauty are impersonally operating bipolar forces creating nature's harmonies and constitute the two givens of environmental ethics. Both are polar expressions of the relatively inaccessible Sacred in space-time. Or so it seems to Taoist and Buddhist sages, and now seems to many sages of Western process, liberation, and feminist theologies.

The principal insight of liberation and feminist thought relevant to this chapter—also supported by Taoists, Buddhists,[8] and Christian process theology—is that whatever else "redemption" or "liberation" means, it is not limited to the final rescue of selected human beings for eternal life in another existence. As Sallie McFague notes from a Christian feminist point of view, liberation involves the fulfillment of all humanity in the fulfillment of the social and political realities of this world.[9]

Process theology and feminist theology expand this notion in ways similar to Buddhist and Eastern views of nature: liberation must include the fulfillment of everything in nature, for nature is the context in which all particular forms of fulfillment must take place. Human beings, like all things, are not separate, static, substantial individuals relating in external ways to other individuals, mainly human ones, and in minor ways to other forms of life. We belong—from the cells of our bodies to the finest creations of our minds—to the intricate, constantly changing cosmos. We belong to the ecosystem—everything does: rocks, water, atmosphere, plants, animals, and human beings interact in mutually supportive ways.

By what ethical principles, then, should human beings guide interaction with the environment that is the context of all life? What is the character of a primordial environmental ethic conceived in awareness of the mutual relatedness and interdependency of all things and events at every moment of space-time? How does living in accord with such principles contribute to the liberation of life?

Some General Principles
of a Life-Centered Primordial Ethic[10]

Norman Myers, who is a consultant to the World Council of Churches and a conservation biologist, notes a frightening fact: of the five to ten million species that share this planet, the Earth is likely to lose at least one-quarter, and possibly one-third to one-half within the next century. Such a loss "will represent the biggest setback to the planetary complement of species since the first flickering of life almost four billion years ago."[11] Once more, this loss will be caused not by climatic or geophysical disasters but by a single species, *Homo sapiens*–us, the species that is this universe looking at itself.

If humanity does have the power to destroy itself and other forms of life, is it possible to think that humanity possesses sufficient power to prevent worldwide destruction of itself and other forms of life? We have the power to destroy life; do we have the power to creatively sustain life? Much depends on the meaning of power. Power understood as sovereignty over the earth, given to humanity by a transcendent deity possessing absolute sovereignty, has proved counterproductive. Traditional Jewish, Christian, and Islamic teaching grants such power only to God, with human beings exercising derived power over nature given by God. But this model of power, as Sallie McFague convincingly notes, has three flaws that make it an outmoded and self-destructive mode of exercising power.[12]

First, God is portrayed as worldless and the world as godless; the world is empty of God's presence because it is too lowly to be the royal abode of God. Time and space are a yawning void empty of God's presence; the places we love on the earth as well as the infinite space of the universe are without God, for God is a totally other creator-king on whose power everything is dependent. God's power as creator extends over everything in the universe at every moment of space-time, of course, but God's being does not. God relates to the universe externally, not internally; he is not part of the universe, but is essentially different and apart, for there is nothing in nature to which we can liken God.

Second, while traditional Jewish, Christian, and Islamic models of God portray God as a benevolent ruler of the universe, God's benevolence usually extends only to human beings. In such a "monarchical model," as McFague notes, God has little concern for the cosmos, for the nonhuman world. Nature is simply blank in terms of what lies beyond the human sphere.

Third, in this model not only is God distant from the world, relating only to human beings; God controls the universe through a combination of domination and benevolence. God's action is on the world, not in the world, and it is the kind of action that inhibits human growth and responsibility. Thus, while it is simplistic, for example, to blame the Jewish-Christian tradition for the current ecological crisis–on the grounds that in Genesis God instructs human beings to have "domination" over nature–this imagery nonetheless supports attitudes of external control over the natural world in imitation of God's external relation to nature.

In cruder traditional Christian views of God's creating power as dominance, for example, God is a king who fights on the side of his chosen ones to bring their enemies down; nature is one of these enemies. In more refined views of the same model of power, God is the father who will not let his children suffer; nature is a created order under God's control. From the vantage point of environmental ethics, the first view supports exploitation of nature as an instrumental means created to serve humanity's and God's purposes. The second view supports escapism; nature is good, but now is in a state of sin; whatever liberation it might experience must be created by God and is of secondary importance to the liberation God has planned for some of humanity, when God finally establishes his kingdom.

An ecological worldview contradicts models of power as dominance. If the human species is indeed now directing the course of its evolution along with nonhuman species inhabiting this planet—because we are so intrinsically and extrinsically interdependent—our choice is to accept this power, but not as dominance and control. In other words, power must be conceived differently from traditional Jewish-Christian-Islamic understandings of power. For the evolutionary-ecological perspective for which I have been arguing renders impossible any understanding of our relation with nature or with the Sacred as an external relationship to an outside power exercising total control over anything.[13]

Accordingly, a primordial environmental ethic rests on metaphors of power that are relational. In Christian process thought and Christian feminist theologies of nature, for example, God's power is understood through the metaphor of "loving" persuasion that empowers and recognizes the freedom of all things and events in space-time as God "lures" all individuals to realize their own creative potential. Buddhist metaphors of power stress the power of cooperative co-origination and co-creation in the mutual becoming of all things and events in space-time. Consequently, "enlightened compassion"—awareness of the interrelation of all things and events to such a degree that the suffering of any "sentient being" is experienced as one's own suffering—ideally guides Buddhist interaction with nature. The sages of Taoism stressed nature's interdependent balancing act through harmonious tension between the bipolar forces of *yin* and *yang* that constitute the Tao, which is experienced and reenacted by the sage through "actionless action" (*wu-wei*) in his or her dealings with life.

These sources, and contemporary process thought, in conjunction with current scientific ecological notions, provide a resource for metaphorically revisioning a life-centered primordial ethic as the practice of "loving/compassionate wisdom." By "love" I mean passionate concern for the welfare of all living beings; "compassion" is the experience of empathy—for the suffering of all living things—that accompanies the "wisdom" that reveals that we are mutually interrelated and interdependent with all living beings because we are life looking at itself.

The first question of a life-centered ethic based on loving/compassionate wisdom is, Why should we work to save species now in danger of extinction and work to preserve as much biological diversity as possible? Because, among other reasons, it is in our and their self-interest to do so, since we are as mutually implicated in their lives as their lives are in ours. Through their genetic constituents, species of animals and plants are natural resources. For example, in the interests of agriculture, medicine, and industry, human beings may need to draw upon the variety of species of life as a support, just as we have done in the past. We may rely on genetic diversity for our survival in ways that are uniquely human, but such reliance mirrors the fact that all species of life survive because of genetic diversity that originates in the plurality of life forms.

However, self-interest is not the only reason for spending time on preserving biological diversity. In addition to the instrumental value plants and animals have for our species, all species of life have their own intrinsic value—value for themselves. In a mutually interdependent world, all life forms, not just human beings, have intrinsic value.

A primordial ethic of compassionate/loving wisdom thus requires respect for and affirmation of the intrinsic value of all living things: the value that each and every living thing has in and for itself. There is nothing new in this affirmation. The intention of any life-centered ethic—whether in Christian, Buddhist, Taoist, secular, or primordial form—is to revere life. While our application of a life-centered ethic in practice will also recognize a need to balance considerations of intrinsic value with extrinsic value for us, life-centered ethics starts with recognizing that all living things have value in their own right.[14]

There are numerous resources from which to draw in envisioning a primordial life-centered ethic, and all should be considered: neglected traditions within Judaism and the Christian Way, contemporary feminist thought, the religious traditions of humanity, and contemporary developments in the arts and sciences. Numerous starting points are available, but two good places to begin consideration of the application of the principle of loving/compassionate wisdom to practical environmental issues is what some Western environmental philosophers call the "land ethics" movement and the "animal rights" movement.[15] While this does not exhaust the issues with which environmental ethics is concerned, the remainder of this chapter will focus on land ethics and animal rights in order to illustrate how a primordial ethic of compassionate/loving wisdom might be applied to specific environmental issues involving the liberation of life.

Land Ethics

The forerunner of environmental ethics in Western philosophy was Aldo Leopold (1887-1948). He was not a professional philosopher, but worked as a forest and game manager for the U.S. Forest Service, and later as professor of game management at the University of Wisconsin. His book *Sand Country Almanac* resounds with ideas that resonate with similarities to Western process philosophy, and Buddhist and Taoist views of nature. The argument around which his views revolve is that environmental ethics should move beyond anthropomorphism toward a land ethic.[16] The issue is that "there is as yet no ethic dealing with [humanity's] relation to land and to animals and plants which grow upon it. . . . The land relation is still strictly economic, entailing privileges but not obligations."[17]

Environmental philosophers who stress land ethics are communitarian and systematic in their views. The basic idea is that the good of the "biotic community" is the ultimate measure of the moral rightness or wrongness of human actions affecting and effecting the environment. To J. Baird Callicott, this principle means that the effect upon ecological "systems" is the decisive factor in deciding the ethical character of actions.[18]

Jay McDaniel notes two issues that have evolved from this point of view. First, in what sense is land valuable apart from its usefulness to human purposes? Or, more generally, does nature have value in and of itself apart from human purposes? Second, given the emphasis on ecosystems and biotic communities, what is the ethical status of individual living organisms?

A number of environmental philosophers have thought long and hard about the issue of value in nature. Among the most important are Holmes Rolston III. In his *Environmental Ethics*, he sharply criticized the mechanistic worldview of industrialized civilizations that characterize nonhuman life forms and all inorganic forms of nature as devoid of value other than what is assigned by human beings.[19] In place of seeing nature as that which has extrinsic, instrumental value to human purposes—a secularized version of the creation mythology of Genesis—he proposes that nature has value in and of itself independent of its value to human beings. As evidence for this view, he cited occasions of human experience in which we experience nature as a carrier of value, not as a recipient of assigned human valuation.

Rolston's argument is Kantian; all human experience of anything, in this case, our experience of nature, is interpretative. In some of these interpretations there is a receptive element: often in our experience of plants and animals, we experience a kind of "givenness" that discloses value. Some of these values are aesthetic: the snowy white clouds cascading over the northern summit of Mount Rainier like an inverted fan. Some of these values are signs of the unity within the diversity of life: the web of a spider flashing silver in a winter morning's sun. Some are even indications of the presence of the Sacred: the great blue heron gliding under the bridge spanning the creek running in front of my house that November morning two years ago, but which still seems to me like only yesterday. When we attend to these experiences, we discover that value is actualized in human interrelation with nature, sometimes by conscious design, sometimes quite suddenly apart from human expectations.

What Leopold, Callicott, and Rolston warn us to avoid is thinking of nature in excessively individualistic terms. They are suspicious of ethical preoccupation with individual nonhuman life forms because they view this as expressive of Western bias toward individualism. They do not deny that individuals can have a place in our ethical concern, but it is not their well-being as individuals that is important. Rather, it is the well-being of the biological community of which they are a part and to which they contribute that is of highest ethical importance. This is why land ethics approaches tend to mistrust ethical views that stress animal rights or arguments for the intrinsic value of individual natural entities. Their point is that even though individual mountains or plants or animals do indeed have value apart from their usefulness to human beings, they are valueless intrinsically and extrinsically in isolation from their environments. A natural entity's value is inseparable from its being an organic part of wider biotic communities, and ultimately, the entirety of nature.

However, the presuppositions of an environmental ethic stressing nature as a whole—as does the land ethic approach—engender questions land ethics is unable to confront. What, if anything, is the value of individual nonhuman life forms as they intrinsically exist in and for themselves apart from their extrinsic value to the environmental system of which they are a part? In what sense can land be valuable apart from its usefulness to human ends? Given the emphasis on ecosystems or biological communities that is central to land ethic orientations, what is the ethical status of individual living entities? Questions such as these are central to animal rights ethics.

Animal Rights

McDaniel traces the beginning of the contemporary animal rights movement to Albert Schweitzer's (1875–1965) principle of reverence for life.[20]

> When abuse of animals is widespread, when the bellowing of thirsty animals in cattle cars is heard and ignored, when cruelty still prevails in many slaughterhouses, when animals are clumsily and painfully butchered in our kitchens, when brutish people inflict unimaginable torments upon animals, and when some animals are exposed to the cruel games of children, all of us share in the guilt.[21]

For Schweitzer the primary ethical imperative was to eliminate the unnecessary suffering of all animals at the hands of human beings. This imperative is also the central goal of the contemporary animal rights movement.

Peter Singer is probably the animal rights movement's leading spokesperson. His *Animal Liberation: A New Ethics for Our Treatment of Animals* zeros in specifically on the suffering human beings inflict on animals in scientific experimentation, agriculture, and business.[22] He argues that in principle no reason exists why the welfare or suffering of nonhuman animals should matter less than our own. The fact that many animals cannot reason or communicate in languages similar to human speech ought to be as ethically irrelevant to us as the fact that some human beings to whom we have ethical obligations cannot reason or communicate, for example, severely retarded children. For Singer, the question is not whether animals can reason and talk, but whether they can suffer and experience themselves suffering.

Singer's answer is, of course, that nonhuman animals not only experience suffering and pain; many are equipped with neurophysiological systems similar to our own, and, like us, they expend a great deal of energy avoiding pain and suffering. Because animals do suffer—just as human beings do—human beings as apparently the most highly evolved species of life on this planet at this time are obliged not to inflict more pain on animals than we would inflict on members of our own species.

However, animal rights ethics does not demand that we treat all creatures equally. But we are obliged to grant all creatures equal ethical consideration in our interaction with them. The human neglect of such equal moral consideration Singer calls "speciesism."

In order to avoid the ethical pitfalls of speciesism, Singer advises several forms of action. First, we should immediately end unnecessary scientific experimentation on animals and all forms of unnecessary infliction of pain on animals in agriculture and business. This requires that human beings cease, for example, hunting for sport; farming mink, fox, and other animals for their fur; capturing wild animals and imprisoning them in cages for human beings to stare at; forcing animals, either kindly or through painful behavioral modification techniques, to entertain people at rodeos and circuses; slaughtering whales with exploding harpoons; and generally ignoring the interests of wild animals as the human community spreads concrete and urban industrialized pollution over their habitats.

Finally, Singer argues that human beings should become vegetarians on two grounds: (1) the meat available for human consumption comes from animals who suffer while being reared for market; and (2) the agricultural-industrial complex that profits through animal exploitation from animals' being reared on factory farms to their assembly line deaths in slaughterhouses wants our money, not our approval. Boycotting meat is the only way to end the suffering animals encounter under the conditions of modern factory farming.

Clearly, the ethical foci of land ethics advocates and animal rights advocates sharply differ. Land ethics is system oriented, whereas animal rights ethics is individual oriented; land ethics is concerned with the stability, integrity, and beauty of ecosystems, whereas animal rights ethics is concerned with the suffering of particular creatures; land ethics is concerned with the value of rivers, valleys, and mountains, whereas animal rights ethics emphasizes other animals.

Must we choose between these two forms of environmental ethical orientations, or can these two viewpoints be synthesized into a larger life-centered ethic that is responsive to both the abuse of animals under human domination and to the degradation of larger environmental wholes, which are themselves habitats for countless living human beings? Surely wisdom dictates synthesis. For is not the real issue this: In a world of mutual interrelationship and interdependency, how can we balance the needs of the human and nonhuman communities against the needs of the environment that nourishes all living communities on this planet? Spelling out the principles of such a synthesis will involve an ethical shift from anthropocentrism with respect to individual animals to an emphasis on the ecological systems nurturing life. Eliminating anthropocentrism also means affirming the intrinsic value of all life forms.

The Practice of Loving/Compassionate Wisdom

Anthropomorphic thought centers on human life, purposes, and achievements as the model for measuring value and worth. Protagoras's assertion, "man is the measure of all things," is the defining character of anthropomorphism. However, while a life-centered ethic guided by the principle of loving/compassionate wisdom is non-anthropomorphic, this does not imply that all types of anthropomorphic thought are inappropriate or ethically reprehensible. At this juncture of the evolution of our present cosmic epoch, humanity seems to be the only species with the capacity and corresponding responsibility to develop any sort of ethical stance about the environment. Human beings seem to be the only animals to have evolved with sufficient capacity and freedom to destroy the environment and all the life it supports, since we are the culprits, the blot on nature, performing criminal acts on the environment. This form of anthropomorphism is not inappropriate.

Recognizing human responsibility for the environmental crisis facing this planet simultaneously entails recognizing that our species is not the center of the environmental processes that engender and nourish all forms of life. Placing ourselves at the center of nature—an anthropomorphism that is a direct consequence of traditional Christian, and to a secondary extent traditional Jewish and Islamic anthropomorphic readings of the biblical creation mythology—is the primary cause of the environmental destruction now occurring on the Earth. A life-centered ethic of living/compassionate wisdom must renounce this form of anthropomorphism.

All life, human and nonhuman, has both intrinsic value—value for itself—and extrinsic value—value for other forms of life—in a universe of dynamic, processive, and mutual interdependency and interrelationships. The pain of one species is the pain of all; the welfare of one species is the welfare of all. The life of all species is the life of each. As Jesus is reported to have said, God's compassionate care extends to sparrows; as Mahayana Buddhists say it, there are no fully enlightened Buddhas unless every blade of grass is enlightened. We are all in this together, and we—the human species—are not the center, for the center of life is everywhere and nowhere.

The practice of loving/compassionate wisdom is the application of the principle of nonviolence in our relationships with all life forms and all environmental systems that nourish life. Evil is understood as that which injures or destroys interrelationships on which life depends. Yet in our environmental system, noninjury is never completely possible. Life forms must eat other life forms to stay alive, and apparently human beings are the top of the food chain; the practice of life-centered nonviolence will not eradicate suffering or death from nature. All that can be realistically hoped for is to lessen the suffering our species inflicts on the natural order in the hope that environmental stability and balances can be maintained and in some cases reestablished. But we must raise our collective consciousness by training ourselves to see nature—in all its forms and processes—as the place where we catch glimpses of the relatively inaccessible ox.

If we see the Sacred "in, with, and under" the processes of nature, from the American bison of the Lakota to sacred mountains and rivers to forest groves to my great blue heron—even in the very processes that cause the death and suffering of one animal so that another can live—our relation to the natural order suddenly changes. We become compassionate, not from altruism that sees the suffering of another life form as different from one's own but through recognition that the suffering of others, in part, *is* one's own since, in part, the other *is* an element of one's own selfhood. But experiencing the suffering or welfare of another life as one's own demands compassionate wisdom—the experiential insight and awareness of the nondual, mutually interconnected dependency of all life forms as expressions of the processes of universal co-origination and interdependency that constitute all things and events in the universe at every moment of space-time. But just as faith without works is dead, so too is compassionate wisdom without love—the active affirmation of the right to life of all life forms expressed through caring application of compassionate wisdom in our daily interaction with all life forms, including those life forms on which we depend for food.

How does one practice the principle of love compassionately and wisely? We must, of course, practice compassionate/wise love on a case-by-case basis. However, McDaniel suggests five guidelines:[23]

(1) It is always wrong to kill animals needlessly or for entertainment or to cause animals pain or torment; it is always wrong to destroy the habitat of animals needlessly.

(2) It is never morally acceptable to fail to provide food, shelter, and care for animals for which we have accepted responsibility.

(3) It is always wrong to oppress animals for research and medical experimentation unless absolute need can be demonstrated and unless research and experimentation can be done without inflicting suffering on animals.

(4) It is always reprehensible to rear animals for food in any way that causes them pain or suffering or denies them the ability to live in conditions that are reasonably natural for them.

(5) It is wrong to imprison animals for display for any reason other than to preserve a species near extinction or preserve biological diversity.

Certainly, this is not an exhaustive list of principles. But their serious application would enormously reduce the suffering inflicted by human beings on other life forms by greatly lessening damage to the environment. Such principles, and perhaps others, assume that our lives are instances of, rather than exceptions to, the forces generating life. Therefore, we should behave toward the processes of nature, the environmental systems that constitute nature, and each specific life form accordingly. They are principles of ecological balance in which we participate, not dominate. They are guidelines that seek always to balance the needs of the human community with the needs of the environmental forces that nourish all life in all ecosystems.

A number of examples come to mind that illustrate that determining the wisest life-affirming action is not always easy. For example, how should the economic needs of loggers and other forestry-related industries in the Pacific Northwest be balanced against environmental concern to maintain remaining old-growth forests and endangered species of animals like the spotted owl and plants like the Pacific yew. Since the corporate greed of the timber interests of this region of the United States has for over a hundred years depleted the forests, both old growth and second growth, through unwise environmental practices and greedy economic policies, the needs of the ecosystems that constitute forest lands must be preserved even if this means the loss of timber-related jobs. No logging in old-growth forests should be permitted, to preserve not only endangered species like spotted owls but the forest ecosystem that nourishes all life forms—deer, elk, salmon, eagles, great blue heron, Douglas firs, Western hemlocks, Pacific yew (whose bark may provide medicine for the treatment of some forms of cancer), and human beings—that depend on forest ecosystems.

This decision will cause suffering to those whose economic livelihood lies in timber-related occupations. But human suffering in this instance is short term. Human beings are the most adaptable species of life inhabiting this planet; we can learn other trades, find other ways to make a living. But overharvesting forest lands kills the life of the forest ecosystem. This is long-term damage and suffering that also damage human life.

The pollution of the Earth's atmosphere provides another example. Air quality must be protected at all costs. In part, this means overcoming our collective addiction to the automobile. Until we do, we must force automobile manufacturers to maintain high emission control standards and build more efficient engines that consume less gasoline. In part, this means also forbidding the emission of industrial waste into the atmosphere and the waterways of the planet. In part, this means finding alternative sources of energy to replace fossil fuels and nuclear generated power. It part, this means placing strict controls on urban development by insisting that all development plans, industrial expansion, road building, mass transportation construction, and technological expansion cause minimal environmental damage. The burden of proof must rest on our species to demonstrate that our needs and the needs of the environment and other life forms the environment supports are in harmony.

Living by loving/compassionate wisdom will require harsh medicine. Sometimes successful treatment of a disease is necessarily painful. Willingness to swallow our collective medicine will require some profound collective consciousness raising, but we have the resources. Luckily for us, some scientists, poets, artists, philosophers, and theologians have a habit of waking us up, grabbing us by the collar and saying, "Will you please pay attention! You wouldn't think something as completely there, so completely busy, as life would be so easy to overlook."

I have a suggestion about how to raise our environmental consciousness. Over twenty years ago, American lunar astronauts saw an earth rise from the surface of the moon. It knocked them breathless. We should send regularly scheduled shuttles to the moon filled with a flurry of artists and naturalists, photographers and painters to see what the astronauts saw; they will then turn their mirrors upon ourselves and show us Earth as a single planet, a single organism that's buoyant, fragile, blooming, buzzing, full of spectacle, full of fascinating human beings, something to cherish. Learning our full address may not end all wars or solve all problems, but it will enrich our sense of wonder. It will remind us that the human context is not as tight as a noose but as large as the universe we have the privilege to inhabit. It will change our sense of what a neighbor is. It will persuade us that we are citizens of the planet, Earth's joy riders and caretakers, who would do well to work on the planet's problems together.

Seeing Earth this way, we would also understand how empty the world would be without animal sounds and without us: blackbirds quibbling like druids; horses galloping on soft tracks; crows sounding as if they are choking on tree bark; burbling swallows hanging like clothespins from the branches of trees; elk bugling like the sound of distant war games; the metallic ping of night hawks; the kindergarten band of crickets; the electric whine of female mosquitoes; the Morse code of red-headed woodpeckers; the joyous laughter of human beings.

However, some of us, perhaps most of us, are not in a position for this sort of consciousness raising because we have more immediate concerns about personal survival. Many of us are poor because of economic exploitation. Many of us are politically oppressed. Many of us are in a state of war with our neighbors. Many of us are uneducated and exploited by power structures over which we have no control. Many of us are oppressed because of gender and race and domestic violence. Many of us require liberation from more immediate forms of human oppression before we can afford to be interested in consciousness raising about our interrelation with the Earth and all life, human and nonhuman. Hence the topic of chapter 7, "The Ox Forgotten, Leaving the Man Alone," is "liberation," specifically the connection between the liberation of life and the liberation of women from patriarchal forms of oppression. Chapter 8, "The Ox and the Man Both Gone Out of Sight," continues the discussion of women's liberation by focusing on the interrelation between liberation from patriarchy and liberation from political, economic, and racial forms of human oppression. Chapter 9, "Returning to the Origin, Back to the Source," concentrates on the interconnection between the liberation of life portrayed in chapters 6 and 7, the liberation of women from patriarchal oppression portrayed in chapter 8, and the need for political and economic liberation portrayed in chapter 9 with "final liberation" understood as the possibility of liberation from death. That is, the topic of chapter 9 is, to employ a Christian theological term, "soteriology."

Notes

1. D. T. Suzuki, *Manual of Zen Buddhism* (New York: Grove Press, 1960), 132.
2. Annie Dillard, *Holy the Firm* (New York: Harper & Row, 1977), 41–42.
3. See chapter 5.
4. Charles Birch and John B. Cobb, Jr., eds., *The Liberation of Life* (Denton, Tex.: Environmental Books, 1990), chap. 3.
5. I have in mind here Mircea Eliade's notion of "sacred place" as a space in the natural order where human beings experience *hierophany*—encounter with the Sacred—at a sacred time. See Mircea Eliade, *The Sacred and the Profane* (New York: Harper Torchbooks, 1957), 22–63; idem, *Patterns in Comparative Religion* (New York: World Publishing Company, 1963), 1–37.
6. See Peter Berger, *A Rumor of Angels: Modern Society and the Rediscovery of the Supernatural* (Garden City, N.Y.: Doubleday, 1969).
7. See Jay B. McDaniel, *Of God and Pelicans: A Theology of Reverence for Life* (Louisville, Ky.: Westminster/John Knox Press, 1989), 13–17.
8. See Roger T. Ames, "Putting the *Te* Back into Taoism," in *Nature in Asian Traditions of Thought*, ed. J. Baird Callicott and Roger T. Ames (Albany: State University of New York Press), 116–17.
9. Sallie McFague, *Models of God: A Theology for an Ecological, Nuclear Age* (Philadelphia: Fortress Press, 1987), 12–17.
10. The phrase "life-centered ethic" is Charles Birch's and John Cobb's (see the introduction to *Liberation of Life*).
11. Norman Myers, "The Environmental Crisis: How Big, How Important?" in *Report and Background Papers of the Working Group, GDR, July* (Geneva: WCC Publications, 1986), 101, cited by McDaniel, *Of God and Pelicans*, 51.

12. McFague, *Models of God*, 65–69.
13. This is a fundamental point in current Jewish and Christian feminist views of power and nature, as well as in Christian process theology. See Judith Plaskow, *Standing Again at Sinai: Judaism from a Feminist Perspective* (San Francisco: HarperSanFrancisco, 1990), 145–50, 154–55; and McFague, *Models of God*, 17–27 and chap. 3.
14. Jay McDaniel makes this point eloquently from the perspective of Christian process theology; see *Of God and Pelicans*, 52–53.
15. I have followed McDaniel's lead in this regard, and his views and insights have inspired formation of my own. Although I draw different theoretical conclusions from him, I find myself in agreement with many of his observations about land ethics and the rights of animals (ibid., 84–90).
16. Leopold was among the earliest environmentalists to use this phrase (*Sand Country Almanac* [New York: Oxford University Press, 1949]).
17. Ibid., 201, cited in McDaniel, *Of God and Pelicans*, 55.
18. J. Baird Callicott, "Animal Liberation: A Triangular Affair," *Environmental Ethics* 2 (1980): 311–38.
19. Holmes Rolston III, *Environmental Ethics: Duties to and Values in the Natural World* (Philadelphia: Temple University Press, 1988), 113–20.
20. McDaniel, *Of God and Pelicans*, 58.
21. Cited by McDaniel, ibid.
22. Peter Singer, *Animal Liberation: A New Ethics for Our Treatment of Animals* (New York: Avon Books, 1975).
23. McDaniel, *Of God and Pelicans*, 70.

7
The Ox Forgotten,
Leaving the Man Alone

THE SEVENTH OX-HERDING PICTURE, "THE OX FORGOTTEN, LEAVING THE MAN ALONE," portrays a transitional state on the Buddhist journey to enlightenment. The man sits in solitude, quiet and at leisure, reflecting on what has happened in his struggle with the ox, unsure of what is later in store for him. Still, something has been achieved:

> Riding on the ox, he is at last back in his home,
> When lo! The ox is no more; the man alone sits serenely.
> Though the red sun is high up in the sky, he is still quietly dreaming;
> Under a straw-thatched roof his whip and rope are idly lying.[1]

In their proper Buddhist context, the first seven Ox-Herding pictures portray in step-by-step progression the successive phases of Zen practice: training in meditation, ethical self-discipline, study of scripture, and, in picture 7, the blissful experience of the unity underlying the diversity of all things and events at every moment of space-time. But the attainment the man realizes at this stage is not the "true Self that is no Self," because the man is still in transit and must not remain at home. He needs to understand that self-liberation is not attained apart from the liberation of other selves. Accordingly, chapter 7 begins a dialogue with the meaning of liberation for other selves that is simultaneously bound up with one's own self-liberation by concentrating on women's liberation. My thesis is that the liberation of women engenders other forms of liberation taken up in chapter 9: liberation from political, social, and economic oppression.

The seventh Ox-Herding picture, then, tells us that wrestling with the ox is as intellectually demanding as it is spiritually and physically exhausting; the ox is always wild and free and cannot be tamed. We must rest every once in a while and mull over what we have experienced, lick our wounds, regroup, and adjust strategy, preferably in "a room of one's own," as Virginia Woolf wrote. So here I am, home alone in my room, haunted by a thought.

The thought is this. Everything I have written thus far has been from a male point of view. Not surprising in and of itself, since I am male. But if we are constantly being mutually created by the interrelationships we consciously and unconsciously experience with other human beings as well as with everything else in the universe at every moment of space-time, surely masculinity does not define all that I am. I have in mind something Taoist: as *yin* creates *yang*, femininity and masculinity are not dualities but interdependent polarities. If so, surely, masculinity is constituted by femininity within my own nature as male, as well as by the quality of my interrelationships with actual women and other men. Surely, similar interrelationships with actual men and other women partly define femininity for women, although admittedly much hangs on cultural and social definitions of "masculinity" and "femininity." Some contemporary feminists tell us that gender is a social construction and a deceit invented by patriarchy to control and dominate both nature and women, that we—men and women—need liberation from patriarchy.[2]

While contemporary feminist thought has sharpened my sense that most of our self-identity as human beings is created by how we experience and understand our interrelationships with nature and with each other as male and female within the contexts of the cultures in which we dwell, feminism is not the earliest source of my encounter with this way of seeing human self-identity. I have learned much also from Buddhist thought and Taoist mysticism in this regard. But there was an earlier teacher.

When I was eighteen years old and full of juice, trying to figure out what it meant to "be a man," I met a Mescalero Apache "singer" named Billy Begaye. His grandson, Antonio, my best friend, invited me to spend two weeks in July with him on the Apache reservation in New Mexico. I jumped at the chance, because at that time Native Americans were one of my "hobbies," and I believed all the romantic white stereotypes about Apache men: all were warriors, hunters, trackers, who knew how to walk the land like unseen spirits as they lived on whatever nature gave them. If anyone could tell me about being a man, I thought, it would be an Apache singer.

"You ask about something important," I remember Billy Begaye saying when I brought the subject up. "It's good that you do. The knowledge you wish is sacred. We must first go to the sweat lodge and prepare. I will tell you there."

"Good," I thought, caught up in the old man's ways. "I'm going to get some answers."

I did, but not as quickly as I expected, nor what I expected. The three of us sat in the sweat lodge for what seemed like hours, soaking in our own and each other's fluids, listening to Billy Begaye chanting in a language neither Antonio nor I understood.

"The thing that makes us male is temporary," he finally began as he poured more water from a gourd over hot stones in the center of the lodge. "Men die and must be remade. The thing that makes women female is found in hard things like minerals, crystals, and stones, and in soft things like water. That is permanent. The female controls and creates. She owns breath, air and wind, bird and feather, and the hard flint from which we used to make weapons. She is earth, sun, moon, sky, and water. She is the forms we see and the cycles of corn we eat. She is the mother of the deer and the bringer of fire and light. That is why Apache women are the keepers of fire. Men come and go; women continue and stay. Honor all women and you will find out what it means to be a man."[3]

That night Antonio explained that he had heard his grandfather speak these words many times, but did not understand them any better than I. My friend never did learn their meaning. He was blown apart by a mine in Vietnam ten years later—one more casualty of white Anglo-Saxon macho idealism. Nor am I completely certain of Billy Begaye's meaning. Yet years later I am beginning to pick up clues, many from feminist colleagues in religious studies. This chapter is about these clues.

A Word on Feminist Methodology

I suspect it will seem problematic at best, and absurd at worst, for a white male to write about feminism, feminist theology, feminist analysis of the patriarchal oppression of women by humanity's male-dominated religious traditions, and feminist visions of women's and men's postpatriarchal liberation, through the filter of a primordial theology that is intentionally pluralistic and not specifically identified with any particular religious Way. There are good reasons for suspicion. The world's religious Ways are patriarchal, and I am, indeed, a white male trained in patriarchy. But as Billy Begaye tried to teach me in 1957, and feminist colleagues continue to teach me now, nothing remains as it is, and not everything is as it seems.

Of course, what "patriarchy" means is a crucial question, as are other terms feminists employ. Therefore, it is important at the outset that the meaning of "patriarchy" and other important related terms be specified. The feminist scholar who has helped me most in this regard is Rita M. Gross, principally because her "feminist Buddhist theology" is grounded in careful and meticulous scholarship in the history of religions. She is a master of both history of religions and theology, so I follow her lead.[4]

"Androcentrism" and "patriarchy" usually go together in feminist writing. "Androcentrism" is a mode of consciousness, a thought-form, a method of gathering information and classifying women's place in a male-defined scheme of reality. Androcentric thought assumes that men represent the normal, ideal, and central kind of human being, while women are seen as somehow peripheral and marginal to this norm. It pretends that humanity has only one center, that masculinity is the sole model of humanity.[5] It also occurs in both masculine and feminine heads. "Patriarchy" is the social and institutional expression of androcentrism. Patriarchy always involves a gender hierarchy of men over women. Men control women, or at least like to think they do.

Androcentrism and patriarchy will be expressed and experienced differently from religious community to religious community. In the context of my being a historian of religions thinking theologically and pluralistically, my encounter with feminist theology has engendered three questions. First, are the world's religious Ways solely a projection of male concerns, experiences, and imagery, coupled with male desire to subjugate women and to legitimate their male claims over women? Second, does "patriarchy" refer only to a system of social organization in which descent and succession are traced through the male line? Or, third, does "patriarchy" refer to more complex social and historical realities that involve not only the differentiation of the sexes but also the symbolization of the natural environment and its relation to the social organization of sex roles with reference to such factors as geography, economics, and psychology? There are many other questions relevant to feminist thought. However, this chapter will relate these specific questions to an overview of the role of women and the images of the feminine in the world's religious Ways. But first, some more preliminary observations and definitions.

It is probably safe to assume that all feminist theology is liberation theology, but not all feminist thought is theological or a species of liberation theology. Some feminist theologies reject existing religious Ways as irredeemably patriarchal. However, the working assumptions of this chapter are: (1) Christian feminist theology is a species of liberation theology, because like other liberation theologies, feminist theology arises out of specific experiences of oppression; (2) its origins lie in biblical tradition in general, and women's experience of oppression in particular; and (3) feminist and liberation theologies that occur in non-Christian traditions are often inspired by, but nevertheless remain distinct from, Christian feminist liberation theologies. Accordingly, there are Christian feminist theologies, Jewish feminist theologies, Islamic feminist theologies, Buddhist feminist theologies, Native American feminist theologies, black feminist theologies, and white feminist theologies.

The theme of liberation is not new in Jewish or Christian tradition. It is a central theme of the exodus story and the central message of Jesus in the Gospel of Luke. God sent Jesus, Luke writes, "to set at liberty those who are oppressed, to proclaim the acceptable year of the Lord" (4:18c). However, because liberation theologies arise out of particular circumstances of oppression, liberation thought possesses a pluralistic nature relative to the nature of the oppression experienced. Yet in spite of the pluralistic nature of liberation theology, the theologies share common methods, goals, beliefs, and problems.

Methodologically, liberation theologies are written by those experiencing oppression—women, blacks, Hispanics, Latin Americans, Asians, Africans, Middle Easterners. They stress experiential/inductive methods. That is, they begin with concrete situations and experiences and try to come to understand where the Sacred is in relation to these situations. For women, it is the experience of patriarchal sexism—the treatment of women as secondary human beings because of female gender—that provides the basic object of concern of feminist theologians.

According to Gross, this means that feminist theologians choosing to work within specific religious traditions are faced with "working through a quadruple Androcentrism" in order to find "an accurate and usable past for women" in the religious tradition in which they participate in order to reconstruct these traditions accordingly. Otherwise, women have no reason to participate in these traditions.[6] First, whenever a religious tradition—in Gross's case Buddhism—chooses which literature to keep and whose experiences to preserve in their historical records, it usually operates with a male-centered or "androcentric consciousness and set of values." Stories about men and the thought and practices of men are far more likely to be recorded than stories about women or what women said or did.

Second, even when a religious tradition preserves significant records about women, later developments within that tradition tend to ignore these stories and stress stories about male heroes as models of practice and attainment. Third, most Western scholarship on the world's religious Ways is androcentric and often agrees with the male-centered biases of the world's religious traditions, to the point of further ignoring the few existing records about women or even ridiculing women. Finally, all contemporary expressions of humanity's religious traditions, both Western and Asian, continue to maintain an unrelenting, ongoing androcentrism.

Accordingly, Gross believes that feminists are faced with working through this quadruple androcentrism to reconstruct their respective traditions according to an accurate and usable past that focuses on women's experience. "Accuracy" has to do with feminism as an academic, historical methodology, while "usability" refers to the feminist agenda for liberation. If feminist scholarship cannot reconstruct an accurate and useful history of humanity's religious Ways that includes women's experience as a constructive element of religious history, there is no reason for women to remain in their respective religious traditions. In Gross's view, such a reconstruction, if possible, will be liberating for both women and men.[7]

The feminist quest for an accurate history stems from the conviction that androcentric history cannot, by definition, be accurate.[8] It is filled with omissions about women as historical actors and in most cases "whitewashes many negativities about the patriarchal past."[9] But a past recounted as normative that ignores or stereotypes data about the female half of the human species cannot be accurate. Accurate history is always better than inaccurate history, not only because of its accuracy but also because one of the forces engendering oppression is the inaccurate historical portrayal of oppressed communities. Accordingly, part of the reason feminists spend time investigating the history of the roles and images of women in the history of their respective religious traditions is to recover and recount what is usually not included in the histories of their religious Ways.

Related to an accurate history is a usable history. All historical records and interpretations of the past are selections. That is, history is never an unbiased, neutral recounting of past events. The question is *how* historians choose "relevant" data. Feminists also usually recognize that history is written and rewritten to reinforce values and perspectives a community deems important. That is, historians seek pasts that are not only accurate but usable. Feminist historians seek historical models, mostly ignored in androcentric historiography, of events that empower, rather than disempower, women. As Eleanor McLaughlin writes on this issue in connection with Christian history, androgynous scholars seek a past that is

> at once *responsible*—that is, grounded in the historicist rubric of dealing with the past on its own terms—and *usable*. I mean by the search for a usable past . . . an examination of . . . history with a new set of questions that arise out of commitments to wholeness for woman and all humanity. Following from new questions, this is a history that redresses omissions and recasts interpretations.[10]

A usable past is important because a religious community constitutes itself by its collective memory of the normative past it recalls and emulates. This is as necessary for Buddhists and Hindus, for whom the past *is not* normative or revelatory, as it is for Judaism, Christianity, or Islam, for whom the past *is* revelatory. Accuracy is especially important when justice issues are involved. When historical records and interpretations ignore women, a community is telling itself something negative about women's potential and place in the community. Likewise, if feminists can recover an accurate, usable past for women, the communities in which they participate are reshaped. The stories people tell, the history they remember, are crucial for empowering or disempowering whole segments of a community. Bringing the stories of women into a community's collective memory liberates both women and men who are shaped by that community's history of oppression.

Of course, feminist methodology includes more than I have described. But Gross's notions of accurate history and usable past are particularly germane to a historian of religions' thinking about the pluralities of humanity's religious traditions. In her case, she is an American historian of religions and a Buddhist feminist attempting to reconstruct Buddhist history into an accurate and usable past for Buddhist women and men. For this reason, her perspective has inspired me to examine how feminists choosing to participate in other patriarchal religious communities are trying to reconstruct accurate and usable postpatriarchal forms of their community's past. That is, I contend that identifying the historical roots of patriarchy might provide a useful resource for reconstructing a community's past, one that is more accurate and usable in the sense specified by Gross. How and why did religious traditions of humanity become systems of patriarchy?

On Women's Experience in the World's Religions

Reconstructing a religious community's history that includes the experiences of women as forces that shaped it requires analysis of how women's experience has been silenced by the androcentric forces of patriarchy. At present, no male historian is qualified to undertake such an analysis. Nor shall I attempt such a reconstruction. But there are qualified feminist voices to whom men need to listen. One such voice is Judith Plaskow. She notes how "women's experience" names an element missing in Jewish sources and communal life that Jewish women need to recover and make a constructive part of Judaism.[11] However, while accurate accounts of women's experience are missing from most of humanity's religious Ways, Plaskow points out that "women's experience"— the daily, lived, conscious events, thoughts, and feelings that constitute women's daily reality—is pluralistic, both in a single tradition and among the traditions.[12] This pluralism takes different forms in different religious traditions. So the fact that there are no women's accounts of Jewish history is not unique to Judaism.[13] Except for some tribal traditions,[14] the same is true for each of humanity's religious Ways.

But why are the experiences of women not included in the defining histories of most of the world's religious communities? Plaskow believes part of the reason lies in the fact that the pluralism of women's experience is distinct from the pluralism of men's, even though both women and men share common experiences as human beings. This implies that the reasons for exclusion of women's experience from the defining pasts of a religious community must be primarily historical and social.[15] In her words:

> The different socialization of men and women . . . nurtures divergent capacities and divergent experiences of the world. But also, insofar as women are projected as Other, women's experience is doubled in a peculiar way. Knowing she is just herself, a woman must nonetheless deal with the imposition of Otherness. She must forever measure herself against a standard that comes from outside.[16]

While patriarchal imposition of "Otherness" on women is a fundamental part of the history of religions, the term "women's experience" is often ambiguous; it has often implied a uniform "nature" that defines all women, when in fact there is great diversity. Indeed, there are common elements in the situation of women, as there are of men: shared biological experiences, the common imposition of otherness, exclusion from positions of empowerment and authority. But women have appropriated and responded to these elements differently in different religious communities, both as individuals and as members of different religious cultures. Women's experience, as well as men's experience, is like a tapestry of many designs and colors.[17]

But the question still remains: Why are male dominance and misogyny so prevalent? What are their historical sources? One surprising fact is that an overview of the world religions does *not* suggest that male dominance is correlated with supreme male deities.[18] Transcendence in the world religions has been and is imagined in a plurality of ways; male, female, and androgynous deities are experienced as unique, dual, or multiple, while transcendence is beyond name, form, gender, and number altogether. Further, the imagery of transcendence occasionally changed in the histories of the world's religious Ways, along with its images of women.

At the same time, however, the world's religious Ways, except for some tribal communities, maintained male social dominance in the prevailing social-political structures. Even so, the lack of correlation between the gender of deities and male dominance in humanity's religious Ways is fairly easy to illustrate.

For example, early Buddhism—Buddhism in its first two hundred years—experienced and conceptualized *nibbāna*, or "enlightenment," as transcendent and refused to characterize it in either its doctrines or meditational disciplines with reference to gender. Enlightenment is quite literally beyond gender distinction since it is beyond all distinctions, and its liberating attainment is available for both men and women. Yet early Buddhism reflected the patriarchal social structure of the culture of its birth from its very origins. Monastic institutions were patriarchal organizations, and Buddhist lay disciples, both female and male, had to defer to male monastic authority.[19] However, the antecedents of Buddhism—early Brahmanic Hindu traditions—posited a predominantly male pantheon of deities and a hierarchy of supreme male deities along with male social dominance. It is possible to argue, therefore, that Buddhist tradition inherited its form of male dominance from Brahmanic Hinduism, while transforming Hindu understanding of transcendence.[20]

Another illustration is the Taoist Way. Its origins lay in ancient Chinese agricultural folk tradition and its reliance on female deities. Yet, according to Barbara E. Reed, Taoist institutions and teachings were also formed in interaction with the male dominance of Confucian tradition.[21] Behind Confucian teaching and practice lurked Shang Ti, the male ancestral *shen* ("spirit" or "deity") of the Shang dynasty kings, which was transformed by the Chou dynasty kings into a supreme male deity associated with heaven (*t'ien*), which is also *yang* and masculine.

This is the probable historical context of the earliest text of Taoist tradition, the *Tao Te Ching*, edited in its present form between 250 and 150 B.C.E.

This text balances Confucian male dominance (*yang*) by the what the editors believed was the feminine trait of passivity (*yin*) to create an androgynous, balanced harmony of opposites.[22] However, the third century was also the era in which Confucian tradition was instituted as the state philosophy of the Han dynasty as a method of stabilizing social order after a long civil war.

"Order" according to this official state Confucian view placed women in "three submissions": to her father, husband, and sons, coupled with regulation "by the *yang* qualities of the male." According to Han Confucian thought, this would guarantee the all-important harmony of the family and the cosmos.[23] Because this particular Confucian concept of social order prevailed in Chinese society, the Taoist Way managed to challenge neither the patriarchal organization of Chinese culture nor its own later institutions, all of which took on the Confucian patriarchal forms of the society in which it existed.

But if there is no direct correlation between male deities and male dominance in the world's religions, what are the historical origins of patriarchy? Peggy Reeves Sanday offers an intriguing suggestion. Since male dominance is not universal in tribal religious Ways, she concludes that male dominance must have evolved wherever there existed the antecedent conditions of an "outer orientation" and separation of the sexes according to "situations of stress."[24] These factors conjointly resulted in male aggression as a response to stress in a negative environment.

An "outer orientation," according to Sanday, exists in an environment in which a culture perceives and pursues power as if it were "out there," be this in the primary food animals of hunting societies, in the land fertility of agricultural societies, or in the activity of war. Primary religious symbols in such cultures are related to the sky, the stars, primary food animals, or some expression of sacred power transcendent to nature. Because pursuing this "outer-power" takes men away from the camp or the farm or the home, there developed male separation of the sexes. Since male bonding is particularly strong during the stress of warfare because of the possibility of death in battle, the separation of the sexes becomes more intensified. In conditions of war, men rely more on one another than on the women in their lives. Sanday reads these historical factors to mean that male dominance developed at a rather late date in human history.

> [However, by contrast, simpler societies] have a rather conceptual symmetry, which is grounded in primary sex differences. Women give birth and grow children; men kill and make weapons. Men display their kills (be it an animal, a human head, or a scalp) with the same pride that women hold up the newly born. If birth and death are among the necessities of existence,

then men and women contribute equally but in quite different ways to the continuance of life and hence of culture. The evidence . . . suggests that all other things being equal, the power to give life is as highly valued as the power to take it away.[25]

According to Sanday's theory, then, if a religious tradition or its antecedent tradition has an "outer orientation" involving strong separation of the sexes in times of stress—especially the stress of war—there will also occur male dominance. That is exactly the case. The formative periods of the oldest world religions (Judaism, Brahmanic Hinduism, and Confucianism)—which themselves provided the historical contexts of later religious ways (Christianity, Buddhism, Taoism)—all involved outer orientations under conditions of great stress in times of war.

Eli Sagan carries this idea further. Her cross-cultural study of societies engaged in warfare and empire building provide important clues about why we find supreme male deities and male dominance in the histories of the world religions. According to her, cultures evolve through stages of development, from the cohesion provided from kinship and the confederating of tribes to a centralized monarchy, which is essentially a system organized by loyalty to a king and fear of his power to oppress.[26] These societies developed hierarchically ordered social systems that were rich in art and culture, and religious systems based on sacrifice.

For example, Indian history from about the ninth to the third century B.C.E. reflects historical forces and features similar to a number of Polynesian and African societies evolving from a collection of loosely connected tribes to a system based on kinship established by war. While the creation of kingdoms arose earlier in China and ancient Israel, warfare was a fact of life in both societies; ancient Chinese and Hebrew kingdoms were fragile structures and were easily collapsed by wars with their neighbors. When Jews returned to their homeland from exile in Babylonia in the sixth century B.C.E. to reestablish their kingdom, there was—if the books of Ezra and Nehemiah are to be believed—increasing anxiety about women coupled with rigid attempts to define women's roles in Israelite society. Similarly, China's classical age was militaristic, masculine oriented, and characterized by interstate rivalries that often used women as political instruments of alliance or subversion.[27]

Katherine K. Young extends Sagan's thesis. If the initial rise of kingdoms, she writes, leads to an increase in male dominance, this should shed some light on the origins of patriarchy in the world religions.[28] Religious taboos evolved in regard to women's sexuality and eating. Men and women must be kept separate, should not eat together, and should remain apart, except under strictly defined and controlled circumstances.[29] The development of schools was also part of the rise of kingdoms, and male dominance extended segregation of the sexes to education; the schools became exclusively male institutions and developed male specialization. Women were kept at home, "barefoot, pregnant, and in the kitchen," the protected property of men, with little or no authority, even over their sexuality and reproductive functions as mothers.

The relation between men and women and the status of women in tribal religious traditions seems, from a psychoanalytical point of view, quite different. What seems different is that male envy and anxiety about women's power are mythically expressed and ritually enacted in tribal religions, which Rita Gross thinks contributed to women's greater evaluation as women and male recognition of women's power.[30] But in the actual lives of tribal males and females, the power of women relative to their biological sphere and the power of men relative to theirs was different, but equally treasured by both males and females. However, this same envy is repressed in the world religions, the psychological corollary of which evolved into male dominance and deep ambivalence about women.

The historical and psychological source of male ambiguity regarding women can be traced to the conflicts created by male experimentation with war and death related to the rise of kingdoms. Women bear children and are the source of stability and order in the home, while men fighting and dying in war are the source of instability. For a kingdom to survive, children must be produced to replace those killed in war and those who die of "natural causes." Woman's chief social value and function become tied to her peculiar biology. To the degree she is outside of her domestic sphere, her value diminishes, for she enters into the sphere and responsibility of men as protectors and orderers of society beyond the family. Since she reproduces and maintains order in the home and family, she must be protected, controlled, and placed in the domestic sphere for the survival of her family and society at large.

Of course, it is a biological fact that women alone can bear children. But it is, and always has been, fallacious to assume from this fact that the religious and social position of women is biologically rather than culturally determined. For women's roles and values in the world religions are related not only to the fact that they bear children but also to male evaluation of this fact. It is also true that, for the most part, women have not had to subject themselves to the possibility of death in armed conflict, because of male protection of women—although there exist traditions of female warriors. The problem for women—and for men—continues to be the restriction of female social and cultural roles because of women's distinctive biology, along with the male misogyny these restrictions have too often engendered.

Why Stay?

Theories about the possible historical or psychological origins of patriarchy have little value in and of themselves, unless they provide resources for addressing and ending male oppression of women. What is certain is that the actual history of women's oppression in all the religious Ways of humanity is bleak indeed—so bleak that one may wonder why *anyone* would bother reconstructing a religious tradition's past to include an accurate and usable history of women's experience. Given the history of women's oppression, why would any woman knowingly choose to stay and fight the hard battle against patriarchy required for accurate reconstruction of the tradition that oppresses her?

For that matter, why would any man participate in a religious tradition that oppresses women? Is it not immoral and theologically wrong for any human being to stay under such conditions? For if reality, the way things really are, is a pluralistic, organic system of interrelationships that constantly form and inform the existence of every thing and event in space-time—as Whitehead believed, Buddhist philosophy and contemporary physics confirm, and the parables of Jesus teach—women's oppression is simultaneously men's oppression, even if the injury to women is more immediately evident. What happens to any thing or event in the universe affects and effects all things and events; what any thing or event does affects and effects all things and events. Male oppression of women breaks interrelationships that are absolutely required for the fulfillment of both women's and men's lives. Suffering and injury imposed on any human being by any community are simultaneously the suffering, oppression, and injury of all. Male oppression also breaks humanity's interrelation with the relatively inaccessible ox, because the Sacred is the chief metaphysical example of the process of harmonizing the pluralities that constitute the universe. For this reason alone, just as white racism oppresses both people of color and white oppressors, as Martin Luther King and Mahatma Gandhi noted, so patriarchal oppression of women, who constitute over half the human race, oppresses male oppressors.

Why *should* women stay and fight to reconstruct the religious traditions that oppress them? Indeed, why should *men* stay and appropriate feminist reconstruction of their particular religious traditions? Why not just leave? Some important radical feminist voices—the classical voice is Mary Daly's—assert that leaving is the only morally viable and theologically possible option for women.

Daly's writings focus mostly on Christian forms of patriarchy. She is certain that no woman in her right mind should stay within the Christian tradition, since the structures of Christian patriarchy are completely beyond redemption. All Christian images of God, all Christian religious practices, all Christian institutions are *necessarily* male oriented and of necessity oppress women. For women to relate themselves to male-oriented images of any kind is anti-woman and anti-feminist, because there is an "ontological logic"

> which says first and foremost "Yes" to ourselves as verbs, as participators in the cosmic Verb, as be-ing, which is becoming. This ontological logic means that we are *seeking* our life force, not losing it. We are finding it, reclaiming it. This logic requires the courage to leave the Christian myth and the societal structures which are its supporting infrastructures, and the courage to leave is very much a matter of self-interest. To use the image of the mental hospital, radical feminism means exiting from the Christian cuckoo's nest. It means naming the self as good and sane, which will of course elicit labels of "evil" and "insane." Radical feminism therefore means exorcism of these labels (which are applied to all women anyway), refusal to internalize them. It means unlearning the lesson of self-crucifixion, taking a qualitative leap beyond the depth-centered processions of patriarchal religion.[31]

Daly's formulations of the power that patriarchy gives men over women and her description of how the "power of naming has been stolen from women" are among the most influential in feminist thought.[32] I also think they bear enough truth to pose a serious challenge to anyone, female or male, choosing to stay in any of the traditional religious Ways of humanity. Her critique focuses not merely on the ways in which men have traditionally held power over women but also on the centrality of power over others that characterizes any patriarchal social structure. That is, male power over females may be the basic structure of all forms of social hierarchy and oppression. Even nonradical feminists seem to agree with Daly at this point; many move on to link patriarchy with militarism and with ecological destruction of the environment.[33]

There is more truth to this analysis than most men are willing to admit. Why should anyone who has been on the exploited end of the oppressive power of patriarchy choose to remain in any patriarchal religious Way, if staying is a barrier to a full and creatively transforming relation with the ox, with nature, and with the human community?

It is perhaps fortunate for both women and men that there are feminist voices in each of the religious Ways who think Daly's analysis does not sufficiently clarify the essential aspirations of modern feminism. For example, according to Rita Gross, the most basic vision of contemporary feminism is not equality or total lack of hierarchy, even though these goals are aspects of feminist vision. She thinks "freedom of gender roles" is much more fundamental. On this, she thinks, depend all other aspects of various feminist programs. "If people are forced to fit themselves into their social places on the basis of their physiological sex, then there will be suffering and injustice even in a situation of 'gender equality'—whatever that might mean."[34] The question for reformist feminists like Gross is whether the patriarchal structures of the religious Way in which they find themselves can be (1) deconstructed so as to (2) engender their reconstruction into nonoppressive postpatriarchal forms that allow equal and full participation of both women and men who interdependently search for the ox.

In fact, there are numerous reformist feminist voices *within* the world's religious Ways who make the case that their religious traditions are capable of feminist reconstruction into postpatriarchal forms. They do not agree with radical feminist views that the best the traditional religious traditions can become is compost for postpatriarchal consciousness.[35] Some, like Lina Gupta and Riffat Hassan seek to reappropriate what they believe to be the liberating elements of their respective Hindu and Islamic scriptures and traditions that have been illegitimately suppressed, forgotten, or erased by men.

In common with her Christian sisters, Lina Gupta notes that male subjugation of women is sanctioned by the myths, symbols, and images of the world's religious traditions. But she thinks that at this point of history it is not enough merely to recognize and analyze the structures of patriarchy and its effects on the religious and social lives of women and men. She calls for seeking new forms of religious experience and practice, either through reinterpretation and reconstruction of the various religious Ways, or through alternative images of the Sacred that will emphasize female experience. She believes that her own Hindu tradition provides an image that can be used to fit the needs of contemporary women, the image of the goddess Kālī and her many incarnations.[36]

According to Gupta's deconstructive and reconstructive analysis of Hinduism, which she claims is similar to Rosemary Ruether's methodology,[37] there are scriptural resources within Hinduism that support the well-being of women and men. In fact, in her view Hinduism is not inherently patriarchal; the equal importance of gods and goddesses in the Hindu scripture (the *Veda*) supports this.[38] Even so, she acknowledges that traditional Hinduism has by and large remained patriarchal. The sources of the discrepancy between scriptural images (*śruti*, "that which is heard," i.e., "scripture") and actual Hindu practice lie, in her view, in what Hindus call "tradition" (*smṛti*, "that which is remembered"). She cites the *Manu Śāstra* ("Treatise of Manu," sometimes called "The Laws of Manu") as an illustration.

The *Manu Śāstra* portrays the ideal woman as the virtuous wife, and there are clear expectations about what this means.

> Though destitute of virtue, or seeking pleasure (elsewhere) or devoid of good qualities, (yet) a husband must be constantly worshiped as a god by a faithful wife. (Manu 154)
>
> Day and night women must be kept in dependence by the males (of) their (families), and, if they attach themselves to sensual enjoyments, they must be kept under one's control. (Manu 2)
>
> By a girl, by a young woman, or even by an aged one, nothing must be done independently, even in her own house. (Manu 147)
>
> In childhood a female must be subject to her father, in youth to her husband, when her lord is dead to her sons; a woman must never be independent. (Manu 148)[39]

Gupta's point is that traditional patriarchal readings of Hindu scriptures—of which the *Manu Śāstra* is the classical illustration—are the sources of the patriarchal structures of the Hindu Way. But since "tradition" (*smṛti*) does not have the authority of "scripture" (*śruti*), Hindu women possess a source for deconstructing traditional Hindu patriarchy. What scripture has taught Gupta is that behind the diverse incarnations of the Hindu mother goddess as the wife and consort of the God Śiva—Sāti, Sīta, Durgā, and Pārvartī—lies the wrathful presence of the goddess Kālī, the savior. Hindu women can identify with the mythological images of Kālī because,

> there is an interaction between a contemporary woman's psyche and the mythic behavior patterns of the goddess, patterns that inform and are played out in a woman's life. For example, when a woman is outraged by her husband's lack of understanding or refusal to follow through on her request, her acting out is comparable at some level to the story of outraged Sāti, who appears as Kālī to confront and terrify the uncooperative Śiva. When a woman feels a tremendous need to subordinate her welfare to the welfare of another, she is encountering self-sacrificing Sīta. By identifying themselves with the ways Kālī acts on the mythic level, with the actual potential embodiments of Kālī, we begin to find a transpersonal source of liberation within her character and nature.[40]

In other words, through her numerous incarnations, Kālī, the consort and "power" (*shakti*) of the god Śiva the Destroyer, incarnates herself within the behavioral reality of Hindu women subjugated by patriarchal readings of "scripture" (*śruti*) through the lenses of "tradition" (*smṛti*). Since all Hindus acknowledge the authority of the Vedas as primary and revelatory, and since all Hindus regard tradition as secondary to the authority of the Vedas, Gupta's conclusion is clear: patriarchal traditions as they now stand have no authority because they are not supported by the Vedas. That is, traditional readings of the Vedas, such as the *Manu Śāstra*, read patriarchy *into* the sacred texts of the Vedas that is not in the Vedas. In order to stay within the Hindu Way, women must: (1) deconstruct and reject this traditional reading of the Vedas in its entirety, and (2) reconstruct Hindu faith and practice through the creation of a new tradition (*smṛti*) that faithfully and accurately reflects the equality of women and men portrayed in the Vedas.

Riffat Hassan's method of deconstruction and reconstruction of Islamic patriarchal structures is similar to Gupta's, except that she does not appeal to the goddess image. Like Gupta, Hassan believes "tradition," not "scripture," is the source of Islamic male oppression of Muslim women. The two most important sources of Islamic faith and practice are the *Qurʾān* and the Ḥadith. Of these two, the *Qurʾān* is the more important because it is regarded by all Muslims as the primary source for figuring out how to practice "surrender" (*ʿislām*) to the will of Allah. As "a guidance sure, without doubt" (Sura 2, *Baqara*, or "The Heifer"), the *Qurʾān* is the "scripture" against which Muslims test and measure their *ʿislām*. It has absolute authority and is believed to be God's unadulterated final revelation conveyed through the agency of the archangel Gabriel to God's last prophet, Muhammad.

Along with the *Qurʾān*, the Ḥadith ("report," "event," or "news"), a literary form that preserves the *sunna* ("custom," "usual procedure," or "way of acting" of Muhammad), has also played a central role in identifying what constitutes "surrender" to the will of God for Muslims. Essentially, the Ḥadith is a collection of stories about what Muhammad was observed to have done or heard to have said during his lifetime. This means that for Muslims, "Scripture" (the *Qurʾān*) and "custom" or "tradition (the Sunna) are the primary sources of Islamic faith and practice. That is, the Ḥadith literature constitutes the Sunna ("custom") that is the lens through which Muslims have read and interpreted the *Qurʾān*.

Hassan notes, however, that every part of the Ḥadith literature is surrounded by controversy. The question of the authenticity of individual *ahidith* (plural of *hadith*), as well as the Ḥadith literature as a whole, originated in the earliest years of Islam after Muhammad's death. As noted by Fazlur Rahman, "a very large proportion of the Ḥadith were judged to be spurious and forged by classical Muslims themselves."[41] Yet as Rahman also notes, "if the Ḥadith literature *as a whole* is cast away, the basis for the historicity of the *Qurʾān* is removed at one stroke."[42]

Consequently, the problem for Muslim women is that the assertion of the historic importance of the *Qurʾān* and the Ḥadith as primary sources of Islamic tradition has created a massive problem for Islamic women. Throughout Muslim history, these sources have been interpreted only by Muslim men, "who have arrogated to themselves the task of defining the ontological, theological, sociological, and eschatological status of Muslim women."[43] Except for the wives of Muhammad and a few outstanding women in the Sufi movement in early Islam, Islamic tradition has remained rigidly patriarchal, particularly in promoting the growth of scholarship among women in the realm of religious thought and practice. Furthermore, the historical source of traditional Islamic patriarchy is not the *Qurʾān*, but the Sunna, which contains numerous traditions of the Prophet Muhammad invented by men, but which have no support whatsoever in the *Qurʾān*, particularly in reference to the place of women in the Islamic community.[44]

That the *Qurʾān*, the most authoritative source of Islam, is thoroughly nonpatriarchal and does not discriminate against women has been clearly demonstrated by "modernist" Islamic and Western scholarship. Not only does the *Qurʾān* emphasize that standards of righteousness apply in identical ways to both women and men, it also consistently affirms the equality of women and men and the fundamental right to actualize the human potential that women share equally with men before God. It is the Ḥadith literature that has undermined the intent of the *Qurʾān* to liberate women from the status of inferior creatures to make them free and equal to men.[45]

Consequently, women who choose to stay within the "House of Islam" (*dār al-ʿislām*) must deconstruct patriarchal readings of the *Qurʾān* and replace these with new, reconstructed interpretations of the *Qurʾān* that faithfully and accurately reflect the *Qurʾān*. The God who encounters humanity in the *Qurʾān* is characterized by justice and compassion toward all human beings, without regard to gender. Patriarchal injustice against Islamic women that lies at the heart of the Ḥadith cannot be regarded as God-derived. In Hassan's view, patriarchy is not integral to the ʿislām enjoined on humanity by the *Qurʾān*. Rejection of patriarchal *hadith* literature does not mean rejection of God, for any form of human oppression is rebellion against the will of God.[46]

Other feminists also emphasize reconstructing, rethinking, and reformulating aspects of their traditions on the basis of deconstructive analysis of teachings and practices that have legitimated oppression. Judith Plaskow stresses historical assessment of the status of women within the history of Judaism. According to her, Jewish subordination of women is based on rabbinic tradition's understanding of women as "other than the norm" and as "less than fully human."[47] It is women's otherness that is the central presupposition of Jewish law (*halakah*) as defined by rabbinic tradition throughout Jewish history. Consequently, any attempt to improve the status of women through revision or rejection of rabbinic legal decisions is certain to fail, given the historical weight of patriarchal tradition. Furthermore, Plaskow insists that so long as Jewish women are seen as "other" whose lives must be lived parallel to and governed by men, Judaism will continue to be shaped by the experiences of men as the normative definition of Jewish life.

While Plaskow refuses to search for the liberation of women through rabbinic tradition stripped of historical deviations, she does lay bare the patriarchal foundations of Jewish history and thought. For example, rather than viewing Jewish law as the cause of women's subordination, she maintains that *halakah* itself is a product of Judaism's traditional view of women as other, reinforced through a theology that continues to symbolize God as exclusively male. She writes:

> If God is male and we are in God's image, how can maleness *not* be the norm
> of Jewish humanity? If maleness is normative, how can women not be
> Other? And if women are Other, how can we not speak of God in language
> drawn from the male norm?[48]

But Israelite tradition did not always imagine God as exclusively male. Plaskow notes that the ancient Israelites worshiped both gods and goddesses, and that the exclusive worship of Yahweh was the result of a long, drawn-out struggle. This is not an argument for Jewish return to paganism, but she believes this fact does call Jewish women and men to reimagine the goddess through the lens of Jewish monotheism in order to acknowledge the many names of the goddess among the names of God.[49]

> [Accordingly, Jewish] feminists need to assert that the full range of images
> for God we have tested and will test are also different guises of the same
> One. Indeed, the capacity to see the One in and through the changing forms
> of the many, to glimpse the whole in and through its infinite images, is
> finally what monotheism is truly about.[50]

As Plaskow centers her reconstruction of Judaism on what she identifies as the nonpatriarchal, most authentic core of Jewish tradition, so Paula Cooey stresses what she believes is the nonpatriarchal core of Christian revelation. Specifically, she stresses a "post-patriarchal image of the incarnation" that "affirms the full integrity of women as women . . . the human poor and the powerless whatever their sex and gender identification, as well as the earth and other sentient creatures."[51] In her view, a postpatriarchal image of the incarnation is one that "refers to an immanent, ongoing divine creation, preservation, and regeneration of life. Wherever there is healing and affirmation of life, there is the redeeming body of God."[52]

According to Cooey, the trouble with traditional christological images is that they are exclusively male. They also generate rigid spirit–matter, spirit–body, male–female, spirit–nature dualities that have made life very hard for women, have been very hard on the poor and powerless, and have been ecologically disastrous. The body has especially served and still serves as a symbolic and actual focus for much that is oppressive in patriarchy."[53] Identified by traditional Christian thought with property, finitude, nature, and human female sexuality, the body provides a major symbolic focus for what Western culture permits and what it prohibits. The body determines the dividing line between public and private; and, extended metaphorically, the body engenders social attitudes toward nature. This in turn tends to create a battleground, where

> the human body reflects ongoing struggles for political power through social institutions of slavery, torture, warfare, and marriage. Those who achieve power further maintain it by regulation of sexual interaction, reproduction, childbearing, medical practices, and work roles, often justified or rationalized on religious grounds. The powerful, as makers of culture, likewise elicit the tacit support of the relatively powerless through the social consequences of gender, of class, and of the significance of the racial and ethnic differences.[54]

Postpatriarchal images of incarnation, therefore, must recognize that the "transfiguration of pain begins with giving voice or bearing witness to injustice with a view to healing and nurture."[55] "Giving voice" and "bearing witness" need not imply rejection of traditional christological statements like those of the Nicene Creed or the formulations of Chalcedon. But Christian images of incarnation will acquire new meanings as Christians reread them through the spectacles of biblical, especially New Testament, images of the body and incarnation in the Pauline epistles and the Synoptic Gospels. In this scriptural tradition, Christians will find that the incarnation is imaged as "ongoing divine creativity characterized as self-emptying imagination, continually making relations, things, and events from the flesh, making these real in the flesh, and repairing broken relations and things by making them differently—creatively, from the inside out rather than from the top down, so to speak."[56]

In other words, Christians will find that "Jesus saves us through directing our attention through the events of his life and resurrection" in a way that "reconciles and restores all life, including especially life usually considered the least noteworthy."[57] Reconciliation and restoration found in Jesus of Nazareth have nothing to do with patriarchy.

On Learning the Neighborhood

Feminism is not only a system of thought that challenges patriarchal control of women. As are all liberation theologies, feminist theology is a "practice," similar to the Catholic sense of *praxis*, that intends to put faith into deliberate action to the end of liberating women from all forms of patriarchal oppression. Which in turn comes full circle to the liberation of men. This last observation feels like certainty to me whenever I invite feminists into my room, either in person or in their writings.

I sit here, she sits there. Our eyes meet, or our minds if it is only her writing on my desk; a consciousness snaps back and forth, and then what I know, at least for starters, is this: here we—so incontrovertibly—are. This is our life, these are our seasons, and then we die. In the meantime, in between time, I am learning how to catch feminist glimpses of the ox, to see in new ways that transform old ways of seeing and old ways of consciousness. Scales fall from my eyes, as if cataracts are cut away, and I can work at making sense of the color patches *we both* see in an effort to discover *where we* so incontrovertibly *are*. It's common sense. When you move into a new neighborhood, you try to learn the territory, which, as it turns out, is another way of wrestling with the ox. Here are some of the lessons I think learning the neighborhood is teaching me.

Writing about the relation of feminism to the Christian Way, Mary Daly takes the stand that there is radical incompatibility. She holds that all Christian images of the relatively inaccessible ox are necessarily male-oriented and anti-woman. She suspects correctly that this is the case in all of the mainline religious Ways of humanity. The incompatibility to which Daly refers is not superficial. Nor does it have to do only, or even primarily, with male dominance in church institutions or with the prevalence of sexist language. These are but symptoms of something more fundamental—the maleness of all Christian images of God. Daly's radical critique of the Christian Way can be, and has been, extended to other non-Christian religious Ways by many feminists even if they do not follow her critique to her conclusions.

In my judgment, however, Daly is *almost* correct. Gupta, Gross, Plaskow, Cooey, Hassan, and others have taught me another lesson: it may be possible for women and men to deconstruct and reconstruct their religious traditions, in dialogue with one another, into postpatriarchal forms that liberate both women and men from patriarchal oppression. Daly teaches me that if this is not possible, Christian women (and men) should leave if the Christian Way can be defined only according to past patriarchal forms. For now the most viable option is for women and men to reconstruct their religious traditions, using not only their particular religious tradition's legacy but also scientific discovery, contemporary postmodern theologies of religious pluralism, and contemporary social and political analyses of the sources of oppression.

In summary, my dispute with Daly and other radical feminists is about whether what has been is, in fact, necessary. Certainly, if all religious traditions are patriarchally beyond redemption, none is capable of freeing us from oppression. Women are thus driven, it seems, to create their own independent religious Ways of thought and practice exclusive of male participation. Many thoughtful women have chosen this route. The problem with this choice is that it requires "invention" of a new feminist religious Way. But as every historian of religion knows, including feminist historians of religion, no one has ever "invented" a religious Way, because as are all symbols and myths, religious traditions are "discovered" as human beings experience and interact with the ox in the specific cultural and historical contexts within which all human experience must happen.[58]

Accordingly, my view is that any definition of the Christian Way is false that forces Christians to define their faith and practice solely in terms of past forms. Furthermore, any definition of any religious Way is false that defines its distinctive traditions solely in terms of what has been and is now the case. Religious Ways are not static entities embodying unchangeable essences, unless they are "dead religions" like those of ancient Egypt or the Bon tradition of Tibet. Religious traditions live and die; those that are alive are processes of change, just as is everything in the universe.

Therefore, not only Christian women but Christian men should leave if the Christian Way can be defined only in terms of its past forms. I believe the same conclusion applies to Buddhist, Islamic, Jewish, or Hindu women and men: they should leave if their respective religious Ways can only be defined in terms of their past forms. If, for example, Christians are necessarily bound to understandings of Jesus or the Bible that predate the rise of Western critical historical scholarship, Christian women and men informed by this scholarship should leave. If Christians are bound to supernaturalist understandings of the world and God in reaction to Newtonian science or Darwin's theory of evolution or contemporary relativity or quantum theory, then Christians informed by contemporary scientific worldviews should leave. If today the Christian Way is identified with what Christians have predominantly believed thus far about their exclusive relation to salvation, then Christians who recognize truths of ultimate importance in non-Christian religious Ways should leave. If the Christian Way must be defined only in terms of its past patriarchal forms, then Daly is right. Women should leave. So should men.

Fortunately, leaving is not necessary. To see this, we, men and women, must listen hard to what feminists who deconstruct and reconstruct their particular religious Ways are saying and doing. My listening has led me to a hunch, which some feminists might find unsatisfactory. It is this. Feminist theology is not merely one species among others that constitute the collective pluralism of liberation theology, although it is that; feminist theology is the central, most important form of liberation theology. After all, women comprise over half the human population on this planet. The liberation of women from patriarchal forms of exploitation and oppression is interdependent with humanity's liberation from social, political, and economic forms of oppression, since women are generally the most socially, politically, and economically exploited human beings in every cultural and religious context. Women's liberation from patriarchy is also, I believe, interdependent with liberation of the environment. In other words, to the degree that women achieve liberation from patriarchal oppression, to that degree do we all achieve social, political, and economic liberation; to that degree does the earth achieve liberation from human oppression; to that degree is life itself liberated from the threat of human-caused environmental destruction. The interconnection between the liberation of women and other forms of liberation is the topic of the next chapter, "The Ox and the Man, Both Gone Out of Sight."

Notes

1. D. T. Suzuki, *Manual of Zen Buddhism* (New York: Grove Press, 1960), 132.
2. For example, see Judith Plaskow, *Standing Again at Sinai: Judaism from a Feminist Perspective* (San Francisco: HarperSanFrancisco, 1990), 1-15; Sallie McFague, *Models of God* (Philadelphia: Westminster Press, 1987), chap. 1; Rita M. Gross, *Buddhism After Patriarchy* (Albany: State University of New York Press, 1993), 125-30; and Rosemary Radford Ruether, *Sexism and God Talk: Toward a Feminist Theology* (Boston: Beacon Press, 1983), chap. 1.
3. For the importance of the feminine principle in Apache religious tradition, see Ines Talamantez, "Images of the Feminine in Apache Religious Tradition," in *After Patriarchy: Feminist Transformations of the World Religions*, ed. Paula M. Cooey, William R. Eakin, and Jay B. McDaniel (Maryknoll, N.Y.: Orbis Books, 1993), 131-45.
4. Gross, *Buddhism After Patriarchy*, 20. Also see Cooey, Eakin, and McDaniel, "Introduction," in *After Patriarchy*, xi-xii.
5. See Rita M. Gross, "Tribal Religion: Aboriginal Australia," in *Women in World Religions*, ed. Arvind Sharma (Albany: State University of New York Press, 1987), 38.
6. Gross, *Buddhism After Patriarchy*, 18.
7. Ibid., 19.
8. This same point is made from a Jewish feminist perspective by Judith Plaskow when she writes about the need to reshape Jewish history (see *Standing Again*

at Sinai, 28–56). Also see Jo Ann Hacket, "In the Days of Jael: Reclaiming the History of Women in Ancient Israel," in *Immaculate and Powerful: The Feminine in Sacred Image and Social Reality*, ed. Clarissa W. Atkinson, Constance H. Buchanan, and Margaret R. Miles (Boston: Beacon Press, 1985), 15–38; and Rosemary Radford Ruether, "Sexism and God-Language," in *Weaving the Visions: New Patterns in Feminist Spirituality*, ed. Judith Plaskow and Carol P. Christ (San Francisco: HarperSanFrancisco, 1989), 149–62.

9. Gross, *Buddhism After Patriarchy*, 19.

10. Eleanor McLaughlin, "The Christian Past: Does It Hold a Future for Women," in *Womanspirit Rising: A Feminist Reader in Religion*, ed. Carol P. Christ and Judith Plaskow (San Francisco: Harper & Row, 1979), 94–95, cited in Gross, *Buddhism After Patriarchy*, 20.

11. Plaskow, *Standing Again at Sinai*, 10.

12. As are the methodologies that feminist theologians employ to interpret women's experience as the foundation for reconstructing the traditional religious Ways in which they choose to participate more meaningfully. See Judith Plaskow and Carol P. Christ, "Introduction," in *Weaving the Visions*, 4–8.

13. Ibid., 11.

14. See Paula Gunn Allen, *The Sacred Hoop: Recovering the Feminine in American Indian Traditions* (Boston: Beacon Press, 1986), 102–17.

15. Plaskow, *Standing Again At Sinai*, 11.

16. Ibid.

17. Ibid., 12.

18. Katherine K. Young, "Introduction," in *Women in World Religions*, 6–7.

19. Gross, *Buddhism After Patriarchy*, 31–48.

20. For an expanded version of this argument, see Gross, *Buddhism After Patriarchy*, 41–59.

21. Barbara E. Reed, "Taoism," in *Women in World Religions*, 160–81; also see Theresa Kekkeher, "Confucianism," ibid., 135–59.

22. See Roger T. Ames, "Taoism and the Androgynous Ideal," in *Women in China: Current Directions in Historical Scholarship*, ed. Richard W. Guisso and Stanley Johannsen (Youngstown, Oh.: Philo Press, 1981), 21–47.

23. Ibid., 53.

24. Peggy Reeves Sanday, *Female Power and Male Dominance: On the Origins of Sexual Inequality* (London: Cambridge University Press, 1981), 110.

25. Ibid., 5. Also see Allen, *Sacred Hoop*, 12–50; eadem, *Grandmothers of the Light: A Medicine Woman's Sourcebook* (Boston: Beacon Press, 1991).

26. Eli Sagan, *At the Dawn of Tyranny: The Origins of Individualism, Oppression, and the State* (New York: Alfred A. Knopf, 1985), 320.

27. Ibid.

28. Young, "Introduction," in *Women in World Religions*, 10.

29. Sagan, *At the Dawn of Tyranny*, 90.

30. See Rita M. Gross, "Menstruation and Childhood as Ritual and Religious Experience Among Native Americans," in *Unspoken Worlds: Women's Religious Lives*

in Northwestern Cultures, ed. Nancy A. Falk and Rita M. Gross (San Francisco: Harper & Row, 1980); and Bruno Bettlelheim, *Symbolic Wounds: Puberty Rites and the Envious Male* (Glencoe, Ill.: Free Press, 1954).

31. Mary Daly, "The Courage to Leave: A Response to John Cobb's Theology," in *John Cobb's Theology in Process*, ed. David Ray Griffin and Thomas J. J. Altizer (Philadelphia: Westminster Press, 1977), 85–86. Also see Daly, *Beyond God the Father* (Boston: Beacon Press, 1973) and *The Church and the Second Sex, With an Autobiographical Preface and Postchristian Introduction by the Author*, rev. ed. (New York: Harper & Row, 1975).

32. Daly, *Beyond God the Father*, 8.

33. For example, see McFague, *Models of God*, 3–28.

34. Gross, *Buddhism After Patriarchy*, 300.

35. See Emily Culpepper, "The Spiritual, Political Journey of a Feminist Freethinker," in *After Patriarchy*, 146–63.

36. Lina Gupta, "Kālī, the Savior," in *After Patriarchy*, 16.

37. Ibid.

38. Ibid., 16–17.

39. All citations of the *Manu Śāstra* are from *A Sourcebook in Indian Philosophy*, ed. S. Radhakrishnan and Charles A. Moore (Princeton: Princeton University Press, 1957), 190–91.

40. Gupta, "Kālī, the Savior," 36.

41. Fazlur Rahman, *Islam* (Chicago: University of Chicago Press, 1966), 64.

42. Ibid., 66.

43. Riffat Hassan, "Muslim Women and Post-Patriarchal Islam," in *After Patriarchy*, 41.

44. For Hassan's analysis and arguments for this assertion, see ibid., 43–59.

45. Ibid., 59.

46. Ibid., 60–61.

47. Plaskow, *Standing Again at Sinai*, 11-12.

48. Judith Plaskow, "God and Feminism," *Menorah* 3 (February 1982): 2, cited by Ellen M. Umansky, "Creating a Jewish Feminist Theology, in *Weaving the Visions*, 188.

49. Plaskow, *Standing Again At Sinai*, 152.

50. Ibid.

51. Paula Cooey, "The Redemption of the Body: Post Patriarchal Reconstruction of Inherited Christian Doctrine," in *After Patriarchy*, 106.

52. Ibid., 107.

53. Ibid., 108.

54. Ibid., 108-9.

55. Ibid., 109.

56. Ibid., 120.

57. Ibid., 121.

58. For example, see Gross, *Buddhism After Patriarchy*, 305-17; and Elisabeth Schüssler Fiorenza, "In Search of Women's Heritage," in *Weaving the Visions*, 29–38.

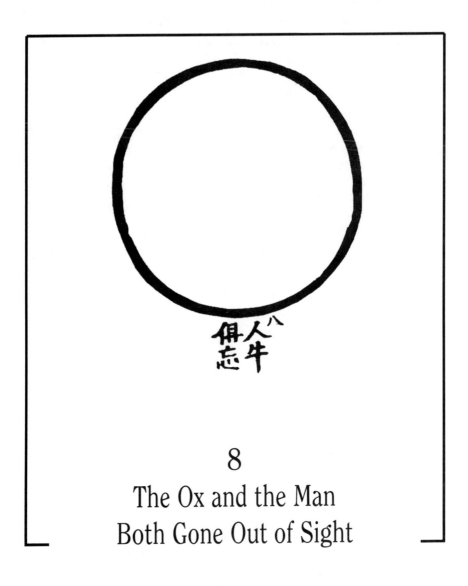

俱忘人牛 八

8
The Ox and the Man
Both Gone Out of Sight

THE EIGHTH OX-HERDING PICTURE PORTRAYS THIS STAGE OF THE MAN'S RELIGIOUS quest by a curious drawing—an empty circle. In Mahayana Buddhist teaching, Emptiness or, truer to Buddhist experience, "Emptying" (*śūnyatā*), does not imply that things and events are nonexistent. "Emptying" means that nothing exists independently of other things and events, that every thing and event is interdependent with every thing and event. Nothing is substantially permanent, including our experience of self and world, self and community. Or, as the *Heart Sutra* explains, "Form is Emptiness; Emptiness is form."[1] Or, in the words of the accompanying poem:

All is empty—the whip, the rope, the man, and the Ox;
Who can survey the infinity of heaven?
Over a furnace burning hot, not a flake of snow can fall;
When emptiness is experienced, manifest is the spirit of the ancient
masters.[2]

The thesis of chapter 8 is in complete agreement with the Vietnamese Zen monk Thich Nhat Hanh:[3] in an emptying, interdependent universe—here symbolized by an empty circle in the eighth Ox-Herding picture—our religious quest and experience do not separate us *from* the world. Rather, they throw us *into* the world's suffering rough-and-tumble and force us to wrestle with it and work for peace and justice, often with the desperation of a hungry rat running a maze. Any religious practice or theology that refuses to wrestle with the world, that refuses to focus on issues of liberation from injustice and poverty, is impotent and self-serving.

Yet, like many academics, I must confess that the ideas to which I have committed my life have required of me no more effort than frequent trips to the library. My life has set me at little risk, put me under few hardships. In this, I and most Anglo-American male professors my age differ from most of the world's people. Too many human beings are made poor by institutionalized forms of economic exploitation. Too many human beings suffer political and military oppression. Too many human beings are racially oppressed. Too many human beings are forced to expend their energy simply trying to survive the exploitation of their lives by the powerful, and have neither time nor inclination to revel in the beauty of ideas or in the arts or in theological reflection about religious pluralism.

Furthermore, many human beings who commit themselves to the liberation of oppressed peoples often do so at great personal risk. They are witnesses who speak and write with authority that white Anglo-Saxon middle class scholars and writers like me need to hear, internalize, and act upon so that we may become witnesses ourselves.

We need such witnesses. They help us see the ox more clearly. A witness is someone who looks, who does not turn away, who wrestles with the ox and does not despair or give up even when there is every reason to do so, who is willing to be called upon, who will speak and testify in public, who will take an oath bound to the truth "so help you God" for the sake of the community, for without witnesses, there can be no community. The history of religions is full of past and present witnesses who speak for their communities from within the midst of suffering, poverty, exploitation, and oppression: the civil disobedience of Mahatma Gandhi (Hindu); the interdependent American civil rights movements of Martin Luther King, Jr. (Baptist Christian), and his contemporary, Malcolm X (Muslim); the Buddhist socialism of Sulak Sivaraksa (Thai Buddhist); the "engaged Buddhism" of the Vietnamese monk Thich Nhat Hanh; the liberation theology of the Peruvian priest Gustavo Gutierrez (Roman Catholic); to name only a few contemporary examples.

That there have always been witnesses makes the history of religions not altogether dismal, but fairly consistent. For generally speaking, most theology is used as a stone wall against witnesses who wrestle with the relatively inaccessible ox. Theology too often becomes a buffer that justifies the economically and politically powerful's exploitation of the poor and the weak. Conventionally religious persons tend to erect doctrinal walls between themselves, between themselves and the ox, as well as between the rich and poor, the powerful and the impotent. Yet witnesses show us that Karl Marx was at least half right: religion *can be and often is* an opiate; witnesses show us that it does not have to be this way, that walls can be breached, that theologically induced injustice can be defeated. But the price can be high.

Among the "signs of the times" that challenge sensitive witnesses in all the world's religious Ways are the experience of religious pluralism and the experience of the many poor. These signs have taught me that the three most creative and vital contemporary forms of theology are: theologies of religions that respond to the issues of religious pluralism; theologies of nature that respond to the environmental dangers threatening life on planet Earth; and theologies of liberation that respond to the urgent problems of human suffering and injustice.

Of course, the specific concerns of each of these types of theologies are interdependent, and the neighborhoods of the advocates of each overlap. Even so, religious pluralists, environmental theologians, and liberation theologians tend to live in their respective neighborhoods as if they were separate turfs. In recent years, however, the old theological neighborhoods have been changing and expanding as theologians from all three camps meet together, learn from one another, and work collaboratively in their different projects.[4]

In chapters 6 and 7, I described how my primordial theology of religious pluralism is interdependent with a theology of nature that envisions the liberation of life. This chapter follows lines of thought begun in chapter 7. There I proposed that dialogue between theological pluralists and feminist liberation theologians is an opportunity for mutual transformation. Chapter 8 shows what theologies of religious pluralism can learn from theologies of liberation and demonstrates how the principles and practices of liberation theologies can contribute to the pluralistic theology of religions I have named "primordial theology."

On Dialogue between Liberation Theologians
and Religious Pluralists

Much of my dialogue with liberation theologians has been with feminists working to reform the patriarchal power structures of their respective religious Ways. They have clarified for me that religious pluralists and liberation theologians of all varieties urgently need each other. First, the history of religions reveals just how important a force religious faith is and has always been, for better or for worse, in engendering social, political, and economic change. Contemporary evidence abounds: the role of Shiʾah Islam in the Iranian revolution and its policy of genocide against the followers of Bahaʾi; the defense of the Reagan administration by the American Christian right; the role of basic Christian communities in implementing the revolution in Nicaragua and struggling for it in El Salvador; the terrorism of Catholic-Protestant communal violence in Northern Ireland; the revolt of the Tamil-speaking Hindu minority against the majority Buddhist government of Sri Lanka; Hindu-Muslim violence at the time of India's partition in 1948; the Sikh community's violent attempt to create their own independent state in India; mutual Israeli-Palestinian terrorism.

Events such as these have convinced me of the truth behind the broad philosophical claims of historians such as Arnold Toynbee and Wilfred Cantwell Smith: only a vision that originates from humanity's religious symbols and experience can empower us to end the wars human communities wage against themselves and planet Earth.[5] It is through the hope and self-sacrificing love born of religious experience, faith, and practice—wherever we find it—that human beings "muster the energy, devotion, vision, resolution, capacity to survive disappointment that will be necessary—that *is* necessary—for the challenge of creating a just and peaceful world."[6]

Accordingly, liberation theologians need to see that all movements of liberation—the liberation of nature *and* the liberation of human beings from poverty, racism, and political oppression—require not just *a particular* religious tradition but the participation and support of *all* religious traditions. As Paul Knitter wisely writes, "Economic, political, and especially nuclear liberation is too big a job for any one nation, culture *or* religion. A cross-cultural, interreligious cooperation in liberative praxis and a sharing of liberative theory is called for."[7]

In short, for the plurality of liberation theologies to become relevant and effective, they must plant themselves within the global contexts of the world's religious communities, East and West. This point has been made strikingly clear by Aloysius Pieris. Writing as a Sri Lankan Christian liberation theologian, he reminds us:

The irruption of the Third World [with its demands for liberation] is also the irruption of the non-Christian world. The vast majority of God's poor perceive their ultimate concern and symbolize their struggle for liberation in the idiom of non-Christian religions and cultures. Therefore, a theology that does not speak to or speak through this non-Christian peoplehood [and its religions] is a luxury of a Christian minority.[8]

Pieris's warning must be taken seriously. Apart from dialogue with the plurality of humanity's religious traditions, a purely Christian or Buddhist or Islamic or Jewish or black or feminist liberation theology runs the risk of inbreeding and irrelevant scholasticism, of drawing an overly ideological vision of liberation. In a universe of interdependence and process, we suffer together, experience injustice together, die together, achieve liberation together, whatever "liberation" might finally be. Dialogue with the liberating visions of Hindu tradition, Buddhist tradition, Islam, or Judaism might teach Christian liberation theologians that they have tended to be too influenced by the negative caricatures of religious faith in the thought of Karl Barth and Karl Marx. Like Barth, and for different reasons, Marx, many Christian liberation theologians, especially in Latin America, too hastily deny the liberating potential of non-Christian religious Ways.[9] The need for liberation is global and requires a global interreligious dialogue.

Second, my dialogue with feminists and other liberation theologians has taught me how imperative dialogue between theologians of religions, Christian and non-Christian, and theologies of liberation, Christian and non-Christian, really is. Growing numbers of western European mainline Christians have been deeply shaken by liberation thought's notion of preferential treatment of the poor.[10] Liberation theologians have clarified just how much interreligious dialogue has taken place in academic ivory towers overlooking the activities of death squads. Globally, theologians engaging in interreligious dialogue are gradually realizing that every religious idea and practice that fails to address the varieties of poverty and oppression that pollute all human communities are irrelevant. As David Tracy notes, interreligious dialogue without serious encounter with the challenges of liberation thought in all its varieties too easily becomes a mystical pursuit divorced from "real life" in the "real world," of interest and affordable only to a few ultra-academic dilettantes.[11]

Third, religious pluralists in dialogue with liberation theologies are being forced to recognize the dangers of uncritical, overenthusiastic affirmation of religious pluralism. While pluralism is, I believe, a metaphysical fact of our universe, uncritical understanding of this "fact" too easily leads to acceptance of "the intolerable," as Langdon Gilkey phrased it—"virulently nationalistic Shinto, Nazism, aspects of Stalinism and Marxism, Maoism, Khomenei's

Islamic fundamentalism"—where "in each of these situations an absolute religion sanctions an oppressive class, race, or national power."[12] Dialogue has limits, and there are things that should never be tolerated. The limits of tolerance are set by the victims of society, wherever human beings are unjustly crippled by economic and political oppression, deprived of dignity, destroyed, raped, or injured by what students during the 1960s called "the system." Or, in the words of Paul Knitter, who has thought long about this issue, liberation theologians urge us to "encounter other religions, not *primarily* to enjoy diversity and dialogue but to eliminate suffering and oppression," and most of all, "to work for justice."[13]

Consequently, the basic humanitarian concerns and the visions of "salvation" of most of humanity's religious Ways demand that preferential option for the poor and the nonperson constitute a primary purpose of interreligious dialogue. All religious persons seeing the relatively inaccessible ox from the perspectives of humanity's numerous religious Ways must speak and work together to remove the forces of oppression that contaminate planet Earth like the Black Death that devastated medieval Europe. Interreligious dialogue is also essential to—because it is interdependent with—the liberation of life as I discussed this idea in chapters 6 and 7.

Accordingly, the remainder of this chapter will focus on how dialogue with the methodologies of liberation theology can: (1) help pluralist theologians avoid absolutist positions, while respecting the genuine validity and differences of religious traditions other than one's own, and (2) avoid the debilitating relativism for which religious pluralists are often criticized. Since the notion of "practice" (*praxis*) is a fundamental category for both primordial theology and liberation thought, I shall begin my particular pluralist dialogue with a comparative analysis of this notion as a possible hermeneutical principle of dialogue between religious pluralists and liberation theologians.

On the Meaning of Practice (Praxis)

Normally, whenever we hear the word "practice," the meaning we are likely to understand is the popular meaning that predominates in the West: "practice" names something opposed to "theory." In this sense, "theory" and "theoretical knowledge" are ends in themselves, while "practice" is a means to achieve a theoretical end outside itself.[14] Seen from this perspective, then, practice most often appears as something one does to achieve a goal, theoretically formulated, one has not yet achieved, as in practicing the piano to achieve skilled concert performance.

This view of practice is an instrumental view. Thus, athletes practice tennis to win matches and tournaments; Buddhists practice meditation to achieve enlightenment; Christian nuns practice contemplative prayer to achieve union with Christ; Muslims practice "surrender to the will of God" (ʿislām) to attain eternal life with God in paradise. In other words, religious disciplines are practiced to achieve theoretical ends outside practice.

That instrumental views that separate practice from theory are oversimplifications has been demonstrated by John C. Maraldo. According to him, there is another consideration which precludes the view of religious practice as a means to achieve an end one does not yet have.

> This is the fact that theory, by way of its Latin translation, has been associated with contemplation and the purely contemplative, that is, apolitical life—the life later associated with religious meditation. Thus we are confronted with a view which would take the theoretical life paradoxically as the life of religious practice."[15]

In other words, practice and attainment of a theoretically formulated end are not separate in the experience of religious persons. "Practice" *is* "attainment"; "attainment *is* "practice."

What Maraldo has in mind is similar to the Greek idea of *askēsis*, from which the English word "asceticism" is derived.[16] The original meaning of *askēsis* had nothing to do with self-mortification of the body or the subjugation of our natural senses and desires in order to achieve supposedly higher spiritual ends. The context within which the Greeks understood practice was athletic training. *Askēsis* was an affirmation and positive evaluation of bodily existence and the repeated practice of exertion and training for athletic accomplishment.

It is this sense of practice that supports what religious persons experience when they practice their religious faith. Any activity that takes practice to be performed efficiently and creatively can serve as an illustration of the meaning of religious practice. One can, for example, think of learning to play the piano, or learning a foreign language, or learning a martial art, or Japanese flower arranging, or the tea ceremony. To say that mastery of these arts takes practice means that repeated effort and concentrated performance are absolute requirements in the process of learning. Such activities are daily performances and disciplines practiced for no other goal than their performance. That is, when a tea master conducts a tea ceremony, she is performing the same kind of activity she did when she was a novice beginning her study of this art. For her, there is no difference between practice and skilled performance. Her "performance" is her practice; her practice is her performance. For her, if she is a master and not a novice, practice and performance are nondual and noninstrumental; no gaps exist between what she wills to do and what she attains as she practices the art of tea.

The same is experientially true for the masters of any art or discipline demanding skilled performance. It is only novices who experience a gap between practice and skilled performance. A novice's sense of practice is understood according to the *theoria–praxis* ("theory-practice") duality: practice is an instrumental means, something one does to achieve an end one desires but has not yet attained. Thus, a novice pianist practices to attain skilled performance. The novice perceives his or her lack of skill and practices to become skilled. But for the master, there is never a time when practice is not skilled performance or skilled performance not practice.

It is this sense of practice that is emphasized in contemplative and meditative forms of religious discipline. Thus, novices at the beginning stages of religious practice often experience a separation between their performance and their theoretically formulated attainment. Novice Buddhist monks and nuns, for example, practice their disciplines as an instrumental means to achieve enlightenment. They perceive themselves as unenlightened and practice to become enlightened. But for Buddhas, there is no gap between practice and attainment; for them, practice is enlightened attainment; attainment is enlightened practice. Or, as the Soto Zen master Dogen instructed the monks under his care:

> This Dharma is amply present in every person, but unless one practices, it is not manifested, unless there is realization, it is not attained. . . . As it is already realization in practice, realization is endless; as sitting is practice in realization, practice is beginningless.[17]

Likewise, Western contemplative religious practice is structurally similar to the meaning of Buddhist practice that Maraldo illustrates with Dogen's notion of the non-duality of practice and enlightenment. Maraldo illustrates this with the example of the contemplative practice of Francis of Assisi, which had four interrelated dimensions: (1) it is learned by following a normative Rule with specific injunctions; (2) it is actualized in ordinary, everyday actions and situations; (3) it is persistently and consistently applied; and (4) it is itself the proclamation of the "gospel life"—living in obedience and chastity, without property, in order to imitate the teachings and practices of Christ.[18] In other words, "practice—contemplative prayer, the life of poverty, labor on behalf of others—*is* the "gospel life"; the gospel life *is* practice. Practice and attainment are nondual.[19]

Maraldo's analysis of religious practice raises important questions for pluralists for whom interreligious dialogue is itself a form of religious practice, as well as for notions of practice that are central to liberation theologies. For example, must a religious pluralist wrestling with the ox practice *zazen* ("seated meditation") to understand Dogen's encounter with the ox? Must we take Franciscan vows to understand and appreciate what Francis's *Canticle of Brother Sun* can contribute to our experience and understanding of the relatively inaccessible Sacred? Is it not also possible, perhaps likely, that we could practice *zazen* all our lives and never understand Dogen or the Enlightenment he tried to teach his monks to attain through practice? Is it possible that even if we gave away all our possessions, lived without sex, obeyed superiors even when we thought they were muddleheaded, we could still not be practicing the Franciscan Rule? Or from the context of liberation thought, does it make any sense to think of "practice" and "attainment" non-dualistically in the struggle of the poor against institutionalized forms of economic and political exploitation? The poor are poor because they have not attained liberation from forces of economic and political exploitation. From a poor person's perspective, practice and attainment *are* dual.

The issues these questions pose become clearer as we examine what liberation theologians generally mean by "liberation." From what do human beings need "liberation" and what "practices" best lead to it? Seen from a liberation context, human beings need liberation from economic, political, and social oppression engendered by economic, political, and social institutions— often justified and supported by a culture's dominant religious tradition. Such liberation has not been achieved, and needs to be, through practice. For this reason, Gustavo Gutierrez thinks the meaning of "liberation" has two interdependent features.[20]

First, "liberation" refers to the aspirations of oppressed human beings and social classes. As such, liberation names a process of conflict, a struggle that places oppressed people at odds with oppressive national, social, economic, and political forces. Liberation *praxis* means working in the struggle to overcome the forces of oppression. Second, "liberation" implies a certain understanding of history. Liberation thinkers tend to see history as a process in which human beings gradually assume conscious responsibility for their own individual and collective future. The focus of this responsibility is reflection on the meaning and struggle for social and political changes that have occurred in the past and are occurring in the present. "Accurate and usable history," to borrow a term from feminist thought, is the major source for creative struggle to establish political and economic justice and equity. It is such struggle that liberation thinkers identify as "practice."[21]

Of course, the meaning of liberation practice will be conceived within the theological language and worldview of the religious Way within which a liberation thinker struggles for liberation. For a Christian, the central image of liberation is Christ as the savior who brings liberation to human beings not only from the bondage of sin and death but also from the social, economic, and political sins of oppression. "Christ makes [humanity] truly free," writes Gutierrez, because "he enables [humanity] to live in communion with him; this is the basis for all human brotherhood."[22]

For a Muslim, to practice "surrender" (*ʿislām*) to the will of Allah means to follow the *Qurʾān's* injunctions and the *sharīʾa's* (law) admonition to struggle in the rough-and-tumble of historical and political existence for the liberation of all of humanity from economic and political oppression. This means working to establish the "House of Islam" (*dār al-ʿislām*)–human community established on justice, compassion, and "peace" (*salam*) that originates only in the practice of *ʿislām*.[23] Therefore, the practice of *ʿislām* is liberation *praxis*; there is no such thing as nonliberation practice in Islam's call to surrender to the will of God.

Similarly, the chief model of practice for Theravada Buddhists is the enlightened practice of Gautama the Buddha, and for Mahayana Buddhists, all Buddhas and Bodhisattvas. Enlightenment must engender compassionate action "skillfully" applied (*upāya*) to help liberate all sentient beings from suffering. Since much suffering that human beings and other life forms experience is institutionalized within the political and economic structures of human communities, a necessary part of Buddhist practice is nonviolent struggle to liberate all humanity, all existence, from these structures of violent exploitation.[24]

Likewise, the symbol of liberation for Jews is the exodus from slavery in Egypt and God's demand for justice and compassion within the human community. For Jews, following God's "instructions" (Torah) exemplified by the prophetic call for justice *is* "liberation practice."[25] Finally, Mahatma Gandhi's Hindu religious vision and practice had important political and economic consequences for the liberation of India from the oppression of British colonialism.

Still, at least on the surface, notions of practice derived from contemplative traditions of the religious Ways of humanity and liberation views of practice seem completely opposite. Traditional forms of religious practice derived from the meditative and contemplative *praxis* of mystics seem to encourage religious elites to withdraw from the world to seek their own private visions of union with the relatively inaccessible ox. Often "the world"–its responsibilities, cares, and injustices–are seen as hindrances that get in the way of one's private spiritual growth and progress. One must withdraw from the world, not get involved with the world's institutionalized violence from which the vast majority of human beings cannot escape, and seek a private "salvation" within the solitude of small monastic communities.

From a liberation perspective, this notion of practice seems selfish, immoral, and religiously irrelevant. It fails to recognize the interdependency of all human beings. It ignores the institutionalized forms of human suffering and oppression, fails to recognize that such privatized religious practice cooperates with, indeed, contributes to, the forces of injustice. Human beings need liberation from such ego-centered, elitist forms of religious practice and experience.

But need we see contemplative traditions of practice and liberation practice as dualistic opposites? They certainly have been seen this way, but is it necessary to do so? Do not liberation practices too easily degenerate into uninspired and dry political and economic ideologies when torn apart from the religious vision and experience of the Sacred that is so treasured by contemplatives and mystics East and West? Oppressed human beings don't need another ideology; there are too many of these. Oppressed human beings need vision. Liberation theologians would do well, therefore, to enter into dialogue with the plurality of contemplative traditions of religious practice as a means of energizing liberation practice.

Experience of the Sacred, furthermore, so treasured and sought after in the practice of mystics and contemplatives, has practical application to the issues of human liberation from oppression. Dialogue with liberation thought can help religious pluralists see more clearly the practical implications of religious insight and vision to the quest for liberation from political and economic oppression. In the remainder of this chapter, I will describe the "bare bones" of what such a dialogue with liberation notions of practice can contribute to this particular primordial theology. This description assumes the following hermeneutical principle: interreligious dialogue *is* a form of religious practice. But while what I mean by "practice" is rooted in contemplative and meditative traditions of *praxis*, liberation notions of practice need not be seen as opposite or contradictory to contemplative traditions of practice. Understanding this hypothesis requires closer examination of two forms of liberation *praxis:* the "hermeneutics of suspicion" and "the preferential option for the poor."

Interreligious Dialogue and the Hermeneutics of Suspicion

There are Buddhists and Christians who argue that their respective religious traditions require new methods of encountering other religious Ways on the basis of a genuinely pluralistic interreligious dialogue. Such a dialogue is one that avoids preestablished absolutist claims in order to let all the participants have an equal voice, so that each participant can fully hear, as much as possible, what the other is saying.[26] Similar encounters are also occurring between Hindus and Christians, Jews and Christians, Muslims and Christians, and Muslims and Jews.

At the same time, those of us engaged in interreligious dialogue also know that this kind of conversation can easily lead to a debilitating relativism in which no one can make any normative judgments about anyone's faith and practice except one's own. Dialogue with liberation theologies of practice can help us maintain the richness of religious pluralism while avoiding debilitating relativism.

This is so because liberation theologians usually enter their "hermeneutical circle"–the process by which they try to interpret their particular religious tradition's vision of the ox–with a "hermeneutics of suspicion." They are suspicious of how easily, and perhaps unavoidably, religious teachings and practices become ideology, that is, a means of promoting one's own or one's own community's interest at the expense of others. For example, Christian liberation theologians point out that the truths proposed as God's will too often degenerate into disguised attempts to maintain the status quo or to protect Western cultural and economic superiority.[27] Buddhist, Islamic, and Jewish liberation writers note similar tendencies in their own traditions.[28]

Such ideological abuse of tradition has been a lurking danger in the histories of every religious Way, but this danger has been most evident in the history of the Christian Way. Historically, the Christian Way has proved to be more ideological and monological than any other religious Way, which means it has fostered more violence than any other. For this reason alone, the practice of hermeneutics of suspicion, which originated in Christian liberation thought, is relevant. How much theology, how much doctrine in all religious Ways, has served to cloak and to justify conscious and unconscious ideological attempts to dominate and control, or to devalue other traditions, culturally or religiously?

Accordingly, liberation practice means being suspicious of and sniffing out any ideologies that are operating in a given tradition of faith and practice, including, or especially, one's own. Systems of faith and practice transformed into ideologies must be detected and either revised or rejected before we can see the relatively inaccessible ox well enough to wrestle with it.

Pluralist theologians have much to learn from the hermeneutics of suspicion. It would first of all require that we be hermeneutically suspicious of our own tradition's claims about outsiders. Why have Catholic Christians, for example, been so eager to maintain the doctrine of *extra ecclesiam nulla salus* ("outside the Church, there is no salvation")? Why have Protestants been so eager to maintain the doctrine that outside explicit belief in Jesus as the Christ, there is no salvation? Is it really necessary for Christians to assert that Christ is the final norm for all other religions? It is certainly the case such doctrines have been, and still are, used to justify the often violent subordination and exploitation of nature, non-Western cultures, and non-Christian religious Ways.[29]

Even if Christians do not consciously or unconsciously employ their tradition to make other cultures subordinate or to violate their religious sensitivities, whenever such effects occur, then these teachings and practices must fall under the hermeneutics of suspicion. "Orthodox" teachings and practices that cause suffering to human beings are always highly suspicious. For the most part, it is in dialogue with the voices of other religious traditions and cultures that Western Christians can begin to feel suspicion. For example, Third World Asian theologians have forcefully exposed the pain and suffering caused by Christian missions in non-European cultures. Western Christians are now increasingly aware that even inclusive models of Christian dialogue with non-Christian religious Ways—for example, Karl Rahner's "anonymous Christianity" and Hans Küng's "critical catalyst" models—promote colonialist theologies of religions and Western cultural imperialism.[30]

This is inevitable, Christian liberation thinkers warn, because inclusive models of religious pluralism are very similar to First World development models for promoting economic progress in the Third World. Gustavo Gutierrez, Herman E. Daly, and John Cobb, for example, have pointed out how First World notions of "development" create further economic dependence and control of the Third World by the industrialized West.[31] There is indeed cause for suspicion. Can any form of Christian self-understanding that legitimizes sexist, racist, classist, and religious oppression be a theologically adequate expression of Christian encounter with the ox revealed in the life, death, and resurrection of the historical Jesus as the Christ?

Similar suspicions can be raised in the histories of non-Christian religious Ways as well. Although its history is not as bloody as the Christian Way, does traditional Islamic self-understanding that legitimizes male oppression of women and the oppression of non-Islamic religious Ways—for example, the Muslim conquest of India and its oppression of Hinduism and Buddhism, or Shiʔah Muslim persecution of Bahaʔi in Iran—truly reflect the call to "surrender" to the will of God to which the *Qurʔān* calls all human beings?[32] It is the hermeneutics of suspicion, central to the *praxis* of liberation thinkers in whatever religious Way they work and struggle, that has motivated many Christians and non-Christians to acknowledge the reality of religious pluralism and to engage in interreligious dialogue as a primary form of liberation *praxis*.

Interreligious Dialogue: Preference for the Poor

As the hermeneutics of suspicion can clear away ideological obstacles to authentic interreligious dialogue, so liberation practice of preferential option for the poor can help resolve several complex and controversial questions concerning both the presuppositions and procedures of interreligious dialogue. Much scholarly energy has been expended on these questions. How *should* we understand religious pluralism and engage in interreligious encounter so that everyone has not only the right to speak, but genuine ability to hear what is spoken? This is not an easy question. The traditional view is that fruitful interreligious dialogue requires the hypothesis of some kind of "common ground" shared by all religious Ways. Several examples of "common ground" notions have been suggested: the "common essence" of Arnold Toynbee; the "universal faith" suggested by Wilfred Cantwell Smith and Bernard Lonergan; or a common "mystical center," as suggested by Walter T. Stace and Thomas Merton.[33]

But numerous critics think that positing anything common between the religious Ways of humanity as a basis for dialogue is unwarranted and dangerous. Some philosophers, such as Francis Schüssler Fiorenza and Richard Rorty, are troubled by what they perceive to be the danger of "objectivism" or "foundationalism." By this they seem to mean the conviction that there must be some permanent ahistorical essence or framework to which we can finally appeal in determining the nature of rationality, knowledge, truth, reality, rightness, or religious experience.[34] Rather than looking for a common ground above or beyond the plurality of religious faith and practice, Fiorenza and Rorty enjoin us to accept all knowledge as "theory-laden." Different societies have different "plausibility structures." Therefore every religious Way is plausible only within its own "language game," so that there can be no "common ground, that is, no way "from outside" a religious tradition to assess the meaning and truth claims made "within it." Different religious beliefs are, in other words, "incommensurable."

Theologians such as John Cobb and Raimundo Panikkar are also highly critical of "objectivism." If we really take religious pluralism seriously, they warn, the search for a "universal theory" or a "common source" of religious experience should be abandoned, including my notion of one sacred reality or "Relatively Inaccessible Sacred Ox" seen differently from the contexts of all religious Ways. Panikkar's critique is especially harsh. A genuine religious pluralism, he thinks, cannot and should not imagine a universal system of thought. For him, a pluralist "system" is a contradiction and the "incommensurability" of ultimate systems is unbridgeable."[35] For similar reasons, John Cobb is highly critical of John Hick, Wilfred Cantwell Smith, Paul Knitter, and me. He thinks that looking for something common to all religious Ways is to abandon religious pluralism to ahistorical reductionism. To accept religious pluralism is to abandon this quest and simply be open. But openness is inhibited unnecessarily if we state in advance what all religious human beings have in common.[36] The danger is, of course, that we will miss what is genuinely different, and therefore what is genuinely challenging, in religious traditions other than our own.

In fact, Cobb regards this danger as so likely that he has suggested that there is no one "ultimate" within or beyond the world's religious Ways. Instead, he thinks there might be multiple ultimates behind all the religious Ways of the world, and that religious pluralists like Huston Smith, Wilfred Cantwell Smith, John Hick, Paul Knitter and me are afraid to face this possibility.[37] I am, in fact, forced to admit that proposing the relatively inaccessible Sacred as the ox seen and experienced from the historical and cultural contexts all religious traditions occupy does indeed run the risk of imperialistically imposing my conception of the Sacred on religious traditions other than my own. Many serious Buddhists, many serious Jews or Muslims or Christians, will not wish to speak about what they experience as a "common ground" at the center of all religious ways, even if it is called "relatively inaccessible."

Still, even as critics forcefully warn against the pitfalls of objectivism, they just as forcefully warn against the pitfalls of radical skepticism based on a relativism that so locks religious Ways and cultures within their own language games or plausibility structures as to make communication among them impossible. Fiorenza, Rorty, Panikkar, and Cobb all, paradoxically, assert the possibility and value of communication and dialogue between "incommensurable" traditions. In doing so, they look for a path between objectivism and relativism, and assert that even though there is no preestablished common ground among religious traditions, religious persons inhabiting different religious worlds can still, and should, talk to and understand one another.

How this is possible is not often clear. Cobb and Panikkar simply trust the *praxis* of communication to reveal common ground or shared problems and viewpoints, and plunge into dialogue. They believe that whatever "common ground" evolves in the dialogue can suffice to overcome incommensurability (e.g., between *śūnyatā* and God in Cobb's theology) and to lead to mutual understanding and "mutual transformation."[38] Similarly, even as Panikkar disavows universal theories of religion and the idea of a common ground shared by all, he still invokes a single "aspiration" or a single "inspiration" for all religious Ways.[39]

What Cobb and Panikkar have seen is that different religious traditions cannot be ultimately different, as, say, apples are different from granite, in an interconnected, interdependent universe. If they are, how or why or should or could interreligious dialogue even happen? The point is, anyone who affirms the value of interreligious dialogue, anyone who undertakes interreligious dialogue as a *praxis*, tacitly implies that there *is* something that bonds together the religious Ways of humanity. In other words, there *is* a common ground underlying the plurality of religious faith and practice, and it serves no purpose to deny it. Even those who do deny it, tacitly at least, presuppose a common ground whenever they engage in interreligious dialogue. The problem is, how do we indicate this common ground explicitly? How to come clean about it? How to discover what it is? How to work creatively in awareness of it, as we allow it to empower us?

I have tried to be explicit about what I perceive to be the common ground underlying the plurality of religious faith and practice: what I metaphorically refer to as "the relatively inaccessible ox." I do not claim that this metaphor is the only one suitable for conceiving what the common ground between religious traditions is, or even that it is the best metaphor; I remain convinced, however, of its possibilities until I am shown otherwise. So while it is possible, perhaps likely–I am writing about the Sacred, after all–that my metaphor might be a mistake, what is not likely is the nonexistence of a common ground underlying the historical and cultural diversity of the religious Ways of humanity.

At this juncture, a suggestion by Paul Knitter becomes relevant. Even if one remains unconvinced about a common ground of religious faith and practice, there is a common "approach" or a common "context" with which religious persons can begin dialogue. "For liberation theologians, this common context or approach would be the *preferential option for the poor and nonperson*–that is, the option to work with and for the *victims* of this world."[40]

What liberation theologians and feminist theologians are telling us is that without commitment to and identification with the poor and the oppressed, our knowledge–knowledge of self, knowledge of others, knowledge of the relatively inaccessible Sacred–is insufficient and impotent. This does not mean that we can know the ox only in commitment to the poor and the oppressed. But apart from the practice of preference for the poor and the oppressed, whatever truths we may know are incomplete, deficient, and possibly dangerous. For poverty and oppression are not "religion specific" but universal.

Furthermore, the religious Ways of humanity have always recognized poverty and oppression as common problems from which human beings need release, long before it became fashionable in the West to call such release "liberation." It is possible that interreligious dialogue can evolve into a shared commitment, expressed in different ways, for religious persons to reach across boundaries and differences in order to hear and understand each other, and be transformed in the process.

Knitter qualifies this, however:

> It is important to note the differences between what is being proposed here and "objectivism" and "foundationalism." The fundamental option for the poor and non-persons serves not as a "foundation" or "Archimedean point," or a sure-fire criterion for judgment, but as an approach, a context, a starting point that must itself be clarified as it creates new common ground for understanding.[41]

I sympathize with Knitter's qualification, but only up to a point. Unlike him, I think focusing interreligious dialogue on liberation *praxis* for preferential option for the poor does not preclude a common ground among the religious Ways of humanity, but *presupposes* it. In my opinion, a "shared locus of religious experience," like poverty and oppression, points to a common ground unifying humanity's different religious Ways as surely as does mystical-contemplative experience. Thus, along with mystics in monasteries, deserts, or on mountains, the struggle for justice is an arena where Hindus, Muslims, Buddhists, Christians, or Jews can sense and begin to speak about that which unites them. What unites them includes not only the struggle for justice, but the relatively inaccessible ox—however it is named—that underlies and unifies that struggle.

Therefore, contemplative or meditative forms of wrestling with the ox in interreligious dialogue should not be understood as opposite to liberation forms of the *praxis* of preferential treatment of the poor within the rough-and-tumble of historical existence. They are complements, not opposites. They should conjointly inform the practice of interreligious dialogue. If so, however, a further point needs to be made, one I have been suggesting throughout this book.

Interreligious dialogue calls into serious question all doctrinal absolutisms and forms of religious imperialism as strongly and as critically as do the teachings and practices of Western and Eastern mystics of the world's religious Ways. Accordingly, those who engage in liberation dialogue should also move on to more primordial views of religious faith and practice.

For Christians, this means moving from christology as the defining center of faith, practice, and thought to more theocentric forms of theology. Paul Knitter expresses it this way:

> For Christians, that which constitutes the basis and the goal of interreligious dialogue . . . is *not how* they are related to the church (invisibly through "baptism of desire"), or how they are related to Christ (anonymously [Rahner] or normatively [Küng]), or even how they respond to or conceive of God, but rather, to what extent they are engaged in promoting human welfare and bringing about liberation with and for the poor and non-persons.[42]

Of course, most Christians are not willing to move from christocentric to theocentric forms of thought and practice. But I think much contemporary theology, together with increasing interest in interreligious dialogue with non-Christians among Christian laity, is now gradually moving contemporary Christian attitudes in this direction.

Likewise, I can imagine similar transformations occurring in non-Christian religious Ways when the preferential option for the poor is integrated into their distinctive traditions of thought and practice. I stress the word "imagine," because the fact that I am Christian—although not a very traditional one—means that I cannot speak with the authority of witnesses *within* non-Christian traditions. Yet my experience as a working historian of religions leads me to believe similar trends are now evolving in non-Christian religious Ways as well as they increasingly encounter religious pluralism and liberation thought. While these trends may be evident mostly among the elites of these religious Ways, they are nevertheless important. They are mostly, as far as I can tell, found among non-Christian feminist liberation thinkers who also participate in interreligious dialogue.

Accordingly, Muslims who focus their dialogue with non-Muslims on God's call to all human beings to surrender to God's will through struggle for the liberation of all human beings, stress what the *Qurʾān* specifies in this regard apart from traditional patriarchal legal interpretations of the *Qurʾān* by the schools of Islamic law. In fact, if any single scripture in the world's religious Ways is an explicit call for struggle against the forces of oppression, it is the *Qurʾān*. For many contemporary "modernist" feminist Muslims, this implies a reinvention of the Sunna ("tradition"), which was set and defined from the point of view of male experience. Indeed, the *Qurʾān* seems open to such reinterpretation; it specifies explicitly that surrender of the human will to God is the common ground of all authentic religious faith, Muslim or non-Muslim. The quality and authenticity of a person's ʿislām are measured by how that individual struggles in community for the liberation of humanity from human-caused forms of oppression. Only that person is a "Muslim," "one who surrenders to the will of God," even when that person might not wear an institutionalized Muslim label.[43] God's justice and mercy are for everyone, not just "believers" in Islam. Or, restated in the language of liberation thought, being a Muslim means practicing the preferential option for the poor while rejecting the theological and legal absolutes distinctive to patriarchally dominated Islamic religious imperialism as "idolatry" (*shirk*). In the struggle for liberation, one's religious label is of secondary importance.

Similar liberationist trends are now transforming Buddhist thought and practice and informing Buddhist dialogue with non-Buddhists. Rita Gross notes that while historically, basic Buddhist teachings are not misogynist or patriarchal, the institutions and traditional forms of Buddhist faith and practice are male dominated and disadvantageous to women.[44] This fact becomes clear especially when examined through the lens of liberation thought. Buddhist thought focuses on "liberation" from suffering in samsaric (phenomenal) existence. Since institutionalized forms of suffering and exploitation are part of the realm of saṃsāra, Buddhist practice is particularly open to the *praxis* of preferential option for the poor. This means the enlightenment one attains in meditation must be completed and expressed through enlightened compassion (*karuṇā*) toward the poor. Since this is the case, much Buddhist dialogue with Christians has centered on ethical and social issues relating to the liberation of the poor from economic and political exploitation.[45] The "common ground" Buddhists assume in their dialogue with non-Buddhists, therefore, is how the Buddhist quest for liberation can be informed by similar quests in non-Buddhist traditions.

Liberationist *praxis* of preferential regard for the poor is currently occurring within Hindu, Jewish, and even Native American traditions as the point of departure for their interreligious dialogues. Since I have described this trend in reference to feminist liberation thought in chapter 8, I will close this section with two observations.

First, and in disagreement with Knitter, liberation *praxis* of preferential regard for the poor presupposes a common ground among the different religious Ways of humanity. I have called that ground "the relatively inaccessible Sacred." Metaphorically, it is the ox with which all religious human beings wrestle no matter where they are found. Wrestling with the ox occurs not only in the quiet of monasteries, temples, churches, synagogues, mountain tops, deserts, or in a room of one's own. It occurs also in the midst of historical existence as we wrestle with the forces that keep human beings bound to economic and political oppression. We do not see the ox clearly *only* in the *praxis* of meditative-contemplative self-discipline in isolation from the world's suffering.

Nor do we see the ox clearly *only* through *praxis* of preferential regard for the poor apart from meditative and contemplative self-discipline. We see the ox *most* clearly when we unite these two forms of practice in our wrestling with the ox. We see the ox most clearly as we wrestle with it in the quiet of our soul's deepest longings for vision and unity *as we* struggle to be *in* the world, yet *not of* the world, in the practice of the preferential option for the poor.

Second, the criticism of Cobb and others to this approach contains an important warning to which we must pay attention. Posing any common ground for dialogue, Cobb thinks—even preferential regard for the poor— seems to give the appearance that we are open to dialogue only with those who share this viewpoint. But need the preferential option for the poor, or my notion of a common ground called the relatively inaccessible Sacred, neces- sarily be imposed as an absolute condition for interreligious dialogue? My experience tells me this is not the case. Most persons with whom I engage in interreligious dialogue do not share my views, do not care for my metaphors, and have trouble thinking about the Sacred as "relatively inaccessible." I do not demand that they accept my metaphor or my idea of a common ground underlying the diversity of religious pluralism. In fact, dialogue is more inter- esting and informative with those who do not accept my particular formula- tions because they force me to think more critically about other options and possibilities.

Nor do I demand that my dialogical partners accept preferential regard for the poor as a condition for dialogue with me. My ideas are an *invitation*. They are never a demand for acceptance. But I suspect, and suggest, that most per- sons can and want to enter dialogue on this account. What I suspect is strengthened by Pieris's conclusion that the religious Ways of the world share more common ground in their "soteriologies" (quest for liberation) than in their "theologies."[46] It is in the *praxis* of preferential regard for the poor in our search for liberation that tradition-specific similarities and differences that seem theologically and doctrinally important drop away. In place of "theology," "soteriology" clarifies *real* differences: between those whose religious tradi- tions are used to perpetuate domination and oppression, and those whose tra- ditions strengthen them in the fight against domination and oppression.

The Way of Silence and the Way of Action

Mystics and contemplatives of the world's religious Ways tell us how to see the relatively inaccessible ox in the interior silence of our deepest selves and in the silence of nature. Seen from the meditative-contemplative experience of *praxis*, when all is said and done, the silence is all there is. It is the alpha and omega. It is the relatively inaccessible ox brooding over the face of the deep of the Genesis creation story. It is the "emptiness" of the Buddha nature within all things and events of Mahayana Buddhist tradition. It is the blended notes of animals and plants, the whine of wings of Native American spirituality. We take a step in the right direction to pray to this silence, to surrender to it, to become one with it—if we are lucky enough to hear it. Here, distinctions blur. We quit our tents. Prayer becomes meditation, meditation, prayer.

But liberation thought teaches us that we must not isolate ourselves from the world in the *praxis* of silent non-duality with the ox; if we do, we will go deaf to a question the ox whispers to us in the silence. An ancient Israelite psalmist standing in silence in the presence of the ox once heard this question in this form: "Who shall ascend to the hill of the Lord? Or who shall stand in his holy place?"

To which the ox whispered an answer: "He that hath clean hands and a pure heart."

This is the problem addressed by liberation *praxis:* there is no one to send because no one, not even mystics standing in the *praxis* of silent union with the ox, has clean hands or a pure heart. Liberation thought shows us that no such human beings have ever existed on the face of Mother Earth. There is only us, a generation prone to comforting ourselves with the notion that we have come at an awkward time. But there is no one of us. There never has been a generation of men and women who lived well and justly for even one day. Yet some of us have imagined well, with honesty and art, and have ascended with such grace and wisdom that we have mistaken their vision for history, their dreams for description, and fancy that our own lives have evolved to higher states of awareness and justice.

We learn this by studying any history at all, especially the lives of contemplative artists and visionaries. We learn it from Dogen or Śaṇkara or Mother Teresa or Emerson or T. S. Eliot, visionaries who noticed that the meanness of our days is itself worth our thought. We learn it with equal force from liberation visionaries of all religious Ways: the Hebrew Prophets, Jesus of Nazareth, Muhammad, Mahatma Gandhi, Martin Luther King, Jr., who collectively teach us how to see the ox within the rough-and-tumble struggle for justice for all human beings.

Accordingly, religious visionaries and mystics always have this problem: they exert influence mostly on other visionaries, and that influence soon passes because it touches the heart of only a few elites. They require correction from persons of practical wisdom, liberationists ever alert to painful issues of injustice and poverty. Yet liberationists have another problem: they often influence the brain with ideology in their call to struggle against oppression, while leaving the heart untouched. But never in this world has justice been achieved unless the heart, deeply stirred, has played its part.

The conclusion of this chapter, therefore, is that only where mystic faith and *praxis* are yoked to liberationist faith and *praxis* is there a possibility for attaining the liberation that both mystics and liberationists seek. For when it comes down to it, the question is: From what do human beings seek liberation? What mystics and liberationists collectively tell us is that human beings seek liberation from evil in many forms—from anxiety; from illness; from inferiority feelings, from grief; from fear of death; from social and economic injustice. What human beings seek may be healing; the elimination of agents of evil; access to power; the enhancement of status; increase of prosperity; the transformation of the social order; and ultimately, the promise of life after death, resurrection from the grave, or freedom from continual rebirth in the realm of worldly suffering and pain. This ultimate liberation, "soteriology," is the topic of the next chapter.

Notes

1. Donald S. Lopez, Jr., trans., *The Heart Sutra Explained* (Albany: State University of New York Press, 1988), 19.
2. D. T. Suzuki, *Manual of Zen Buddhism* (New York: Grove Press, 1960), 133.
3. Thich Nhat Hanh, *Vietnam: Lotus in a Sea of Fire* (New York: Hill & Wang, 1967), chap. 4; idem, *Zen Keys* (Garden City, N.Y.: Anchor Books), chap. 1.
4. See, for example, Aloysius Pieris, S.J., "The Place of Non-Christian Religions and Cultures in the Evolution of Third World Theology," in *An Asian Theology of Liberation* (Maryknoll, N.Y.: Orbis Books, 1988), 87–110.
5. Arnold Toynbee, "What Should Be the Christian Approach to the Contemporary Non-Christian Faiths," in *Christianity Among the Religions of the World* (New York: Scribner's, 1957), 83–112.
6. Wilfred Cantwell Smith, *The Faith of Other Men* (New York: New American Library, 1962), 101.
7. Paul F. Knitter, "Towards a Liberation Theology of Religions," in *The Myth of Christian Uniqueness: Toward a Pluralistic Theology of Religions*, ed. John Hick and Paul F. Knitter (Maryknoll, N.Y.: Orbis Books, 1989), 179.
8. Aloysius Pieris, "The Place of Non-Christian Religions and Cultures in the Evolution of Third World Theology," 113–14, cited by Paul F. Knitter, "Towards A Liberation Theology of Religions," 180.
9. For example, see Gustavo Gutierrez, *A Theology of Liberation* (Maryknoll, N.Y.: Orbis Books, 1973), 162, 222.
10. See, for example, Langdon Gilkey, *Reaping the Whirlwind: A Christian Interpretation of History* (New York: Seabury Press, 1981), 226–38.
11. David Tracy's warning about this is particularly clear; see *Dialogue With the*

Other: The Inter-Religious Dialogue (Grand Rapids, Mich.: William B. Eerdmans, 1990), 119–23.

12. Langdon Gilkey, "Plurality and Its Theological Implications," in *The Myth of Christian Uniqueness*, 44.

13. Knitter, "Towards a Liberation Theology of Religions," 181.

14. What follows is based on John C. Maraldo's essay on practice in "The Hermeneutics of Practice in Dogen and Francis of Assisi," in *Buddhist-Christian Dialogue: Mutual Renewal and Transformation*, ed. Paul O. Ingram and Frederick J. Streng (Honolulu: University of Hawaii Press, 1986), 53–73.

15. Ibid., 55.

16. Ibid.

17. Dogen, *Bendowa*, Norman Wadell and Masao Abe, trans., *Eastern Buddhist* 4 (May 1971): 129, cited by Maraldo, "Hermeneutics of Practice in Dogen and Francis of Assisi," 58.

18. Ibid., 61.

19. Ibid. Also see Ray Petry, *Francis of Assisi* (New York: AMS Press, 1964), chaps. 1, 7–9.

20. Gutierrez, *Theology of Liberation*, 36.

21. See Pieris, "A Theology of Liberation in Asian Churches," in *An Asian Theology of Liberation*, 111–26.

22. Gutierrez, *Theology of Liberation*, 37.

23. See Fazlur Rahman, *Islam* (Chicago: University of Chicago Press, 1966), 68–84; Yvone Yazbeck Haddad, *Contemporary Islam and the Challenge of History* (Albany: State University of New York Press, 1982), 68–70; and Wilfred Cantwell Smith, *Islam in Modern History* (Princeton: Princeton University, 1957), chap. 1.

24. This is especially emphasized in Pure Land Buddhist tradition, but it is also fundamental to every Buddhist lineage. See Paul O. Ingram, *The Dharma of Faith: An Introduction to Classical Pure Land Buddhism* (Washington, D.C.: University Press of America, 1977); and Minor L. and Ann T. Rogers, *Rennyo: The Second Founder of Shin Buddhism* (Berkeley, Calif.: Asian Humanities Press, 1991).

25. Jacob Neusner, *The Way of Torah* (Belmont, Calif.: Wadsworth, 1988), 1–28.

26. See Paul J. Griffiths, ed., *Christianity Through Non-Christian Eyes* (Maryknoll, N.Y.: Orbis Books, 1990); Roger Corless and Paul F. Knitter, eds., *Buddhist Emptiness and Christian Trinity: Essays and Explorations* (New York: Paulist Press, 1990); John B. Cobb, Jr., and Christopher Ives, eds., *The Emptying God: A Buddhist-Jewish-Christian Conversation* (Maryknoll, N.Y.: Orbis Books, 1990); and John P. Keenan, *The Meaning of Christ: A Mahayana Theology* (Maryknoll, N.Y.: Orbis Books, 1989).

27. See Aloysius Pieris, "Western Models of Inculturation: Applicable to Asia?" in *An Asian Theology of Religions* (Maryknoll, N.Y.: Orbis Books, 1988), 51–58; and Gutierrez, *Theology of Liberation*, 234–39; and Juan Luis Segundo, *The Liberation of Theology* (Maryknoll, N.Y.: Orbis Books, 1976), 7–9.

28. See, for example, Masao Abe, "Self-Awakening and Faith—Zen and Christianity," in *Christianity Through Non-Christian Eyes*, ed. Paul J. Griffiths (Maryknoll,

N.Y.: Orbis Books, 1990), 171–80; Judith Plaskow, *Standing Again at Sinai: Judaism from a Feminist Perspective* (San Francisco: HarperSanFrancisco, 1990), 232–38; and Haddad, *Contemporary Islam and the Challenge of History*, 125–44.

29. I made a similar point years ago without specific reference to liberation theology. See *The Modern Buddhist-Christian Dialogue* (Lewiston, N.Y.: Edwin Mellen Press, 1988), chap. 2.

30. For my extended critique of Rahner's and Küng's theologies of religions, see ibid., 47–51.

31. Gutierrez, *Theology of Liberation*, 21–27; Herman E. Daly and John B. Cobb, *For the Common Good* (Boston: Beacon Press, 1989), 135–37, 162–63.

32. Riffat Hassan, "Equal Before Allah? Woman-Man Equality in Islamic Tradition," *Harvard Divinity Bulletin* 17/2 (January–May 1987): 2–4; Fatima Mernissi, *Beyond the Veil* (Cambridge: Schenkman Publishing Company, 1975); and Ignaz Goldziher, "Catholic Tendencies and Particularism in Islam," in *Studies on Islam*, ed. Merlin L. Swartz (New York: Oxford University Press, 1991), 123–39.

33. See Arnold Toynbee, *An Historian's Approach to Religion* (New York: Oxford University Press, 1956), 261–83; Wilfred Cantwell Smith, *The Meaning and End of Religion* (New York: Minneapolis: Fortress Press, 1991), chaps. 6–7; idem, *Faith and Belief* (Princeton: Princeton University Press, 1979); Bernard J. F. Lonergan, *Method in Theology* (New York: Herder & Herder, 1972), 101–24; Walter T. Stace, *Mysticism and Philosophy* (Philadelphia: Lippincott, 1960); Frithjof Schuon, *The Transcendent Unity of Religions* (New York: Harper & Row, 1975); and Thomas Merton, *The Asian Journals of Thomas Merton*, ed. Naomi Burton et al. (New York: New Directions, 1975), 309–17.

34. See Francis Schüssler Fiorenza, *Foundational Theology: Jesus and the Church* (New York: Crossroad, 1984), 283–311; and Richard Rorty, *Philosophy and the Mirror of Nature* (Princeton: Princeton University Press, 1979.

35. Raimundo Panikkar, "The Jordan, The Tiber, and the Ganges: Three Kairological Moments of Christic Self-consciousness," in *The Myth of Christian Uniqueness*, 110. Also see his *The Silence of God: The Answer of the Buddha* (Maryknoll, N.Y.: Orbis Books, 1990), Introduction.

36. John B. Cobb., Jr., "Beyond Pluralism," in *Christian Uniqueness Reconsidered: The Myth of a Pluralistic Theology of Religions*, ed. Gaven D'Costa (Maryknoll, N.Y.: Orbis Books, 1990), 81–95. Also see *Beyond Dialogue* (Philadelphia: Fortress Press, 1982), 86–90.

37. John B. Cobb, Jr., "Buddhist Emptiness and the Christian God," *Journal of the American Academy of Religion* 45 (1979): 86–90. Also see *Christ in a Pluralistic Age* (Philadelphia: Westminster Press, 1975), 202–29.

38. Cobb, "Buddhist Emptiness and the Christian God," 86–90.

39. Raimundo Panikkar, "A Universal Theory of Religion," in *Toward a World Theology of Religions*, ed. Leonard Swidler (Maryknoll, N.Y.: Orbis Books, 1987).

40. Knitter, "Towards a Liberation Theology of Religions," 185.

41. Ibid., 186.

42. Ibid., 187.
43. See Surah 4:58, 65, 105, 135; Surah 8:29; and 16:90. Also see Riffat Hassan, "Muslim Women and Post-Patriarchal Islam," in *After Patriarchy, Feminist Transformations of the World Religions*, ed. Paula M. Cooey et al. (Maryknoll, N.Y.: Orbis Books, 1993), 39–64; and Asaf A. A. Fyzee, "The Reinterpretation of Islam," in *Islam in Transition: Muslim Perspectives*, ed. John J. Donohue et al. (New York: Oxford University Press, 1982), 188–93.
44. Rita M. Gross, "Buddhism After Patriarchy?" in *After Patriarchy*, 70.
45. For example, see Masao Abe, "Buddhism and Christianity as a Problem of Today, Part I," *Japanese Religions* 3, no. 2 (Summer 1963): 11–22; and "Part II," 3, no. 3 (Autumn 1963): 8–31.
46. Pieris, *Asian Theology of Liberation*, 3–14.

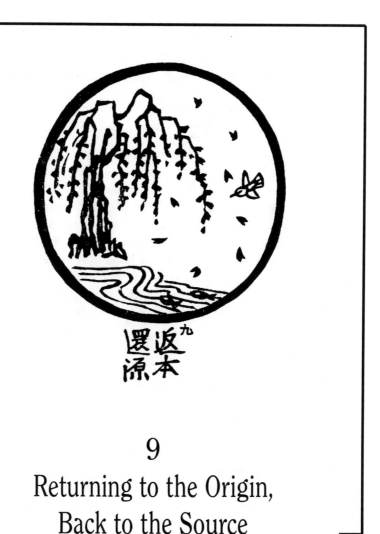

9
Returning to the Origin,
Back to the Source

AS PORTRAYED IN THE FIRST OX-HERDING PICTURE, THE MAN, THE OX, AND THE
world have never been lost or defiled. Now, in the ninth picture, "Returning
to the Origin, Back to the Source," the man has, after much struggle, finally
seen that this is so. Now he watches and participates in the life around him
without inserting his ego into what he sees. He is "natural" (Japanese, *jinen*)
and free, not owning anything, and, thereby, not owned *by* anything. He has
seen reality, the way things really are, not as he wants reality to be, but as it
is. Thereby, he is able to live in harmony with the myriad forms reality
assumes. Or in the words of the picture's poem:

> Returning to the Origin, returning to the Source—already a false step!
> Far better to remain at home, blind and deaf, and without much ado;
> Sitting in the hut, the man takes no notice of things outside.
> Behold the streams flowing—whither nobody knows;
>   and the flowers vividly red—for whom are they?[1]

Indeed, the man is close to final, liberating insight. Yet he has not yet fully arrived. What he is painfully close to achieving is the topic of this chapter— "soteriology," to appropriate a Christian technical term, or "salvation," to use a less technical Western term. After everything is analyzed, said, and done, all religious Ways are about soteriology, because all religious Ways are what Frederick J. Streng called "means to ultimate transformation."[2] However, this chapter is not specifically concerned with Buddhist versions of ultimate transformation. Instead, I shall examine how the pluralism of soteriological experience and conceptions in the world's religious traditions might reveal primordial meanings to which humanity's religious traditions collectively point.

What does "ultimate transformation" mean? At minimum, it seems to entail a fundamental change from being caught up in the troubles of common existence (sin, ignorance, suffering, death) to living in such a way that one can cope at the deepest level with those troubles. This capacity for living allows persons to apprehend the depths of reality—what I have called the relatively inaccessible ox—and live and die accordingly. In the context of religious awareness, ultimacy means the most comprehensive resource and deepest necessity of which a person can be aware. It is one's sense of superlative value that motivates and structures one's life.[3]

Of course, the religious Ways of humanity are as soteriologically pluralistic as they are in every aspect of their teachings and practices. Ultimate transformation and the means to achieve it differ from religious Way to religious Way. Indeed, there can be multiple meanings, often contradictory meanings, of ultimate transformation within the same religious tradition. Does this pluralism itself have something important to teach us? Can even this aspect of religious pluralism help us see traces of the relatively inaccessible ox that we need to see, but might miss, if we focus too narrowly on what our own religious tradition tells us? This chapter's thesis is that soteriological pluralism contains traces of the ox that we can train ourselves to see and appropriate, no matter what our particular religious tradition might be.

It should be evident that the subject of this book—wrestling with the ox— is about "ultimate transformation." Certainly, wrestling with the ox, and all the ways this is symbolized in the ten pictures, portrays a Zen Buddhist means of ultimate transformation. However, I have not emphasized Zen conceptions in the ox metaphor. My goal is to use this metaphor to figure out a pluralistic theology of religions inclusive of, but not limited to, Zen Buddhism. In other words, my work is a thought experiment. Yet I am also aware that whether my particular experiment works is very much up for grabs.

Accordingly, a second goal of this chapter is to relate the issue of ultimate transformation to the issues of liberation discussed in previous chapters: the liberation of life (chapters 5 and 6), the liberation of women (chapter 7), and the liberation of the poor and oppressed (chapter 8). My premise is that what Streng named "ultimate transformation" is indistinguishable from "liberation"; all religious Ways are about "ultimate transformation" because all are about "liberation." Conversely, all religious Ways are about "liberation" because they are about "ultimate transformation." Therefore, the important questions are: Ultimate transformation to what and liberation from what? Is there a final liberating, ultimately transformative state of which every religious Way speaks, in its own distinctively diverse way?

In Christian language, "ultimate transformation" is usually called "salvation." In Christian terms, salvation entails dying to self and living in full relationship with God. Such a state of existence involves turning away from self-centeredness that separates the self from other selves, from nature, and from God, while requiring freely and willfully interrelating with other human beings, with nature, and with God on the basis of compassionate love. Each religious Way of humanity conceptualizes what is wrong with ordinary human existence and how to overcome what is wrong according to its own teachings and practices. I suggest that these different conceptions of salvation or final liberation share a generic commonality: all, in their own historically and culturally specific ways, are concerned with the transformation of human existence from self-centeredness to a new and mutually creative relationship with the relatively inaccessible Sacred.[4]

Another way of stating this is that humanity's religious Ways are what Winston Davis calls "salvation syndromes."[5] Since the evidence of the history of religions suggests that humanity's religious Ways are finally concerned about achieving salvation from suffering in this world as well as from death, this chapter aims to be a dialogical encounter with the plurality of experiences and concepts of death and dying in Hindu, Buddhist, Chinese, Jewish, and Christian traditions. I intend this dialogue to serve as a foundation for some very tentative primordial conclusions about final liberation and ultimate transformation, and how final liberation might interrelate with other forms of liberation. But first some general remarks about death and dying.

On the Plurality of Death and Dying

Sometimes when I think about death and dying, usually when I am alone in my room, thoughts revolve inside my head like a wheel within a wheel, with my room like a third wheel revolving around my head. It's a bizarre feeling because the problem with thinking about death is that we do not know what we are thinking about. Of course, we certainly know *that* death is, that it will happen to us and every living thing, but we do not know *what* death is. Before we can know anything, we must first experience it; but by the time we experience death, it may be too late to know the experience.

I also have a hunch that to the degree we do not know what death is, only that it is, to that degree we do not know what life is, only that it is—provided, of course, that reality is as interdependent and interconnected as great blue herons, Buddhists, Taoists, and Whiteheadian theologians have led me to believe.

It appears, then, that experience gives us at least two conclusions about the fact of death, if not about the experience of death. First, we can see death's traces in life, and life's traces in death. This seems to be what Asian and aboriginal religious Ways see about the fact of death: life and death are nondual, so affirm both. Second, however, we can look at the fact of death through the lenses of traditional Christianity, Judaism, or Islam: death is the dual opposite of whatever constitutes life, a "fall" from eternal life in relationship with God, the penalty for sin, so seek life and avoid death. I have no idea which option is most likely true; both seem to accord with experience. Perhaps there is truth in both. Yet I have heard stories, and have even told some.

Hunters used to tell an old tale in camping places, where human beings lived in the open land among trees and animals. The tale always had to do with messages that the gods sent to them. Someone or some animal always got the message wrong, and the error was impossible to correct. So illness and death intruded into the world.

Most of the time, the animals seemed to understand their mythic roles, but humanity was troubled by the message that they could not quite remember or had gotten wrong. Implied in this is our feeling that life demands answers from us, as if we could stand outside our life looking in and grasp something we do not already have, that an essential part of who we are is our struggle to remember the meaning of the message with which we have been entrusted, that we are message carriers. We are not what we seem. We had a message, even if dimly remembered, and we await further instruction.

My favorite version of this tale is about the creator in the morning of the world. After the creation of the first man and woman, which he named "people," the woman stood by a river and asked, "Shall we always live?"

Apparently, the creator had not considered this and was not willing to grant his new creatures immortality. So the woman picked up a rock and, gesturing toward the stream, said, "If it floats we shall always live. If it sinks, people must die so that they feel pity and compassion."

She tossed in the stone and watched it sink. "You have chosen," said the creator.

Many years ago on a sullen November day in the foothills of the High Sierras I took a long hike that ended at a forgotten cemetery. The weather was threatening, but I was driven by an unusual restlessness. Snow covered the land like a white shroud and clung to the trees like cotton by the time I reached an old cemetery bathed in gray twilight. The community that had placed it there had vanished long ago. Season by season, frost, snow, and heat had cracked the flat stones until none remained upright.

As I stood freezing among the frozen dead, wiping snow from my eyes, I saw the only other living thing in that bleak place—a mule deer showing ribs and hunger beneath its skin. Only the storm contained us. That shrinking, long-eared animal cowering helplessly beside a slab in an abandoned graveyard expected the flash of momentary death. But it did not run. And I, with a rifle I used to carry in that day and time, also stood, while snow—a real blizzard by then—raged over and between us. But I did not fire, and have not fired since.

We both had the power to be fruitful and multiply, I remember thinking. Why was it so, and what was the message that somehow seemed spoken from a long way off, carried by the cold and wind, out of explicit human hearing? The wind swirled the snow around us as the temperature fell. The deer needed that bit of shelter. In its trembling body, in the millions of years of evolution between us, there was no storyteller's aid. It had survived alone, thin, crumpled, and small. But it was alive and that was triumph enough.

I slowly backed away from the mule deer and the dead human beings and their fallen stones. I knew that if I could follow the fence lines, there would be a fire and company for me. It's hard to leave tracks in a snowstorm, and they quickly filled as I made my way back to the house of my friends. Then I suddenly knew: it was out of such desolation that the mule deer and humanity had arisen, and to such desolation to which the mule deer and humanity—along with all things caught in the field of space-time—will return. We are, in essence, belated ghosts of an angry winter searching for springtime; we carry in our hearts winter's death intertwined with yearning for springtime's life.

That mule deer was another of many "hidden teachers" I have encountered. It taught me four lessons. First, the rules of evolution seem to require death. Life grows out of death; death generates life. Life forms must eat other life forms to stay alive; life demands killing, and all living things live on the death of other living things. So death seems to be the necessary condition energizing the evolutionary processes that create and sustain the life of all life forms.

Second, there seems to be one commandment shared by all living things: survive. Life forms and species and groups are armed for survival, fanged for it, timid for it, hungry for it, fierce for it, clever for it, poisonous for it, intelligent for it. This commandment decrees the suffering and death of myriads of individuals for the survival of the whole. Life has one final end, to be alive. All the tricks and mechanisms, all the successes and failures, are aimed to this end. It seems to be the natural order of things that the processes of death that sustain and support life are as diversified as the life forms death sustains and supports; death seems as pluralistic as life.

Third, the interdependency of life and death is a "natural fact of existence." It is neither merciful nor cruel. True, death can seem to come as a welcome friend and bring release from suffering. Yet death is a fact that directly challenges any religious Way's teachings.

Fourth, as if this were not enough, human beings, nature's top predator, add to the pluralism of suffering and death necessitated by evolution. We are one of the few species that consciously kills other living things for reasons other than food. We even kill each other, in extreme instances motivated by rationalizations we invent to justify war, racial hatred, religious competition and conflict, gender oppression, oppression of the poor by the rich and politically powerful. Drug addiction spawns urban violence and crime. We war against other life forms and against the environmental forces that nurture their life and ours.

Here lies the rub. The only species that is a blot on nature, with the ability and will to push the forces of death beyond death's natural capacity to support life, to the point of extinguishing life on this planet, is also the one species that most intimately knows the terror of death, that experiences most acutely the rip that death creates in the human community and the community we share with all living things. Even as human beings have killed or been killed or have died "naturally," sometimes in suffering, sometimes not, our species is haunted by a question: Is this all there is? The religious Ways of humanity, in varying ways, all assert that there is more than this, that there is much more than death. It will be helpful, therefore, to look comparatively at representative examples of the plurality of conceptions about this "more."

Is This All There Is?

Hindu tradition. The oldest religious texts of Hindu tradition, the *Vedas*, give little attention to the experience of death. The traditional authors of the Vedic poetry and the priestly traditions of the *Brāhmaṇas* ("Pertaining to Brahman") seem more concerned with delaying the occurrence of death than with exploring the meaning of death. These traditions speak only vaguely of surviving death, have no developed concept of the "soul" (*ātman*), and fear most what they call "redeath" or "second death," which occurs after the death of the body.[6]

In the concluding portions of the Vedas called the *Upanishads*, however, death and the overcoming of death are the primary concerns of the sages. It is the Upanishadic view of death that became foundational for subsequent Hindu tradition.

The *Upanishads* give prominent attention to the Atman ("Self"), the eternal core of self-identity through time that is the "soul" that dwells within all things and events as "self-forms" of Brahman ("sacred power"), yet which possesses no personal characteristics. Thus, Atman *is* Brahman—birthless, deathless reality that is simultaneously the inmost being of all that exists. "Atman," declares the *Katha Upanishad*, is "smaller than the smallest, greater than the great, is hidden in the hearts of all living creatures" (I, ii, 20).[7] Because Atman is identical with Brahman, it is that which is truly real behind the tangible appearances of the senses that those who suffer from "delusion" (*māyā*) mistake as real.

Death in this conception must be a delusion (*māyā*); Atman, the self-form of Brahman in, with, and under all things, can neither come to an end nor have a beginning. Thus, in the *Bhagavad-gītā*, the deity Krishna consoles Arjuna's grief over the anticipated loss of friends and relatives in a coming battle: "The wise are not sorry for either the living or the dead. Never was a time when I did not exist, or you, or these kings, nor shall any of us cease to exist hereafter."[8] That is, what is born and subsequently dies is not the Atman but an illusory self, a delusion, a *māyā*-form, totally subject to the contingent world. It is therefore carried along by the casual conditions of the world according to which all things and events are endlessly undergoing transformation according to the laws of Karma and *saṃsāra*. So even unliberated souls do not die; they are carried forward by their own habitual deeds into successive births and deaths.

According to Hinduism, then, the goal of religious practice is to be free from what Krishna describes to Arjuna as the "terrible wheel of death and rebirth." That is, Hindu tradition imagines final liberation not as immortality of the soul, for the soul is already immortal. Rather, "liberation" involves the liberation of the soul from the process of death and rebirth through wiping away all those ways of existing in which the "I" is falsely imagined to be the center of one's existence. For insofar as we believe we are such beings, we shall be caught in the repeated casual cycles of rebirth, passing from one death to another, one life to another.

In other words, the standard Hindu view is that it is because people have misunderstood the nondual nature of the interrelationship between the self and the world that they attach themselves to the self as an "I" in separation from the world and other selves. We can only achieve release from the wheel of birth and death if we train ourselves to "see" (*darśan*) that this is not the case: self and world, Atman and Brahman, are not different but identical. It is this knowledge that undercuts the illusion of separate selfhood and frees us from the fear of death because it teaches us that death itself is an illusion. Of what, therefore, is there to be afraid?

Buddhist tradition. Both Theravada and Mahayana notions of death take their distinctive forms from the insight that came to the Buddha on the occasion of his enlightenment. He saw that all existence is rooted in the condition of "suffering" (*duḥkha*) and that suffering is not caused by some external reality over which we have no control, but by our own "desire" (*taṇhā*) for permanence. He also saw that all things exist because of the forces of "interdependent co-origination" (*pratītya-samutpāda*), so that all things are interdependently caused. Nothing is permanent. All things will pass away, which means that human existence, like everything else that lives, is under the power of death.

But the Buddha also taught that ultimate transformation and final liberation from suffering, if not from death, are possible. The Buddhist word for ultimate transformation and liberation is *nirvāṇa* (Pali, *nibbāna*). It is both a Buddhist technical term and an ideal. As a Sanskrit word, *nirvāṇa* primarily refers to the goal of Buddhist practice and is used in much the same way as the standard English word "enlightenment"–a generic word literally translating no particular Asian technical term but used to designate the Buddhist notion of the highest transformative experience of which human beings are capable. However, Buddhist meanings of *nirvāṇa* are as pluralistic as the traditions of Buddhist teachings and practice.

The earliest meanings of *nirvāṇa* are found in early Buddhist textual traditions in the Pali Canon of Theravada tradition. In the Pali Nikayas, first composed two to three centuries after the Buddha's death, there is reticence about discussing the term at all. Indeed, on such speculative issues as the enlightened person's status after death, both Theravada and Mahayana textual traditions admonish that speculation is an obstacle to the achievement of *nirvāṇa*, and should be renounced. The best known version of this idea is found in the *Majjhima-nikāya* (Middle length sayings).

Malunkyaputta once asked the Buddha several philosophical questions, including whether a Buddha continues to exist after death. The Buddha responded that such questions are beside the point; they are comparable to a man struck by a poison arrow worried about the nature and origin of the arrow rather than pulling it out.[9] Such questions do "not tend to edification." Or, as the Buddha is said to have told his disciple Vacca in the *Samyutta-nikāya* (Linked sayings): "The Tathāgata is free from all theories."[10]

In short, early Buddhist texts primarily approached enlightenment as a practical solution to the existential problems of human anguish and suffering. They maintained that by undertaking disciplined practice guided by the Noble Eightfold Path, the seeker could achieve a nondiscursive awakening (*bodhi*) to the interdependent nonsubstantiality of existence, especially of the self. With that insight, one attained release from the insatiable craving for permanence and its resulting suffering through the blissful experience of *nirvāṇa*. Any remaining "speculative" questions would then resolve themselves.

Thus, in most cases, early Buddhist texts describe *nirvāṇa* in negative images such as "extinction," "emancipation," "cessation," "the absence of craving," "detachment," "the absence of delusion," and "the unconditioned." Although there are also positive descriptions of *nirvāṇa* scattered throughout these texts that use such metaphors as "bliss," "peace," and "happiness," negative images predominate. But whether described by negative or positive metaphors, Buddhist texts are not always clear about *what* is "extinguished" and *from what* Buddhas are "emancipated." Still, a central idea seems to be that at minimum, the achievement of enlightenment involves freedom from the karmic forces that keep us recycling in the realm of samsaric suffering. At minimum, then, *nirvāṇa* seems to entail the positive experience of release from the self-created pain of samsaric existence.

Accordingly, enlightenment involves the extinction of what can be reborn, that is, the dissolution of any personal identity after death. This led Buddhists to distinguish between two forms of *nirvāṇa*: (1) enlightenment achieved in this world from suffering caused by craving, or "*nibbāna* with remainder" (*saupadisesa nibbāna*), and (2) perfect enlightenment achieved only after a person dies and is fully released from *saṃsāra*, or "*nibbāna* without remainder" (*anupadisesa nibbāna*). The Mahayana Sanskrit texts refer to these two states simply as "enlightenment" and "complete enlightenment" (Sanskrit *parinirvāṇa*; Pali *parinibbāna*).

The question is, Do these two terms refer to psychological or ontological states? Are *saṃsāra* and *nirvāṇa* states of mind or realms of existence? If *saṃsāra* refers to the psychological experience of suffering because of our ignorance of the way reality really is—impermanent, changing, becoming, non-self—then the transition from samsaric ignorance to nirvanic wisdom engenders a profound change of attitude, perspective, and motivation for action. If, however, *saṃsāra* refers to the phenomenal world of painful experience, then *nirvāṇa* must be somewhere else, another realm of existence different from the world of suffering and death we all experience.

An internal Buddhist reaction against both views of the relation between *saṃsāra* and *nirvāṇa* evolved into Mahayana Buddhist views of enlightenment that differ from Theravada conceptions. Mahayana Buddhist thought minimizes the opposition between *nirvāṇa* and *saṃsāra* by rejecting all suggestions that enlightenment is an escape from the samsaric world of suffering. Instead, *nirvāṇa* involves a wise and compassionate way of living in the realm of samsaric suffering through the Bodhisattva's realization of the absolute interdependency of all things and events in space-time. Such wisdom makes no ontological distinctions between *saṃsāra* and *nirvāṇa*, enlightenment and unenlightenment, pleasure and pain, life and death, for in the experience of the enlightened compassion of Buddhas, they are nondual. The earliest expression of the idea of *saṃsāra's* nonduality with *nirvāṇa*, which also pushes this notion to its furthest conclusions, may be illustrated by the *Heart Sutra:*

> Form is emptiness; emptiness is form. Emptiness is not other than form; form is not other than emptiness. . . .
> There is no ignorance, no extinction of ignorance, up to and including no aging and death and no extinction of aging and death. Similarly, there are no sufferings, no origins, no cessations, no paths, no exalted wisdom, no attainment, and also no non-attainment.[11]

In such an enlightened state, there is no ultimate transformation and final liberation, for all distinctions fall away in the "emptying" (*śūnyatā*) of the experience of enlightened compassion that all Buddhas achieve. Here, both Mahayana and Theravada traditions concur: death is an unavoidable feature of existence. It can cause anguish only when we attempt, in whatever way, to elude it, especially if we speculate on the nature of death or on an eternal soul.

Chinese religions. Of all the religious traditions with which I have had experience, the Chinese ancestor tradition impresses me most with the way it teaches the living to handle the experience of death. Comparatively speaking, the Chinese Way is different from Jewish, Christian, and Islamic tradition:

when loved ones die, they are usually swaddled in heavy shrouds, sometimes put into heavily padded coffins, and returned to the earth, ceremonially unborn. They are dead, no longer part of the living community. Whatever happens to them afterwards, other than becoming food for worms, is something only God can accomplish. They may be granted eternal life with God, or in some more seriously fundamentalist versions be consigned to hell by God, or simply left in death's oblivion. Whatever the case, the dead are dead and no longer part of the living community, except insofar as friends and relatives remember them.

Chinese ancestor tradition asserts the opposite. The rip in the life of the human community caused by death can be healed by the power of ritual (*li*) performed by the living on the dead's behalf. Indeed, Chinese ancestor tradition is as old as the basic Chinese cosmology that underlies both Confucian and Taoist teachings, which the Chinese still wisely combine in their "community religion."[12]

According to the worldview of traditional Chinese religion, the universe is a natural order characterized by a regularity that some forms of nineteenth-century Western philosophy characterized as "natural law." But unlike Western conceptions of natural law, the Chinese observed three interdependent features of nature's regularities: (1) nature is portrayed as an "organism" whose interrelated systems operate cyclically; (2) processes of growth and decline constantly interplay in all things and events; (3) nature's structure is bipolar, that is, all things and events are what they are, and are not, in interrelation with their polar opposites.[13]

In fact, it is the bipolarity of nature which impressed the Chinese most about the regularities they observed in nature. This interest was, as is well known, symbolized through the concepts of *yin* and *yang*. That is, nature is a process of polar forces that continually interplay through opposites in tension—darkness and light, female and male, death and birth, cold and heat—in engendering the things and events constituting this universe. Furthermore, the forces of *yin* and *yang* are not personal forces. Their mutual interplay creates nonpersonal forces operating dynamically in a nonpersonal universe.

Another aspect of the Tao's working through the forces of *yin* and *yang* is that nature always seeks balance, that is, "harmony," between opposites in all things and events. Strictly speaking, "good" is not *yang* and "evil" is not *yin*. Good is balanced harmony between polar opposites, while evil is imbalance between polar opposites. For example, too much justice is a tyranny, while too much compassion is sentimentality that suppresses the need for justice. Extremes, whether of *yin* or *yang*, are always mutually self-destructive. So nature always seeks balance between opposite forces, as symbolized by the

Chinese symbol of the Tao—a circle bisected by a wavy line. Nature never goes in straight lines. Nature wiggles through the harmonizing of polar opposites.

It is this ancient worldview that underlies classical Chinese conceptions of the "soul" and the ancestor tradition that was inherited by classical Confucian and Taoist traditions.[14] The Chinese thought that human nature mirrors the operations of *yin* and *yang*, for like all things, a human being is a product of the balanced harmony of opposites, male and female in the act of reproduction. This means that human beings are not special creations of God. Human beings are part of the universe, and not necessarily the most important part.

So we are alive as a combination of material elements and subtle spiritual elements functioning naturally through the energies of *yin* and *yang*. When a person dies, the material forces of life (*yin*) return to the earth (*yin*), while the subtle spiritual forces of life (*yang*) ascend to the bright region of heaven (*yang*). The *yin* material component is called *p'o* and the *yang* nonmaterial component is called *hun*. If a dead person is properly cared for, with proper burial rites called *li* performed on its behalf by the living, the material side of the soul (*p'o*), returns to the earth and "rests in peace." Simultaneously, the power of ritual transforms the subtle spiritual *yang* soul (*hun*) into a *shin*, a "kindly spirit" or "ancestor deity" that sends blessings to its living family. But if the proper ritual observances are not performed by the living on behalf of the dead, the material form of the soul cannot rest in peace in the earth. The lack of proper ritual transforms it into a *kuei* or "hungry ghost," a caricature of the dead person's mortal form. Such ghosts are hungry for relationships with the living that make life alive: friends, family, sex, food. Cut off from relationship with the living, they are hungry and take revenge against the living.[15]

Four aspects of traditional Chinese ancestor tradition should be noted. First, the condition of the dead depends on what the living do on their behalf. Our status after our death has no relation to the condition or qualities or morality of our lives while we are alive. It is what the living do on behalf of the dead that determines whether they become ancestor deities or hungry ghosts.

Second, it is the power of ritual (*li*) performed by the living on behalf of the dead that transforms the dead into ancestor deities. It is the lack of ritual that transforms the dead into hungry ghosts. Third, normally, families are responsible for the care and welfare of their own living and dead relatives. While one is alive, the quality and conditions of life are the responsibility of the family of which we are members. Likewise, when a relative dies, the family is responsible for maintaining relationship with this dead relative. The dead, in other words, are not cut off from the family at death; their relationship with their family continues, provided the proper ritual observances are performed.

Finally, because Chinese ancestor reverence was confined to lineage or family groups, religious reinforcement was given to the bonds of family lineage. That is, the Chinese lineage group was, and still is, the central "institution" of Chinese religious life, and all other forms of community and state religion were modeled after the family. This made ancestor reverence the one universal Chinese religious institution. As such, by giving religious sanctification to each family or "lineage corporation" (*tsu*), ancestor reverence created a closely knit system of in-group units, each of which claimed the major share of every person's loyalties and obligations. These loyalties and obligations extended to dead relatives, that is, to ancestors.

Chinese ancestor tradition, then, assumed the continuation of a person's life beyond the grave as well as continued relations between living and dead family members. In this sense only ancestors of a family were "deified" through ritual, and this "deification" of ancestors ultimately colored all traditional Chinese religious experience and practice. That is, Chinese religious traditions are an extension of ancestor reverence. This means that ancient ideas that the dead and the living depend on each other, found in many cultures, evolved into their most systematic institutional forms in China.

Jewish tradition. The pluralism of traditional Jewish understandings of death is rooted in the Genesis creation myth, most notably in Genesis 2:4-3:24. God, the narrative states, commanded Adam, the human being God made from the "humus" (*adam*) of the earth, not to eat from the Tree of Knowledge of Good and Evil, though Adam could eat freely from the Tree of Life. Later, when the serpent's temptations had led both Adam and his helpmate, Eve, to eat from the forbidden tree, God punished the first two human beings by driving them from the Garden of Eden. This punishment carried along with it the pain of childbirth for women and—for both men and women—working in toil for their survival, and, eventually, death.

In Jewish thought, death and history are interrelated. While it is true that the Genesis narratives portray death as a punishment for a primordial act of human disobedience to a divine commandment, it is also the case that Jewish thought views death as coming with considerable knowledge and wisdom—the knowledge of good and evil and the power and responsibility to make decisions that have future consequences. This theme—knowledge of good and evil and responsibility for one's actions in community runs throughout the

Hebrew Bible. The God of Israel never rescues his people *from* history, but *for* history. One form of this theme occurs in the patriarchal traditions surrounding Abraham: God's promise is not that God will reward Abraham's faithfulness with immortality or life after death. Instead, God promises to grant Abraham descendants as great in number as the "dust of the earth" (Genesis 13:16).

In the earliest biblical traditions, although the dead are lamented, and although the sufferings of existence in history can lead Job to cry, "I loath life" (Job 7:16), it is nonetheless clear that God's plan for his people does not include saving them from death. Instead, God saves his people from their enemies so that their history might continue. For this reason, God instructed Moses to lead Israel out of Egyptian slavery to a promised land that would give Israel's history meaning. In the exodus traditions, God does not lead his people to a deathless kingdom resembling the Garden of Eden.

Consequently, there is no hint in these earliest traditions of the soul's survival after death, nor is there any hint of resurrection of life from death. However, the Hebrew Bible does mention a place called Sheol, where the dead go. Still, Sheol is neither a heaven nor a hell. It is a vague region where a person gradually slides into oblivion, a place where there is no possibility of relating to God. It is not a place of *afterlife*, but of *afterdeath*.

However, sometime around the third to second centuries B.C.E., Jewish tradition began to increasingly view the soul as immortal, probably because of the influence of Hellenistic tradition in Palestine. Occasionally, life after death is also described in terms of resurrection rather than immortality of the soul, meaning that God raises the dead and brings them to final judgment. The theme of resurrection is found also in the Talmud, although there is only one biblical passage that explicitly states that both the wicked and the righteous will be raised from the dead to face God for final judgment–Daniel 12:2 ff.

Most often, however, the Talmud and later Jewish thought show the influence of Platonic tradition in the way death and the human soul are conceived. For example, Rabbi Leona Modena (1571-1648) admits that it is "frightening" that "we can fail to find in all the words of Moses a single indication pointing to man's spiritual immortality after physical death." Nevertheless, he insists, reason and hope compel us to believe the soul will continue.[16]

Most Jews, but certainly not all, have continued to believe either that God will resurrect the dead after a period of time for a final judgment, after the Messiah appears, or that the soul is deathless and will be judged by God according to its deeds. However, Jewish funeral customs point to the older conception that God does not save us as "individuals" by granting us life after death but saves his people, Israel, for history regardless of death.

This is illustrated in the respect given to a dead person by Jewish rituals of cleansing and strong resistance to embalming and autopsy. These rituals indicate that a human being is not a separable soul that is released from its bodily environment at death. Other funeral rituals reflect the power and loss of death for those who mourn. In many Orthodox communities, those closest to the dead person, for example, are, for a seven-day period following death called *shiva*, forbidden to work, bathe, put on shoes, have sexual intercourse, read the Bible, or have their hair cut. These particular ritual demands symbolically unite the living with the dead by pointing to the solidarity of one's physical existence with one's family, friends, and religious community.

Christian tradition. Traditional Christian views of death are as pluralistic as the New Testament and later Greek philosophical traditions from which they spring. From the sayings attributed to Jesus in the Synoptic Gospels, for example, we can guess that some early Christians thought there was a place to which the dead go, for Jesus often refers to an "outer darkness," where the wicked will be punished for their evil deeds done while they were alive. Although such remarks are rare and rather vague, it is probably true that Jesus had something more than Sheol in mind. But whether he believed there is a place where the righteous go after death seems less certain. On one occasion, Mark records Jesus saying that when the dead are raised they will be like angels in heaven. While there are no explanations about what it means to be "like" an angel, there is a warning against such speculation: God "is not the God of the dead, but of the living" (Mark 12:25 ff.).

Generally speaking, then, the Synoptic Gospels portray Jesus as not especially concerned with the question of death as such. There is no mention of death or the continuing of life after death in the major collection of Jesus' teachings, the Sermon on the Mount. Apparently, it was not a matter of interest to his disciples either, since they asked no questions about life after death. Nor does Jesus often refer to his own death and resurrection. When he does, it is usually related to the appearance of the Son of Man, "who will repay every man for what he has done" (Matthew 24:29 ff.).

The absence of interest in a general resurrection as well as a theory of immortality in the Synoptic Gospels is even more conspicuous in the resurrection narratives themselves. In several accounts of Jesus' appearance to his disciples after his death, he makes no mention of the resurrection of any one except himself. It is not that the Synoptic tradition explicitly denies that general resurrection will occur for those who follow Jesus; the Synoptic traditions simply paint a portrait of Jesus who seems utterly concerned with the living, while content to "let the dead bury their dead" (Matthew 8:22).

The portrayal of Jesus' attitude toward death is somewhat different in the Gospel of John. Like the Synoptic Jesus, the Jesus of John's Gospel does not speak of death directly, nor does he speculate on the soul's survival beyond death. However, Jesus does declare a union between himself and his followers through which they will share his resurrection: "I am the resurrection and the life; he who believes in me, though he die, yet shall he live" (John 11:25).

From John's perspective, then, survival after death does not happen because the soul, as Plato taught, is deathless. Eternal life after death is available only to those who faithfully follow Jesus, who because of their faith, will be raised from the dead with Jesus. The theme of resurrection is even stronger in the writings of Paul. His references to a future resurrection for the faithful are much more explicit: "Lo! I tell you a mystery. We shall not sleep, but we shall all be changed, in a moment, in the twinkling of an eye, at the last trumpet" (1 Corinthians 15:51–52).

Paul also added a theme that is either missing or not stressed elsewhere in the New Testament: for those in a state of faith, the resurrection that is to occur in the future is also a present reality. If by faith we carry the resurrection of Jesus in our bodies, he writes, it follows that the life of Jesus who is the risen Christ will be manifested in us while we are alive. "If anyone is in Christ, he is a new creation; the old has passed away, behold, the new has come" (2 Corinthians 5:17).

Paul is very explicit about the source of the new life Christians have because of their faith: it is Christ who overcomes the death all humanity inherited from Adam's primal act of disobedience of God. All major Christian traditions follow Paul in citing Adam's original sin as the source of death. It is a sin that each human being has subsequently repeated, so death is as much a result of Adam's original sinfulness as it is our sinfulness. This idea has played an important role in Christian theology and doctrine. First, death is not a matter of blind fate, but a consequence of humanity's own doing. Second, sin is so serious a state of affairs that no one can undo it without the saving action of God through the life, death, and resurrection of Jesus as the Christ. In the Platonic conception, in contrast, death is as superfluous as it is in traditional Hindu thought, since the soul is by nature unable to die.

In spite of this, Platonic notions of the soul's immortality had important influence on Christian thought after the biblical period. For example, Origin (third century), actually adopted the complete Platonic teaching that the soul survives both the death of its body and exists before its body's birth, and added to this the idea that all souls would eventually be saved by God—even non-Christian souls.[17] Origin's views were declared heretical by the Council of Constantinople in 553. And in the fourth century, Augustine, troubled by the differences between Plato's teachings and the biblical view that sin is punished by death, proposed a "second death" for those to whom God does not grant salvation in which they do not die once, but endlessly die.[18]

Popular Christian beliefs, both contemporary and ancient, focus on elaborate dwelling places for the saved and the damned. Mainline Christian theologians have, however, resisted preoccupation with the nature of life after death, and have placed emphasis on the eternal life available now through faith. Furthermore, twentieth-century theologians have widely interpreted Christian tradition to hold the view that birth and death are the beginning and end of every human life, just as creation and God's consummation of history stand at the beginning and end of creation. The ultimate destiny of each person depends entirely on God. Accordingly, while Christian tradition has mostly stressed a promised resurrection, how it will occur, when it will occur, and what it will be like are as mysterious to present Christians as they were to the disciples of Jesus, perhaps as they were even to Jesus.

Would It Make Any Difference If This Isn't All There Is?

I know of no religious tradition that does not posit, however vaguely, either the possibility or the actuality of the liberation of life from death's oblivion. Yet the plurality of images and symbols that point to what this state might be like, whether it includes only human beings or all living things, or how it is achieved, is also a striking fact in the history of religions. It's as if we do not know quite where we belong. Especially in times of sorrow, it does not seem to be here, with these silly garden rhododendrons and silent mountains, here with witless insects or hard-eyed birds. In times of sorrow, the innocence of other life forms from whom and with whom we evolve—seems a mockery. Their ways are not our ways; they do not, as far as anyone knows, agonize about death. We seem set among them, lifelike props waiting for a tragedy. It does not seem to be here that we belong, here where space is curved, the earth round. We're all going to die, and sometimes it seems wise to stay in bed.

What are we to make of the plurality of humanity's images and symbols of ultimate transformation? What can all this teach us? What can we learn from the diverse positive answers to the question, Is this all there is? If, indeed, this isn't all there is, if there is something more, so what? What difference does hope for ultimate transformation of life untouched, or at least untarnished, by death make to us here-and-now, where we live in the world's rough-and-tumble?

The first thing to notice in confronting this "so what?" question is that

there is no necessary epistemological connection between the fact that humanity's religious traditions regard life beyond death as a possibility, and the actuality of this possibility. That is, the plurality of views regarding death and dying
in the teachings of humanity's religious Ways does not itself prove that life in
some form actually exists after we die. The sheer fact that all religious Ways are
about ultimate transformation and final liberation is not, in itself, evidence of
anything other than the existence of diverse religious views about the nature
of ultimate transformation and final liberation. We must admit that we simply
do not know what, if anything, happens to us after we die.

Yet the way in which a religious Way conceives of ultimate transformation and final liberation from death is profoundly interrelated with how persons who faithfully practice that religious way experience the meaning of life
in community with other human beings and with other living things while
they are alive. For Hindus, death is an illusion, a form of *māyā*, having no reality in and of itself, because the center of our self-identity-through-time is the
unchanging, eternal imperishable *ātman*. True, Hindus are as frightened of
death as anyone, and death is as painful or as freeing from pain for Hindus as
it is for non-Hindus. But the soul does not die; it transmigrates from life cycle
to life cycle, the quality of its life in any one cycle dependent on its deeds in
previous cycles, until the achievement of *mokṣa*, or "release," of the soul from
the process of rebirth. While recycling, the soul is an entity that experiences
change—suffering, happiness, joy, pain, relationships, everything human
beings experience that makes life alive—but is neither affected nor effected by
the changes it experiences in its transmigratory cycles.

Seen from this perspective—the perspective that whatever "we" are, we
"go around" more than once—traditional Hindu attention seems focused more
on release from the cycles of reincarnation, rather than the ethical, social, economic, or political issues of the living present. Historical space-time, at least
as Jews, Christians, and Muslims understand it, is not the primary concern of
traditional Hindu thought and practice. The structure of traditional Hindu
existence does not, in other words, lead Hindus to focus on issues involving
the liberation of life from human-caused ecological damage.[19] Nor has contemporary Hindu thought, with the possible exception of Mahatma Gandhi
and some of his followers, focused on the need for liberation from the forces
of economic and political oppression or the liberation of women from patriarchy as important parts of its search for final liberation from the cycles of
birth and death.

My point is not that Hindus have not worked and struggled for justice and
fought against poverty and disease and the oppression of women. Such liberation struggles have occurred throughout the history of India, especially in

contemporary times under the influence of Western social and political thought. But "liberation theology" as understood in the West, is not an important structural component of classical Hindu tradition. The quality of life we experience in further rebirths and in overcoming all the karmic factors keeping our permanent souls tied to the processes of reincarnation tend to turn Hindu attention away from the central concerns of Western liberation theologies.

Buddhist views are opposite to Hindu tradition. In spite of numerous parallels with Hindu teaching and practice, the Buddhist teachings of "interdependent co-origination" (*pratītya-samutpāda*) and "nonself" (*anatman*) radically depart from the traditional Indian worldview. To be sure, Buddhists deny the reality of a permanent, unchanging Self (*ātman*), just as they deny that some dimension of reality other than the one we experience through our senses and respond to emotionally is mere appearance or illusion—the Hindu point of view. For Buddhists, there is no reality beyond the successive moments of experience, so understanding ourselves as permanent selves experiencing changes through time is an illusion. Whatever unity the succession of our experiences might have is a function of these experiences themselves. Because this unity cannot be caused by either past or future experiences, the center or ground for the unity or continuity we experience through the moments of our time must be the present realities we experience here-and-now.

Accordingly, to the extent in which in our present moments we believe ourselves to be substantially identical with our pasts and future, to that extent we create a false sense of permanent self-identity through time, i.e., an illusory *ātman*. Once we create a sense that we are permanent souls or selves, we begin to cling to permanent existence in a universe in which interdependent co-origination makes permanent existence metaphysically impossible. Here lies the cause of human suffering: clinging to permanent selfhood in a universe in which permanence is a metaphysical impossibility. It is clinging to permanent selfhood from which we need final liberation.

Final liberation is achieved through the ultimate transformation that occurs with the attainment of *nirvāṇa*. To the extent that through enlightenment we recognize the unreality of permanent selfhood, that we *are* "nonselves," to this extent the moments of our experiences through time are freed from "unsatisfactoriness," "anxiety," "suffering" (*duḥkha*). We achieve peace and serenity in a nontemporal moment. But we are *not* free from death.

Buddhists apply the doctrines of nonself and interdependent co-origination to the environment. While Buddhists do not deny the reality of the world, they assert that the world as given in ordinary reflective consciousness is a product of concepts, hopes, fears, and the human desire (*taṇhā*) for permanent existence. In this way, unenlightened persons falsely perceive the world as substantial, casual, and filled with meanings special to human existence. But the experience of enlightenment reduces the environment to momentary interrelationships lacking all significance for human existence. Thus, enlightened persons are able to disengage their emotional lives from attachment to the world.

Mahayana Buddhist thought carries these teachings to their ultimate conclusions: when nonattachment is attained, those who are enlightened are concurrently filled with compassion. Being unattached to permanence and impermanence, being attached to nothing, they become compassionate toward all sentient beings. Thus, while enlightened beings remain aware of the distinctions occurring within the flux of experience, they do not discriminate among the forms of existence or between themselves and others.

While this is certainly a "beautiful idea," as John Cobb notes, universal compassion in Buddhism does not normally lead to social and economic engagement with the issues of oppression stressed by liberation theologians.[20] Since Buddhist nonattachment to permanence undercuts discrimination among particulars as better or worse, it is difficult from this perspective to engage in critical analysis of the issues of oppression. The point is not that Buddhists have not done so. The point is that stress on the present impermanent moment does not itself engender engagement with issues of injustice created by powerful economic, social, and political institutions which, perhaps because of "unenlightened" views of selfhood, engender so much pain and death for oppressed peoples and for this planet. Such moments may indeed overcome anxiety about death because in this enlightened moment one neither clings to past lives nor desires future life. But such moments do not focus attention on present ethical, social, political, economic, and gender issues of liberation.

Between classical Buddhist and Hindu views lies Chinese ancestor tradition and the religious Ways that dominate the West and Middle East: Judaism, Christianity, and Islam. These traditions have most consistently stressed the interrelation between final liberation and issues of political, economic, and (most recently initiated in Christian circles) women's liberation. Jewish tradition, because it posits that God elected the ancient Hebrew community to a special covenant, has been especially forthright in asserting the interconnection between the liberation of community and final liberation. The result of this election was becoming God's "chosen people" called to live according to the Torah, or God's "instructions" about how human beings should live in relation to each other and to God so as to: (1) realize their fullest potential as persons-in-community, and (2) become "a light to the nations" in order reveal God's "salvation to earth's furthest bounds" (Isaiah 49:6b, *New English Bible*).

One might say, however, that it is the Hebraic prophetic tradition that constitutes the central norm according to which the rabbis of Jewish tradition after 70 C.E. spelled out the foundations of contemporary Judaism. This norm for the Jewish "structure of existence" is summarized in Micah 6:6–8:

> With what shall I come before the Lord,
>   And bow myself before God most high?
> Shall I come before him with burnt offerings,
>   With calves a year old?
> Shall I give my first-born for my transgression,
>   The fruit of my body for the sin of my soul?
> You have been told, O man, what is good,
>   *And what the Lord requires of you:*
> *Only to do justice, and to love kindness,*
> *And to walk humbly with your God.*[21]

Christian tradition also carries on this emphasis of persons-in-community. That is, an individual's relationship with God is intertwined with that person's relationship with community. For Jews this traditionally means following the commandments that lead persons to a life of Torah—a life structured to render loving compassion and justice to the human community as the foundation of one's worship and relationship to God while one is alive, and perhaps in a continued relationship with God in a resurrected life after death.

For Christians, the model for living as persons-in-community is the historical Jesus. Christians assume that Jesus was so open and obedient to God's demand to love all with no strings attached (*agapē*) that he models that for which Christians should strive in their relation with God: love of others and relating to others accordingly, even as God loves humanity and the world God created—a love that continues even after death. In this, Jesus carried on the traditions of the Hebrew prophets. In this understanding, God is on the side of the oppressed of *this* life. What happens *after* death is not as important as working for the liberation of the poor from economic and political oppression.[22] In fact, focusing on what may or may not happen after death is irrelevant in itself, since it too easily anesthetizes us to the hard realities of the life we now experience, most often in the context of noncommunity. In other words, our problem is not what happens after death; our problem is what is happening now while we are alive. Here, in the present social and political realities of our lives, is where we find God. Here, if anywhere, is where we can reasonably hope for a future relation with God uninterrupted by death, here where we live in the midst of struggle for justice in community.

So Jewish teaching and Christian teaching agree that we cut ourselves off from God each time we live unjustly, uncompassionately, egotistically as individuals struggling for our own power and goods apart from consideration of the welfare of the human community or the well-being of other life forms. Jews know better than any other community just how horrible political, religious, and social oppression can be. They, more than any other people, understand the themes of contemporary liberation theology because these are the ancient themes of Hebraic prophetic tradition.

Like Jewish teaching, Christian teaching concludes that our final liberation as persons-in-community is bound up with the need of humanity and the earth for liberation from the powers of oppression that govern this world. Thus Jewish and Christian faith and practice wisely focus on the need for liberation from unjust political and economic forces of oppression while waiting for the Messiah to finally come, or, if Christian, for Christ to return, at which point God will cause justice and righteousness to flow like a perennial stream. In short, what might or might not happen after death is not as important as what happens while we are now alive. We should focus not on death but on what makes life "alive," while trusting God to take care of whatever happens or does not happen afterward.

In a different fashion, traditional Chinese ancestor tradition, assumed by both Confucian and Taoist traditions, comes to similar conclusions. This is especially true in the tradition that originates in the *Analects of Confucius*. The "superior human being" (*ch'ün tzu*), should serve parents when alive according to the rules of filial piety, and when they die, bury them "according to ritual and sacrifice to them according to ritual."[23] The superior human being avoids excessive mourning for the dead because this interferes with filial obligations to the living. Governed by "humanity" (*rin*), the superior human being does not feel anxious about the state of the dead nor about his own death. The present is the object of concern, the rough-and-tumble-here-and-now struggle to create harmonious community grounded in justice and compassion (XVII, 21).[24]

Chinese ancestor tradition has wisely followed the path laid down by Confucius. Living and dead persons constitute a community. Ritual focus (*li*) on what makes life alive for both the living and the dead brings the dead into relation with the living community. But while survivors should maintain relationships with the dead, this should not be overdone. Primary energy must be devoted to the living community because it is the harmony of living persons-in-community that brings "life" to the dead. The dead do not bring "life" to the living. Harmony, meaning justice balanced by compassion, good government, cultivation of the arts, and righteousness as forms of humanity expressed through ritual, keeps the living alive and brings life to the dead. Lack of these virtues brings death to the living and the dead.

Therefore, while the Chinese worry about death as much as anyone, Chinese ancestor reverence focuses attention on this world, on issues of justice and harmony for the living here-and-now. In this way, the focal concerns of the Chinese led to a conclusion shared by Jewish, Christian, and contemporary liberation thought, but arrived at for a different reason: don't focus attention on what might or might not happen after death. Focus on what makes life alive: relationships among persons-in-community and the human community-in-community with the myriad of life forms that constitute the biodiversity of planet Earth. Our problem is the quality of life now. Too much anxiety about our death, or too much concern about the possibility of after-death life, places attention and care where it is not needed. In other words, the Chinese agree with Jesus: "let the dead bury the dead."

Still, we live in a universe in interdependent relation with oxen, blue herons, and all things. Our convictions about final liberation in the future are profoundly interrelated with how we confront the urgent need for the liberation of life now—both human and nonhuman—from economic, political, gender, and racial oppression. The kind of convictions we entertain about final liberation and ultimate transformation, empowers us to hope and work for future possibilities regarding other forms of liberation in ways that are different from those who are convinced that at death, life ends in oblivion.

Of course, convictions do not possess the same epistemological standing as conclusions deduced or induced by the application of methodological arguments and scientific experimentation to evidence. There is no conclusive scientific evidence for life after death, since as far as anyone knows no one who has died has been able to give testimony to the living that life continues. Besides, what possible experimental procedure could be invented to confirm that death is not the end of life? Furthermore, the plurality of views of final liberation and ultimate transformation in the world's religious Ways cannot be counted as evidence to support the conviction that life beyond death—life liberated from death—is an actuality.

Yet my conviction is that it is reasonable to hope for the continuation of life beyond death, and that such hope has a direct bearing on how we understand the nature of the Sacred, our relation to it, to nature, to each-other-in-community, and to the need for life's liberation from the forces of oppression. It is also my conviction that such hope is best understood and maintained within a theocentric perspective that not only recognizes religious pluralism but celebrates it. The question now is, In light of what I have written in the preceding eight chapters of this book, so what? On the basis of these chapters, what conclusions in process can be reasonably drawn? What has my combat with the ox—a wrestling match that still continues, and I suspect will continue until I am dead—taught me? These personal convictions are the subject of the final portion of the last chapter of this book, "Entering the City with Bliss-bestowing Hands."

Notes

1. D. T. Suzuki, *Manual of Zen Buddhism* (New York: Grove Press, 1960), 134.
2. Frederick J. Streng, *Understanding Religious Life* (Belmont, Calif.: Wadsworth Publishing Company, 1985), 2.
3. Ibid., 2-5.
4. I have been, obviously, inspired by John Hick's understanding of the religious Ways of humanity as different, culturally and historically specific means of salvation, all of which possess validity relevant to their particular historical-cultural contexts. See *The Metaphor of God Incarnate: Christology in a Pluralistic Age* (Louisville, Ky.: Westminster/John Knox Press, 1993), 134-39.
5. Winston Davis, *Dōjō: Magic and Exorcism in Modern Japan* (Stanford, Calif.: Stanford University Press, 1980), 129-30.
6. Troy Wilson Organ, *The Hindu Quest for the Perfection of Man* (Athens, Oh.: Ohio University Press, 1970), 119.
7. *The Upanishads*, trans. Swami Nikhilananda (New York: Harper Torchbooks, 1964), 73.
8. *The Bhagavadgita in the Mahabharata*, trans. J. A. B. van Buitenen (Chicago: University of Chicago Press, 1981), 75.
9. *The Collection of Middle Length Sayings*, vol. 1, trans. I. B. Horner (London: Pali Text Society, 1954), 100-101.
10. *Buddhism in Translations*, trans. H. C. Warren (Cambridge, Mass.: Harvard University Press, 1922), 138.
11. *The Heart Sutra Explained*, trans. Donald S. Lopez, Jr. (Albany: State University of New York Press, 1988), 19-20.
12. See C. K. Yang, *Religion in Chinese Society* (Berkeley, Calif.: University of California Press, 1967), 28-57.
13. Laurence G. Thompson, *Chinese Religion: An Introduction* (Belmont, Calif.: Wadsworth, 1989), 1-16.
14. Ibid., 18-22.
15. Yang, *Religion in Chinese Society*, 29-53.
16. *Jewish Reflections on Death*, ed. Jack Reimer (New York: Shocken Books, 1975), 36.

17. Otto W. Heick, *A History of Christian Thought*, vol. 1 (Philadelphia: Fortress Press, 1965), 235 ff.; and J. N. D. Kelly, *Early Christian Doctrines* (New York: Harper & Brothers, 1960), 472–94.

18. Etienne Gilson, *The Christian Philosophy of Saint Augustine* (New York: Random House, 1960), 44–45.

19. See John B. Cobb, Jr., *The Structure of Christian Existence* (Philadelphia: Westminster Press, 1967), 61–65.

20. John B. Cobb, Jr., *Christ in a Pluralistic Age* (Philadelphia: Westminster Press, 1975), 210.

21. J. M. Powis Smith and Edgar J. Goodspeed, *The Complete Bible: An American Translation* (Chicago: University of Chicago Press, 1948).

22. John Dominic Crossan, *The Historical Jesus* (San Francisco: HarperSanFrancisco, 1991), 291–302.

23. *The Analects of Confucius*, trans. Arthur Waley (New York: Random House, 1939), 88–89.

24. Ibid., 214–15.

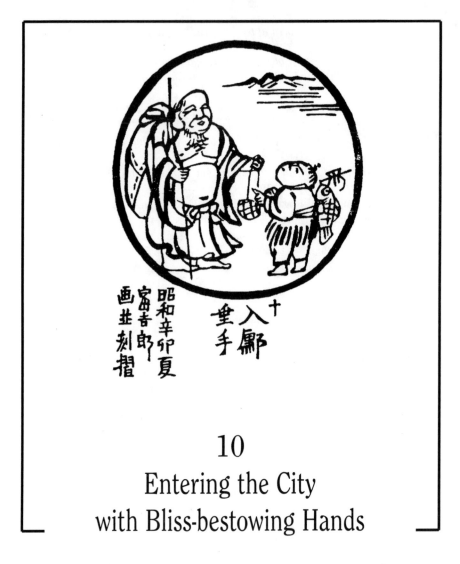

10
Entering the City
with Bliss-bestowing Hands

THE TENTH OX-HERDING PICTURE ELEGANTLY PORTRAYS THE BODHISATTVA'S ENLIGHT-
enment experience. According to the accompanying commentary, the fulfillment of enlightenment means "Entering the City with Bliss-bestowing Hands."
In this "city,"

> His thatched cottage gate is closed, and even the wisest people do not com-
> prehend who he is. No glimpses of his inner life are to be caught; for he goes
> on his way following the path of ancient sages. Carrying a gourd into the
> market place, leaning against his staff, he is at home everywhere. He is
> found in the company of drunkards and thieves, and he and they are all con-
> verted into Buddhas.[1]

Buddhist sages are said to live in the world naturally, at home wherever they are, in the company of the unenlightened, without ego traces, interdependent with all things, even drunkards and thieves. Something here rings familiar, or ought to, to Christian ears; according to the Synoptic Gospels, Jesus too lived naturally, without egoism, in the world among those who were oppressed, preferring the company drunkards and outcasts, enlightened about his and their relation to God. The sage's life-style seems fairly similar in the history of religions. Indeed, the sages of every tradition are very sagacious. The poem that accompanies the tenth picture reads:

Bare chested and bare footed, he comes out into the market place;
Daubed with mud and ashes, how broadly he smiles;
There is no need for the miraculous power of the gods;
For he touches all, and behold, the dead trees are in full bloom.[2]

The Buddhist point of the final Ox-Herding picture is that whatever enlightenment is, it is never final, never complete while the sage is alive. Whatever else enlightened sagehood is, it seems also to be a social event, a process that must be experienced in relation to and deepened by social interaction with other human beings and with nature. So too in the soteriologies of other religious Ways, in spite of their differing conceptualities about the meaning of "salvation."

Still, the topic of this chapter is about neither Buddhist enlightenment nor soteriology in general. It is not even about sagehood, even though I admire sages. I am not a sage, as anyone who knows me will testify. This chapter is about sharing ideas, perhaps occasional insights, that the process of writing this book itself has engendered in my consciousness. It is about loose ends that I hope to tie together in a way that will allow thought and imagination to range freely in new and more challenging directions beyond the specific conclusions I am about to summarize. Some of these conclusions are restatements of previously held assumptions and convictions that I stated in chapter 1, but now seem more firmly confirmed by the process and discipline of writing this book. Others are conclusions about issues and problems I have learned to see, in the sense of *darśan* as described in chapter 2, for the first time. But most of my conclusions are perceptions "in process," demanding from me further reflection, criticism, and meditation.

Accordingly, even though I have not attained sagehood, I think I am beginning to see what "entering the city with bliss-bestowing hands" might be like after years of wrestling with the ox. Of course, I have not seen everything. No one has, not even enlightened sages. I also suspect that in a religiously plural world, entering this city is a different experience for different persons, even for those participating in the same religious tradition.

More on Interreligious Dialogue

In chapter 1 I noted that the primary methodology of what I called "primordial theology of religions" is engagement in interreligious dialogue. I also noted that interreligious dialogue is not just a theoretical enterprise; it is also a form of religious *praxis* of personal engagement with faithful persons participating in religious Ways other than one's own. Aloysius Pieris aptly describes three interdependent levels of the practice of interreligious dialogue: "core-experience, collective memory, and interpretation."[3]

The "core experience" of a religious Way is the "liberative" experience that engendered it and continues to be available to successive generations of human beings. Such experience or collections of experiences function as the "core" of a religious Way, at any given time, at any given place, in the sense that it continually recreates the spiritual mood that broadly and minimally defines it in its unique particularity. This in turn generates a religious Way's peculiar social-cultural expressions according to which it resolves crises and regenerates itself as it confronts new challenges. In fact, the vitality and relevance of any given religious Way depend on its capacity to place each successive generation in touch with its core experience of liberation.

It is a community's "collective memory" that makes the core experiences of a religious Way available to successive generations. Religious movements have "died," often soon after they appeared, because some means of perpetuating or making collectively available their core experiences failed to evolve. Religious beliefs, practices, traditions, and institutions that evolve in a religious Way constitute a communication system that links its adherents to its liberating core experiences. Religious traditions tend to fade from history even after centuries of existence when their symbols and institutions lose the capacity to evoke in their adherents the distinctive core experiences that define them.

Finally, integral to how a religious Way's collective memory functions is "interpretation," or perhaps better, "hermeneutics." To be remembered, a religious Way's core experiences—perpetuated through its symbols, beliefs, and rituals—must be conceptually interpreted and defined by that community's theologians, philosophers, and teachers. For example, the core experiences of Buddhist faith and practice are best classified as "liberative knowledge" (Sanskrit *vidiyā* as opposed to *avidiyā*), while the corresponding liberative core experience of Christian faith and practice is "redemptive love," or *agapē*. The core experiences of Buddhist faith and practice and those of Christian faith and practice are, I think, best seen as salvific because both are self-transcending events that creatively transform persons who have them. Yet there is also definite contrast between Buddhist and Christian experience of liberation, as there is between the core liberating experience of all religious Ways.

However, both liberative knowledge and redemptive love or compassion are equally necessary for creative transformation because each in separation from the other is incomplete. They are, in other words, complementary bipolar idioms that define each other as means of mediating the creative transformation that Buddhists name "enlightenment" and Christians name "salvation."

Accordingly, to appreciate and dialogue about both the differences and the complementarities between the core experiences of one's own religious Way and those of other's requires entering into the collective memories of one's own religious Way as we simultaneously enter the collective memories of religious Ways other than our own. The place of entry into the core experiences of our own tradition in dialogue with the core experiences of others is the place of our own individual wrestling matches with the Ox. So one presupposition of this book is also a primary conclusion about theological method. Christians who desire to enter into a core-on-core dialogue with other religious Ways must be empathetically willing to enter another Way's practices and core experience as deeply as possible—that is, to enter into what Roman Catholic Christian tradition might call a *communicatio in sacris*.[4]

Most of my dialogue with religious traditions other than my own has centered on the core liberative experience of Buddhist and Christian faith and practice. But as a working historian of religions, I have also tried to dialogically encounter the core experiences of Hindu, Islamic, Confucian, Taoist, Jewish, and, of late, Native American traditions. These dialogical encounters are the sources of the conclusions summarized in the remainder of this chapter that are at the heart of the primordial theology here envisioned.

On Living Dialogically with the Ox

What I began to suspect during my first undergraduate course in the history of religions is now a firmly held hypothesis. A good hypothesis has a paradoxical character: it can be both a presupposition for drawing conclusions and a conclusion itself. This means that any hypothesis, if it is a good one, also has a peculiar difficulty. When it is completed and rounded, its corners smooth and its content coherent and cohesive, it is likely to become a thing in itself, a work of art. Then it is too much like a finished sonnet or a painting completed. One hates to disturb it. Even if subsequent information should shoot holes in it, one hates to tear it down because it once was beautiful and whole. This is especially true about theological hypotheses about the ox as one thinks about the Sacred in dialogue with religious traditions other than one's own.

Yet conclusions must be drawn, observations made, about what one thinks one has seen. Hopefully, conclusions will be drawn in a way that leaves room for appreciating and apprehending other ways of seeing the ox, while yet recognizing that one has not seen everything because of the possibility that what one thinks one sees could be an illusion. It may not be quite right to say that *truth* is relative, but our *understanding* of truth, of reality, *is* relative to the cultural, historical, and biological standpoints we must all occupy as we grapple with the ox for understanding. Accordingly, while I believe my conclusions are based on an accurate reading of evidence from history of religions in light of my own personal experiences, I do not claim they are the only conclusions that can be drawn. I cannot even claim that I will hold these conclusions in the future, for they are, as everything is in an interdependent universe, very much in process.

Encountering the relatively inaccessible Sacred. It was Mircea Eliade who trained many historians of religions to employ the word "Sacred" when referring to the object of religious experience, in whatever cultural-historical context such experience happens. In his opinion, "God" was a Western theological-cultural concept that, when applied to non-Christian religious Ways, too easily led scholars to read Western ideas into, say, Buddhist, Hindu, Taoist-Confucian, or primordial tribal traditions. For him, the Sacred was a more neutral word for that transcendent and immanent reality that is the object of *sui generis* religious experience, wherever it is found, that can and should be described phenomenologically.[5] In this way, Eliade hoped to avoid bringing into history of religions an unwanted theological character that compromised his claim that the historian's task was descriptive analysis, not normative value judgment about the religious experience analyzed. In other words, "understanding," not judgment about the truth of what is objectively described, is the historian of religions' task. The latter is best left to theologians and philosophers.

That not importing a theological character into the history of religions has never been possible, and indeed trying to do so rests on an outmoded Cartesian epistemology, is confirmed by anyone who has ever taught a "comparative religions" course to university undergraduates. According to E. Thomas Lawson and Robert N. McCaulley, evidence of a theological character imported into history of religions' claim for the distinctiveness of its method and object of study lies in its use of theoretical concepts pregnant with unavoidable theological notions, such as "the Sacred," or Rudolf Otto's notion, "the Holy."[6] In Eliade's case, he used two terms, "sacred" and "profane," to name two ontologically opposite theologically grounded realities. He then attributed agency, power, and transcendence to this sacred reality he thought all religious experience reflects and that in all respects transcends the profane, meaning the ordinary world we encounter in our everyday experience. In short, there are interesting, unrecognized Christian theological assumptions at work in Eliade's scholarship. So too in the work of many historians of religions, who seem now to be in the process of redefining their academic field of scholarship.[7]

I have employed the term "the Sacred," but not with the intention of avoiding incorporation of an undesirable theological agenda into my work as a historian of religions. Indeed, I have tried hard to be explicit about my theological agenda as a working historian of religions. The sort of Cartesian objectivity sought by Eliade, Otto, and Joachim Wach is neither desirable nor possible. So I have tried to use "the Sacred" in a way that suggests that, while Buddhist, Christian, Jewish, Islamic, Hindu, or Chinese experiences of the ox *are not* identical, they *are* complementary historically and culturally conditioned experiences of one Sacred reality. Hence I interwove two metaphors, one borrowed from the Ten Ox-Herding Pictures and the other from Annie Dillard: the Sacred as relatively inaccessible ox, named and experienced differently according to the perspectives of different religious Ways.

What can be said of the relatively inaccessible ox? Much can be said, yet not everything. We should first understand that the starting point of all conceptualization about the ox is acceptance of a sense of mystery and the rejection of exclusive and inclusive attitudes and theologies as far as matters of ultimate reality are concerned. In this regard, it seems to me that classical Hindu experience and thought have much to teach us. Mystery—the essential character of the relatively inaccessible ox—is not something that can be used to fill in the gaps of our rational knowledge. But it does provide the ontological foundation for critical tolerance and openness to religious Ways other than our own.

This mystery Hindu tradition refers to as "the Truth of the Truth" (*satyasa satyam*). It is both the transcendent center and the immanent center of existence that always remains greater than any particular apprehension of it, even greater than the totality of these apprehensions. In my own case, it is akin to a glimpse of the ox I caught years ago in the natural beauty of a deserted beach on the Olympic Peninsula, or three years ago when a great blue heron first stunned me to silence.[8] On both occasions, as I saw the life pulsating around me, I knew I might never again see so much beauty, the beautiful being something you know added to something you see, in a mysterious whole that is more than the sum its parts.

In religious experience, wherever it happens, mystery and meaning are interrelated, although meaning is awfully difficult to figure out. For unless the ox discloses itself within the particulars of history and human consciousness, it is impossible for us to respond to it. The history of religions shows that human responses are many and varied, even within a single religious tradition. These differences are due to cultural and historical factors. So while each response to the mystery that is the relatively inaccessible ox has a normative character for followers of a particular religious Way, the criteria derived from one religious Way cannot be the norm for judging the responses of other religious traditions. This is not to say that all religious Ways are equally true or valid responses: no one knows enough to either affirm or deny this assertion. However, it is to say that we must be critically open to all possibilities, since it is through these possibilities that we learn to wrestle with the ox. To be sure, not everything will be valuable or useful, but we cannot determine this unless we remain critically open to what we see. Wrestling with the ox demands that we be willing to take our lumps.

The ox as nonpersonal and personal. In chapter 3 I noted that my search for the ox began in the Christian Way; I have passed through several Protestant denominations of this Way. When I was an infant, my United Brethren father and my Presbyterian mother had me baptized by a United Brethren minister. I was baptized again when I joined the Disciples of Christ as a high school student in 1954 because this denomination does not recognize infant baptism. Part of my academic training occurred in an interdenominational seminary operated by the Methodist Church in California. After I married a lifelong Lutheran, I signed up with the American Lutheran Church after moving to Indianola, Iowa, where I assumed my first teaching position at Methodist-affiliated Simpson College, mostly because there were no Lutheran Church in America congregations in town. Later, I became a Methodist and remained so until I was into the third year of my employment at then American Lutheran Church owned and operated Pacific Lutheran University. My wife and I joined a local Lutheran Church in America congregation, which has since merged with the American Lutheran Church to form the present Evangelical Lutheran Church in America. Presently, we are members of my university's student-led University Congregation.

I cite this record of Christian denominational pluralism as evidence that I have never taken the institutionalized forms of the church with the seriousness denominational bureaucrats expect or local clergy hope for. As no single religious Way has a monopoly on truth, so no single Christian denomination has a monopoly on Christian faith. Yet I do take the Christian Way seriously, since I find myself in this tradition, like most Christians, quite by accident; chances are, I would not wear the label "Christian" had I been born and brought up in India or Japan or Sri Lanka. So I must acknowledge that much of my work as a historian of religions, like much of my spiritual struggle with the ox, is grounded in methods and concepts opened up to me by the accident of my birth in a denominationally pluralistic Western nation whose "civil religion" is primarily a secularized Calvinist form of the Christian Way.

Therefore, even though for the moment I participate in a Lutheran version of the Christian Way, I reject all forms of Christian exclusivism and inclusivism as error. What Christians have seen in their encounter with God's incarnation through Christ is, I believe, there to be seen. But it is not all that has been seen or can be seen. This is why, as a Christian historian of religions, I have concluded that a Christian theology of religions should be theocentric rather than christocentric. Asserting in advance of dialogue that Christ is the norm against which the value and truth of non-Christian religious faith and practice must be measured is a monological isolationist and imperialistic blinder that prevents Christians from critically seeing and apprehending the realities of religious pluralism.

The question now is, What do I think my work as a Christian historian of religions who enters into dialogue with religious Ways other than his own has taught me about the relatively inaccessible ox? First, however, the Sacred is named—Ox, God, Allah, Dharma, Emptying, Tao, Brahman, Śiva, Krishna, or Wakan Tanka of Lakota spirituality—all are metaphors that say more about the person naming than the reality named. For God—I shall use this word from now on simply because it is as good as any other metaphor even as I understand that this name may not be adequate in non-Western traditions—is beyond name and forms. God, the Ox, Brahman, Dharma, the Tao are referents that point human beings from limited historical-cultural contexts to a reality that is beyond the limitations of thought, experience, and contexts, while yet being the ontological foundation of all thought, experience, and contexts. We should never confuse referents that point to the Sacred with the Sacred.

However, to affirm that the names human beings use to label the ox say more about human beings than about God is *not* to affirm that naming is unimportant or that all names are equally valuable. Naming is serious business, because it is part of humanity's wrestling with the ox, and much is at stake. How we name the ox, how we conceptualize about the mystery that grapples with us as we grapple with it, profoundly conditions how we relate to nature, to each other, and to persons outside our own particular religious communities. Naming the ox is interconnected with how we affirm life and how we struggle for justice, the liberation of nature, and the liberation of oppressed human beings; it is crucial for how we understand suffering and death in all the forms these realities can assume, as well as whether we can face death with courage and grace in the hope of final liberation beyond death.

What, therefore, do I mean and intend when I name the relatively inaccessible, mysterious ox "God." What follows is based on how I read the history of religions through an admittedly Western philosophical-theological theoretical filter influenced by Whiteheadian process philosophy. I do so because process philosophy has provided me with conceptual aids that allow interpretation of non-Christian ideas and experiences in terms congenial to Western forms of religious experience and thought, while not falsifying non-Christian traditions, which is not to say that process thought is the only Western philosophical tradition capable of providing such a hermeneutical framework. But for me, Whitehead's process philosophy provides a worldview within which I can engage in interreligious dialogue at the conceptual and experiential levels because it helps me understand Christian tradition as well as religious traditions other than my own.

Three Whiteheadian concepts have been especially helpful in this regard: the "category of creativity," the "primordial nature of God," and the "consequent nature of God." Creativity, wrote Whitehead, is the "universal of universals," that process at the heart of reality by which every individual entity in this universe—the "disjunctive diversity" of the universe—enters into complex unity—the conjunctive oneness of the universe. That is, the many actual occasions (all things and events at every moment of space-time) that constitute the disjunctive plurality of the universe become one actual occasion, the universe conjunctively.[9] This implied for Whitehead that creativity is the principle of novelty. All things and events are particular, novel entities distinct from every other entity in the universe that it experientially unifies. Yet, since every actual occasion—every particular thing and event—unifies the many that constitute the universe in itself in its own individual way according to its "subjective aim, creativity always introduces novelty into the content of the many things and events that constitute the universe conjunctively.[10]

What this rather abstract formulation implies is that the creative process at work in the universe has no independent existence apart from actual things and events undergoing process. Therefore, as "categorically ultimate," every actual occasion—all things and events at every moment of space-time—undergoes the process of creativity, including that actual occasion Whitehead called

God. Thus, all things and events, including God, are concrete instances of the "many becoming one and increased by one."[11]

While all things and events exemplify the process of creativity in their own individual ways according to their particular "subjective aims," even if only trivially, Whitehead thought God is the formative element, indeed the chief example of the creative process. Accordingly, Whitehead spoke of God's reality as bipolar, constituted by two interdependent natures: an eternal, unchanging "primordial nature" and a changing, processive "consequent nature." God's primordial nature is what God is in God's own self-nature, that which eternally constitutes God as God, what God always remains, unchanged and eternal. God's "consequent nature" is what God becomes as God had been affected, affects, and will be affected by the multiplicity of past, present, and future things and events at every moment of space-time as God unifies these into God's subjective experience according to God's "subjective aim" that all things and events achieve maximum harmony and intensity of experience.[12] In other words, God's consequent nature is what God becomes as God experiences and interrelates with every entity in the universe, while God's primordial nature is an abstraction from the actual processes of what God is in God's processive consequent nature. However, both natures are interdependent and mutually constitute what God "is" in God's own experience of the universe—and in the universe's experience of God.

What does this imply about humanity's experience of God—the mysterious, relatively inaccessible ox? First, there is never a moment when the ox is not part of a human being's—or anything else's, for example, a blue heron's—experience. Nor is there ever a moment when the ox is not experiencing us and being affected by us from its perspective as God. Of course, not all human experience of the ox is conscious, intense, or constant. Often it is unconscious, momentary, or fleeting. It is often ignored or shoved into the periphery of awareness or distorted by those who claim to know more than they do.

Second, whatever the quality and nature of our experience of the ox are, it is always in relation to and relativized by the cultural-historical-religious traditions we embody and occupy at the moment we experience. We do not experience the ox apart from some point of view, some cultural perspective, some religious ground, some biological embodiment, according to our subjective aim. As finite beings, we cannot experience the ox from all points of view. Therefore, no words, no creeds, no theoretical perspective—not even Whiteheadian categories—no symbols, no particular religious Way can claim normative, absolute insight about the relatively inaccessible ox.

Yet because the ox is relatively inaccessible, it is also *relatively accessible* to the perspectives of the religious Ways of humanity. That is, Christians,

Buddhists, Hindus, Muslims, Jews, Taoists, Confucianists, Native Americans have "seen" the ox, partially and incompletely. What they have experienced of the ox is there to be experienced, but it is never all there is to be experienced.

Third, the ox as relatively inaccessible and accessible mystery—a half empty glass is also half full—points to God's primordial nature, what God is, beyond name and form, that transcends all our experience and conceptualizations. Conceptions, symbols, theologies, rituals, reflect how God affects us as we affect God's consequent nature from the religious standpoints we occupy. Yet even here, words and symbols point, never completely define or denote, what the ox relatively is for us.

Fourth, human beings have experienced the ox as nonpersonal and personal. Most of the religious Ways of East and South Asia have focused on nonpersonal experiences of the ox and have wrestled with and named it accordingly: Brahman, Dharma, Emptying, Tao, the "Supreme Ultimate" (Chinese, *ta'i-ch'i*), best encountered in mystical insight that comes with the practice of meditation. Yet even in these traditions, human beings have experienced the personal nature of the ox as Krishna, Śiva, Kālī, Amida Buddha, Tara.

Those religious Ways that originated in the Middle East—Judaism, Christianity, Islam—have primarily encountered the ox as personal: as God who instructs his people to live by the Torah, as God who incarnated in the life, death, and resurrection of Jesus of Nazareth, as God who fulfills humanity's religion in the *Qurʾān* revealed to Muhammad, best surrendered to in prayer and social-ethical self-discipline in the rough-and-tumble of historical existence. Yet the ox's nonpersonal nature has been celebrated and sought by Western mystics and contemplatives, who tell us that the mysterious nonpersonal character of the ox is the foundational support for whatever personal character of the ox we experience. Both forms of seeing the ox—nonpersonal and personal experience—have much to teach us, and we should be in dialogue with both ways of seeing as these are expressed within our own religious Way in dialogue with persons practicing religious Ways other than our own.

Finally, if Whitehead and the Taoist tradition are right, that God's nature is bipolar and exemplifies the process of creativity constantly occurring in the universe, there is never a time when we are not in some experiential relation with the relatively inaccessible ox, made relatively accessible through whatever religious Way we follow or through whatever "secular" worldview we believe. So whether we see the ox primarily through personal or nonpersonal lenses, whenever we open ourselves to the creative process at the heart of the universe rooted God's consequent nature, the creativity we see is experienced as a process of creative transformation Christians name "grace."

That there is something like "grace" operating in the universe is witnessed to by all of humanity's religious Ways. Even a Hindu's experience of the "great identity" of his or her Ātman (Self) with Brahman, or a Buddhist's experience of enlightenment, or a Christian or Muslim mystic's experience of oneness with God has a gracious character. Our relation to and experience of the ox are given, ongoing processes, because wrestling with the ox reveals a paradox: grace does not come to us *because* we wrestle with the ox. It has always poured over us like a waterfall, a tidal wave, so that we *can* wrestle with the ox. The religious Ways of humanity thus testify that whenever we become aware of the gracious character of the creative transformation going on in the universe that has been there all along, we are rocked and toppled. For the experience of grace shears, looses, launches, winnows, grinds. Grace is never cheap precisely because it never separates us from the world; it thrusts into the world in new ways and understandings because it sharpens our sense of interdependency and interrelation with other human beings and with nature. Consequently, the grace we encounter, when we become consciously aware of it, has practical implications for human interaction with nature, the struggle for women's liberation from patriarchal oppression, and the struggle for humanity's liberation from political, economic, and racial oppression.

The Struggle for Liberation

What I take to be the metaphysical fact that we live in an interrelated universe in which all things and events are mutually implicated provides the major ethical foundation for understanding and participating in the struggle for liberation. I have called this foundation "the principle of interdependency." What happens to any person or community of persons is interdependent with whatever happens in nature, for good or ill; whatever happens in nature, whatever non-human life forms undergo, is interdependent with what happens to the human community. In other words, in an interdependent universe, one aspect of the experience of grace is that it does not isolate us from our interrelationships with nature; it heightens awareness of these relationships as it pulls us into ethically responsible, interdependent interaction with nature.

According to the title of the tenth Ox-Herding picture, the gracious character of enlightenment engenders compassionate entry "into the city with bliss-bestowing hands." This seems to be the testimony of humanity's religious Ways; however "grace" might be conceptualized in these traditions, it is always part of the experience of whatever "enlightenment" or "spiritual release" or "salvation" is. That is, grace is never an unethical event. It always involves "creative transformation" of the individual along with that person's relationships and responsibilities to the human community and to nature.

Accordingly, any political system, economic philosophy, social organization, or environmental policy that disrupts, hinders, breaks, throws out of balance, or exploits interrelationships upon which we all depend is unjust, hermeneutically suspicious, and needs to be resisted. Seen according to the principle of interdependency, as chapter 6 noted, human exploitation of the environmental forces creating and supporting life on this planet is harmful to both human beings and other life forms. It is therefore necessary that we practice an "option for the environment" that is similar to what liberation theologians call the "option for the poor." The main question is, How should human beings live in harmony with the environmental forces nurturing and sustaining all life on this planet? How should we balance the needs of the human community with the needs of the environment upon which all life depends? How best to struggle for the liberation of life?

A good starting point for answering these question is hermeneutical suspicion of any anthropocentric policy that exploits the environment through failure to balance the needs of the human community with the needs of the environment. Such policies are ethically wrong and should be resisted. Accordingly, practicing preference for the environment requires that the burden of proof must rest on any human-initiated economic policy or political decision to demonstrate that it has no negative ecological impact.

The ethical implications of what I think is the metaphysical fact of interdependency, made powerfully clear when we experience the gracious character of reality, may also be applied to the struggle for the liberation of women from patriarchal forms of oppression. The fundamental injustice of the patriarchal oppression of women—religiously, socially, economically, politically, sexually—is that the oppression of women damages both the oppressed and the oppressor; both men and women are hindered from realizing and attaining full personhood and creative transformation. In an interdependent universe, masculine forces and feminine forces—I have in mind how the Chinese imagine and experience universal interdependency through what Taoist tradition calls *yang* and *yin*—are co-equal forces that structure human reality. That is, femininity and masculinity are bipolar forces through which the Tao (Way) interacts in nature. Each requires the other as part of its nature; when in balanced harmony, *yang* defines and creates *yin* as *yin* mutually defines and creates *yang*.

When *yin* and *yang* are in harmonious balance, which the Chinese believed the natural forces of nature always seek, there is justice, peace, and creativity. But whenever there is too much *yin* or *yang*, there arises imbalance, disharmony, non-peace, suffering, injustice. This is because too much of one thing is self-destructive. For example, too much compassion (*yin*) is sentimentality. Compassion needs to be harmonized with justice (*yang*). But too much justice creates tyranny. Justice needs to be balanced by compassion.

Seen from this perspective, patriarchal oppression of women represents an overabundance of *yang*. It thus breaks those interrelationships equally required by both men and women; in so doing, full humanity is denied to both women and men. Stated in a Taoist way, patriarchy is too much *yang* out of balance with *yin*. The result is disruption of the interdependency of masculinity and femininity that mutually creates and constitutes human existence and which is necessary for realizing full humanity—what Confucius called *rin*— for both women and men. This is why patriarchy is stupid; it is self-destructive for men, even as it causes incredible suffering and oppression for women. Patriarchy thus denies the humanity of both men and women, for as men oppress women they oppress themselves.

If it is true that the struggle for women's liberation against the forces of patriarchy and sexism is simultaneously a struggle for men's liberation from these same forces, it is an ethical and theological imperative that men critically listen to feminist critiques of religious and secular forms of patriarchy. Yet men must do more than critically listen. Men must join with women and follow their lead in feminist deconstruction of patriarchy in all its forms in a joint effort to reconstruct new religious, political, and social visions of reality and institutions that assume equality between women and men. It is in men's and women's best interest to do so because the liberation of men is interdependent with the liberation of women, as is the liberation of women interdependent with that of men.

Finally, the principle of interdependency is also the ethical foundation of humanity's quest for liberation from economic, political, and social forms of institutionalized oppression. In this regard, one of the conclusions of chapter 8 is particularly relevant. The quest for liberation needs to be placed in the global context of humanity's religious communities East and West. The liberation of nature, women's liberation, and the liberation of human beings from poverty, economic oppression, and social oppression are too big a task for one religious community. In our present "cosmic epoch," as Whitehead would phrase it, the need for liberation is a universal need that requires global interreligious dialogue. In an interrelating universe, the oppression of any human being oppresses all human beings; no human being is liberated from oppression unless all human beings are liberated from oppression.

Chapter 8 also concluded that religious pluralists need dialogue with liberation theologies in order to face up to the dangers of uncritical, overenthusiastic affirmation of religious pluralism. To be sure, pluralism is, I believe, a metaphysical fact of existence. It is the ground for interrelatedness and inter-dependency between all things and events in this universe at every moment of space-time, including humanity's interrelatedness with the ox. Yet liberation theologies remind us that uncritical affirmation of pluralism can lead to unethical and socially irresponsible relativism. Affirming the principle of inter-dependency as the ethical foundation of liberation does not mean that any-thing goes. It means precisely the opposite: racism, sexism, genocide, exploitation of the poor, the current global resurgence of religious "funda-mentalism," or exploitation of the environment must be resisted because all forms of oppression break the bonds of interdependency that all human beings require for achieving full humanity.

Accordingly, the principle of preferential option for the poor and oppressed and the practice of hermeneutics of suspicion are two aspects of liberation thought that need incorporation into any theology of religious plu-ralism. Mutual interdependency means that there is much that should never be tolerated. The limits of tolerance are set by society's victims, wherever the mutual interdependency and process of creative transformation are crippled by economic, political, and social forms of oppression.

Finally, as mystics and contemplatives of the world's religious Ways help us to see the relatively inaccessible ox in the interior silence of our deepest selves and in the silence of nature, so liberation theologies teach us that we must never isolate ourselves from the world in the practice of silent non-duality with the ox. If we do, we will not hear the groaning of nature's travail or the groaning of oppressed human beings. Yet liberation theologians, always focused on painful issues of injustice, risk transforming their theologies into ideologies that leave our deepest selves untouched by silent encounter with the ox. The contemplative way of mystic practice and the activist way of the liberationist practice are interdependent. Both ways tell us that human beings seek liberation from oppression, that we are in an interdependent search for mutual transformation, and that, ultimately, the search for liberation is a search for mutual transformation involving release from suffering and death.

Final Liberation

John Bowker describes the plurality of religious quests for final liberation as a "religious exploration of how value can be maintained at the limit of life without seeking illusory compensation."[13] This is indeed the soteriological ground that the religious Ways of humanity, in their own distinctive ways, explore: the human capacity for self-delusion; the recognition that life yields to life, part to part; that the attainment of the whole, whether it be the forms of life on a coral reef or human life in a modern city, seems to demand a sacrifice few living things are willing to volunteer on their own account, but which some do nevertheless volunteer, thereby making their death a sacrifice for the benefit of others.

The theme of sacrifice, which Bowker thinks is the earliest category through which religious traditions explore the nature and significance of the experience of death, is fundamentally the theme of not simply life yielding *to* life, but of life yielding *for* life to enable life's possibility.[14] I think Bowker's insight is highly suggestive. Sacrifice is a major category, even if it is not the only category, through which the religious Ways of humanity have explored death. Furthermore, it is the religious exploration of death in all of its plurality that brings us to more sensitive awareness of evil, because how we experience death and think about it flows back into our moral, aesthetic, and political decisions while we are alive.

But, this having been said, it is clear that many of the differing views of the nature death and its relation to the quest for mutual transformation and liberation beyond death cannot possibly be true. All may be false, but they cannot possibly all be true, at least as propositions about matters of fact. That is, it is not possible for both a Hindu and a Buddhist to be correct in their views of human nature. It is not possible for both a Christian and a Muslim to be correct in terms of what they propose about the death and resurrection of Jesus.

Undoubtedly, such propositional differences in the soteriologies of the religious Ways of humanity make a difference, especially to those who believe them. They are not trivial, in the way that a preference for yellow, say, rather than green might be. Thus, Judaism and Islam agree in regarding human beings as teachable: humans can learn from God through Torah or *Qurʾān*. God tells Muslims and instructs Jews what to do, and gives them help to do it, thereby educating those who follow these orders or instructions into salvation. So Judaism and Islam might be said to have relatively optimistic views of human nature. But the Christian Way has a relatively pessimistic view of human nature: subversive egoism and evil lie at the root of every human enterprise, and we cannot be educated into salvation. Salvation, if it is to come at all, comes *in spite of* who we are.

Still, propositional differences between the religious Ways of humanity, especially in relation to death—their pictures of death and what may survive it—may be approximate and mainly wrong as a matter of literal description. They may also be literally wrong yet approximate about some fundamental demand arising from human experience. In this sense, the pictures and concepts of different religious conceptualities may reinforce each other, even though in detail they are incompatible. This does not mean that issues of truth disappear; it is simply that truth issues are not foreclosed in advance. So choices remain to be made, far short of immediate verification or falsification of factual propositions, since in the nature of the case of the possibility of life beyond death, verification cannot be other than eschatological.

So the affirmation of value in all of the religious Ways of humanity *includes* the reality of death, sometimes as a last enemy, but always as a necessary condition of life. Attempts to evade death, or to pretend that it is not serious, or to deny its necessary place in the ordering of life, or to structure one's life ethically and religiously in order to reap the reward of life after death have usually been regarded by the world's religious Ways as false or dangerous or subverting of truth. Furthermore, to the question whether death is as great an evil as most of us suppose, the religious Ways of humanity unanimously answer—no. The category of sacrifice is a dramatic statement of this answer. There can be no other terms on which we can live except those of death.

Reflecting on the category of sacrifice does not mean imposing the fact of sacrifice on others in moments of their suffering. Nor ought we suppose that the fact of death and its necessity can be used as an argument to make the occasions of death benign. Death kills, and grief knows it.

And yet there exists a quality in the humanity of some human beings, in every age, culture, and religious Way that affirms and acquires a sense of sacrifice, who make their lives a sacrifice, a positive acceptance on behalf of others that there are no other terms on which human life can be humanly lived. Such persons show us that we must affirm death without fear because without death we cannot live at all. As it was once reported to have been said by Jesus, "For greater love hath no one than this, that he lay down his life for his friends." Out of compassion for all sentient beings—everything that lives—the Bodhisattva sacrifices his or her own life to relieve their suffering.

The religious traditions of humanity, therefore, seem to teach us in their own distinctive ways that sacrifice is the condition under which all things and events must exist, from galaxies to loved ones who succumb to entropy and death. They instruct us not only to recognize the fact of death but to consciously affirm death's necessity as a required sacrifice through which life itself is enabled, ennobled, and secured.

But to what purpose? Are not death and sacrifice, which interlock us not only with each other but with every thing and event in the universe at every moment of space-time, as pointless as the blood of bulls and goats against which the Jewish prophets fumed? "What are your endless sacrifices to me?"

says the Lord. "I am sick of burnt offerings of rams and the fat of calves; I take no pleasure in the blood of bulls and lambs and goats" (Isaiah 1:2).

Certainly. But not all sacrifices are what they seem. For while we *are* here, humanity's religious Ways teach us, our resistance to the tide of entropy can also establish within us such miracles of relationship as grace and love, and that in this, we can know that the fact of death is, at least in a preliminary way, creatively transformed. That is, in the formation and transformation of character and relationships through which we now live, we are already experiencing levels of experience that reach through death and that transcend the experiences of stones or the lilies of the field in all their glory. For some of us, this is quite sufficient, and there is no need to explore further. But most human beings seem constructed in such a way that they are capable of entering into relationships of love and hate, of acceptance and rejection, not only with each other but with nature itself and with a responsive and interactive relatively inaccessible ox, that is both part of us and transcendent to us.

This way of living—in sacrificial and liberating interrelation with nature and with each other—is a true possibility for all of us. The different religious Ways of humanity—for all their differences, follies, wickedness, evil, and malevolence that their respective histories reveal—could not have survived unless this were so. The religious issue of ultimate transformation rests on whether the human body, which unquestionably owes entropy a death, is simultaneously the foundation from which we climb higher into love and grace so that we can enter into yet other levels of interconnection and possibility—into those levels of interconnection Christians call the communion of saints; whether, in Christian language, that life which is love, which is interconnection, which is interdependency itself, so that we who owe God a death are nevertheless enabled to enter joyfully into ultimately transformed life with God.

The purpose of sacrifice, then, is to affirm the value and worth of the entire universe, which cannot exist on any other terms than death.[15] Affirming that death is a necessary condition for new and creative transformations of life is the heart of the religious category of sacrifice. Each of the religious Ways of humanity affirms sacrifice in this sense. That is why we must love the universe and our life in it, while yet not clinging to it with attachment, as Buddhists might say, because here, as Christians might say, we have no abiding city—because "he is not here. Why seek the living among the dead?" (Luke 24:5). For Christians, the death and resurrection of Jesus constitute the single event that initiates the life attained through his sacrificial death, a new life which we are now able to live. For the Mahayana Buddhists, it is through the enlightened sacrificial compassion of the Bodhisattva that we too can realize and enact interrelationships that create ultimately transformed life beyond entropy and death. Both the Christian affirmation of the crucifixion and the Buddhist notion of enlightened sacrificial compassion are deep affirmations that there cannot be ultimately transformed life in a universe like this without death. Or again in Christian language, God's drawing us to God's selfhood has simultaneously drawn to God the necessity of death as the cost we, and even God, must pay for transformed life.

But there is also another affirmation in the Christian images of the self-sacrifice of God through the death and resurrection of Jesus: there is no death without the consequence of life. All the evidence of nature, all the evidence of the history of the plurality of humanity's religious experience of the ox points to this conclusion: as there is no life without death, there is no death without life. In a universe of this kind, what Jews, Christians, and Muslims call resurrection is not particularly surprising, and it is indeed reasonable to hope for ultimate transformation in the form of resurrection, just as it is reasonable for Buddhists, Taoists, or Native Americans to hope for ultimate transformation in terms of what their respective traditions teach.

How can we picture such ultimate transformation? What might continued existence after our individual deaths look like? To be sure, in the present here-and-now moments of the lives we now live, we cannot know for certain whether there is or is not life after death or what such postmortem life might be like. Much depends on the particular theological and philosophical assumptions through which we look at the reality of life and death. But John Hick's imaginative portrayal of what he believes is the reasonable likelihood that an individual's existence evolves through several stages of life and death culminating in the perfection of human personhood seems consistent with the particular assumptions and themes of the primordial theology I have described in this book.

In contrast to prevailing secular understandings of death, it seems likely to Hick that the universally held religious claim that life is part of a much larger structure of reality that transcends our individual lifetimes is very likely to be true. "Both the survival of the mind without a body," he writes, "and also the reconstruction or 'resurrection' of the psycho-physical person in another environment . . . are realistically conceivable, as is also some form of rebirth on this earth."[16]

The philosophical-theological foundation for this conclusion is Hick's appropriation of Irenaeus's (d. 200) solution to the problem of evil. Irenaeus, who was bishop of Lyons and one of the earliest important Roman Catholic theologians, taught that the purpose of existence is God's intention that human beings should evolve spiritually and morally toward a quality of being that represents the perfection of human nature. Since this world is God's creation, God intends the world to be an environment in which human evolution toward perfected personhood should take place. But if such a process *is* taking place in this world, it is seldom, if ever, completed by the time a human being dies. Furthermore, many human beings die in infancy or well before completing their normal life spans, most often in suffering and oppression. Consequently, *if* the evolution of human life toward perfected personhood is ever to be carried out, it seems that life must necessarily continue in some form after we die. That is, "a real continuation of human life after death as a formative process toward achieving perfected personhood seems required."[17]

But how can we imagine this state of "perfected personhood," since neither Hick nor I nor anyone now alive has yet experienced it? Hick's particular imaginative picture draws heavily on the Christian idea of resurrection and on Buddhist and Hindu notions of reincarnation because he thinks there is a point at which these notions converge and are compatible.

> But they agree more deeply in their view of man as a psycho-physical unity, so that life after death must be in a body, and a body which expresses the inner character of the individual. The [doctrines of resurrection and reincarnation] are thus versions of a common view that man lives again as an appropriately embodied being. If he is "reincarnated" he is thereby resurrected (brought back) to a new embodied life; if he is "resurrected" he is thereby reincarnated, i.e., incarnated (enfleshed) again.[18]

Thus, part of what happens after we die, according to Hick, is that our persisting self-conscious individualities will continue to exist in an embodied form. But we will not, in most cases, immediately attain the state of egoless personhood. Only those whom the religious Ways of humanity call "saints" or Buddhas or Sages or *jivan muktas* ("released selves") have fulfilled the purpose of temporal existence—the gradual creation of perfected personhood. The perfection of such persons consists in a self-transcending state beyond separate ego-existence. Those of us who die without having attained this perfected state must continue further in time as distinct and separate egos.[19]

Hick notes that there are several possible pictures of this final liberative state of perfected egoless personhood. Hick calls these pictures "pareschatologies." Pareschatologies refer to the next stages of human existence after death *before* the achievement of perfected personhood, which he thinks consists of "union"—the final overcoming of "egoity"—with God.[20] "Eschatology" refers in his thought only to this ultimately transformed stage of final liberation from egoism.

According to Hick, Christian, Buddhist, and Hindu pareschatologies are best seen as "open-ended." That is, "They are pointers beyond the known which do profess to delimit the boundaries or describe the contents of that toward which they point."[21] Consequently, if Christian, Buddhist, and Hindu pareschatologies arose from significant experiences at the interface between the human and the Sacred, we should be open to the possibility that these differing pareschatologies offer convergent indications, each pointing beyond our present experiences and yet pointing in the same *eschatological* direction. Hick concludes this is exactly what we find,[22] and so he draws two conclusions based on his distinction between a religious Way's particular "pareschatology" and "eschatology."

First, relative to traditional Christian *pareschatology*, the weight of standard Christian teaching insists that our earthly life is the only environment in which human beings come to salvation by the grace God gives to those whom God chooses to save. Thereafter, individuals exist in perpetual interrelationship with God. However, Hick believes this notion is "unrealistic," both about what happens before death and about what happens after death.

If salvation in its fullness involves the actual transformation of human character, it is an observable fact that this does not take place in the course of our present earthly life. There must, therefore, be further time beyond death in which the process of perfecting can continue.[23]

Consequently, Hick argues that we must live a series of lives, each bounded by something analogous to birth and death, "lived in other worlds in spaces other than that in which we now live,"[24] so that the condition of our lives in these successive worlds or spaces depends on our actions, thoughts, and experiences as we work our way through the process of human perfection.

Second, from the perspective of *eschatology*, all of humanity's religious Ways teach, each in its distinctive way, that there exists a final liberative state in which all human beings are drawn individually and corporately into egoless, selfless interrelationship and interdependency with the Sacred. Hick imagines this final state to be the end of a process in which "as the separate ego-selves attain their human perfection the boundaries between them become transparent and human existence becomes more corporate than individual," so that "as the individual becomes perfected he becomes more and more a person and less and less an ego."[25] Since personality is essentially outward-looking, as a relationship to other persons, while egoism creates boundaries that limit interrelationships with other persons, the perfected individual will be transformed into a "personality without egoity, a living consciousness which is transparent to other consciousnesses in relation to which it lives in a full community of love."[26]

This final liberative state is, then, one in which there exists a plurality of mutually and creatively transformed personal centers without separate ego-boundaries. These personal centers—the authentic selfhood for which all of humanity's religious Ways teach us to strive—will have ceased to be mutually exclusive. They will instead have become mutually *inclusive* and open to one another in a "richly complex shared consciousness."[27] They thus experience an intimacy of personal community that at present we can barely imagine. What *can* be imagined about these perfected human selves, however, is that they *just are* many different selves, each with its own unique character and history, but in this final liberative state so harmoniously interrelated that they form an immensely complex personal unity of humankind—"a unity which perhaps requires all their different unique contributions."[28]

Hick's portrayal of final liberation and mutually creative transformation is elegant, reasonable, and hopeful. Still, we must admit that there may be no necessary connection between elegant, reasonable hope and reality. Much for which human beings have reasonably hoped has been a delusion. Reality will be whatever it will be no matter how reasonable or elegant our hopes. Furthermore, if there is such a thing as final liberation, it must not only be human life that is ultimately transformed. In a universe of interdependency and interrelation, if final liberation is a reality, it must be an inclusive process involving not just all human beings who have lived, now live, or will live, but everything that has lived, now lives, or will live.

Therefore, in the between time of our birth and death, we discover life in interrelationships—with nature, with each other, with the poor and oppressed struggling for liberation and transformation—here and now. Making the struggle for liberation in all its forms our struggle—which is what it is in an interdependent universe—requires that we focus on the life we live in the midst of death here and now.

Such struggle entails a life of self-sacrifice here and now. Whatever happens after we undergo our particular death, whether there is something called ultimate transformation, we can never know for certain in the present here-and-now of our lives. So while we may reasonably hope for ultimate transformation, we should focus on liberating life here and now from unnatural death caused by human oppression of the interdependent evolutionary forces of life and death that together nurture life on planet Earth. We should focus our energy on working for the liberation of women and men from unnatural death caused by patriarchal oppression. We should struggle against economic, political, and racial oppression that collectively engender unnatural deaths before their times of the poor and the oppressed here and now. For when all is said and done, ultimate liberative transformation—if it exists—is up to the relatively inaccessible ox that is also relatively accessible. But *we* find life in *struggle* for liberation, even if hope for the ultimate transformation of life beyond death proves to be an illusion.

Still, I have a suspicion. Struggle for the liberation of life, for the liberation of women and men from patriarchy, for the liberation of the poor and the oppressed, requires a special kind of death of the self, a death we can experience while alive. The death of self of which the religious Ways of humanity speak is not a violent act. It is merely joining with the universe in its roll. It is merely the cessation of the ego's willful spirit and the intellect's chatter. It is waiting like a hollow bell with stilled tongue, for the ox. It's the waiting that's the thing, because not only does the ox come if we wait; we discover it has been here all the time, pouring its grace over us like a waterfall, like a tidal wave. When we wait in all naturalness without expectation or hope, emptied, translucent, then that which comes—the relatively inaccessible ox however we name it—becomes relatively accessible.

Then we understand what Annie Dillard meant when she wrote that there is always an enormous temptation "to diddle around making itsy-bitsy friends, pursuing itsy-bitsy needs, and making itsy-bitsy journeys for years on end until we die." We should not have any of this. Wrestling with the ox will not let us be so conventional, for we will discover that the universe is wilder than this in all directions, more extravagant and bright, more dangerous and bitter. "We should never make hay when we can make whoopee; we should never raise tomatoes when we should be raising Cain, or Lazarus."[29] Wrestling with the ox reveals not only that there is grace operating in the processes of life and death, but that there are also very few guarantees. To be sure, our *needs* are guaranteed, absolutely guaranteed—for liberation—but by the strictest of warranties, in the plainest language: "knock, seek, ask." But, as Annie Dillard and the New Testament warn, there's a catch and we had better read the fine print. "Not as the world gives, I give to you."[30]

Notes

1. D. T. Suzuki, *Manual of Zen Buddhism* (New York: Grove Press, 1960), 134.
2. Ibid.
3. Aloysius Pieris, "The Buddha and the Christ: Mediators of Liberation," in *Asian Faces of Jesus*, ed. R. S. Sugirtharajah (Maryknoll, N.Y.: Orbis Books, 1993), 46–48.
4. Ibid., 47.
5. See Mircea Eliade, *The Sacred and the Profane* (New York: Harcourt, Brace, & World, 1959), chap. 1.

6. E. Thomas Lawson and Robert N. McCaulley, "Crisis of Conscience, Riddle of Identity: Making Space for a Cognitive Approach to Religious Phenomena," *Journal of the American Academy of Religion* 61 (1993): 209-10. Also see Rudolf Otto, *The Idea of the Holy* (London: Oxford University Press, 1956).
7. Ibid., 210-20.
8. See chapters 3 and 5 above.
9. Alfred North Whitehead, *Process and Reality* (New York: Macmillan, 1967), 31.
10. Ibid., 31-32.
11. Ibid., 31.
12. Ibid., 521-33.
13. John Bowker, *The Meanings of Death* (Cambridge: Cambridge University Press, 1991), 41.
14. Ibid.
15. For a Vedic Hindu version of the necessity of sacrificial death as the primordial act that creates the universe, see the "Hymn to Purusa" in *A Sourcebook in Indian Philosophy*, ed. S. Radhakrishnan and Charles E. Moore (Princeton: Princeton University Press, 1957), 10-20.
16. John Hick, *Death and Eternal Life* (Louisville, Ky.: Westminster/John Knox Press, 1994), 15.
17. Ibid., 273-75.
18. Ibid., 371-72.
19. Ibid., 399.
20. Ibid., 425.
21. Ibid., 427.
22. Ibid.
23. Ibid., 455.
24. Ibid., 456.
25. Ibid., 459-60.
26. Ibid., 460.
27. Ibid.
28. Ibid., 463.
29. Annie Dillard, *Pilgrim at Tinker Creek* (New York: Bantam Books, 1974), 276.
30. Ibid., 227.

Selected Bibliography

Abe, Masao. "Buddhism and Christianity as a Problem of Today, Part I." *Japanese Religions* 3 (Summer 1963): 11–22.

———. "Buddhism and Christianity as a Problem of Today, Part II." *Japanese Religions* 3 (Autumn 1963): 8–31.

———. *Zen and Western Thought*. Honolulu: University of Hawaii Press, 1985.

al ʿArabi, Ibn. *The Bezels of Wisdom*. Trans. W. J. Austin. New York: Paulist Press, 1980.

Ali, A. Yusuf, trans. *The Holy Qurʾān*. Brentwood, Md.: Anima Corporation, 1983.

Allen, Paula Gunn. *The Sacred Hoop: Recovering the Feminine in American Indian Traditions*. Boston: Beacon Press, 1986.

Atkinson, Clarissa W., Constance H. Buchanan, and Margaret R. Miles, eds. *Immaculate and Powerful: The Feminine in Sacred Image and Social Reality*. Boston: Beacon Press, 1985.

Barbour, Ian, ed. *That Earth Might Be Fair: Reflections on Ethics, Religion, and Ecology*. Englewood Cliffs, N.J.: Prentice Hall, 1972.

Beare, Frank W. *St. Paul and His Letters*. Nashville: Abingdon Press, 1962.

Berger, Peter. *The Heretical Imperative*. Garden City, N.Y.: Doubleday, 1979.

———. *A Rumor of Angels: Modern Society and the Rediscovery of the Supernatural*. Garden City, N.Y.: Doubleday, 1969.

Bettlelheim, Bruno. *Symbolic Wounds: Puberty Rites and the Envious Male*. Glencoe, Ill.: Free Press, 1954.

Birch, Charles, and John B. Cobb., Jr. *The Liberation of Life*. Denton, Tex.: Environmental Ethics Books, 1990.

Bornkamm, Günther. *Jesus of Nazareth*. New York: Harper & Row, 1960.

———. *Paul*. New York: Harper & Row, 1969.

Boulding, Kenneth. *Ecodynamics*. Beverly Hills, Calif.: Sage Publications, 1981.

———. *The World As A Total System*. Beverly Hills, Calif: Sage Publications, 1985.

Bowden, John. *Jesus: The Unanswered Questions*. Nashville: Abingdon Press, 1989.

Brown, Raymond E., et al., eds. *The New Jerome Biblical Commentary*. Englewood Cliffs, N.J.: Prentice Hall, 1990.

Buber, Martin. *I and Thou*. New York: Charles Scribner's Sons, 1958.

Bultmann, Rudolf. *Theology of the New Testament*. 2 vols. Trans. Kendrick Grobel. New York: Charles Scribner's Sons, 1951.

Burton, Naomi, et al., eds. *The Asian Journals of Thomas Merton.* New York: New Directions, 1975.

Burtt, E. A. *The Metaphysical Foundations of Modern Science.* Garden City, N.Y: Anchor Books, 1954.

Callicott, J. Baird. "Animal Liberation: A Triangular Affair." *Environmental Ethics* 2 (1980): 311-38.

———, and Roger T. Ames, eds. *Nature in Asian Traditions of Thought.* Albany: State University of New York Press, 1989.

Campbell, Joseph, and Bill Moyers. *Joseph Campbell: The Power of Myth.* New York: Doubleday, 1988.

Capra, Fritjof. *The Tao of Physics: An Exploration of the Parallels Between Modern Physics and Eastern Mysticism.* Boulder, Colo.: Shambala, 1975.

———. *The Turning Point.* New York: Bantam Books, 1982.

Christ, Carol P., and Judith Plaskow, eds. *Womanspirit Rising: A Feminist Reader in Religion.* San Francisco: Harper & Row, 1979.

Cobb, John B., Jr. *Beyond Dialogue.* Philadelphia: Fortress Press, 1982.

———. "Buddhist Emptiness and the Christian God." *Journal of the American Academy of Religion* 45 (1977): 11-25.

———. "Can A Christian Be a Buddhist, Too?" *Japanese Religions* 10 (December 1978): 1-20.

———. *Christ in a Pluralistic Age.* Philadelphia: Westminster Press, 1975.

———. "Response to Wiebe." *Buddhist-Christian Studies* 5 (1985): 151-52.

———. *The Structure of Christian Existence.* Philadelphia: Westminster Press, 1967.

———, and David Ray Griffin. *Process Theology: An Introductory Exposition.* Philadelphia: Westminster Press, 1976.

———, and Christopher Ives, eds. *The Emptying God: A Buddhist-Jewish-Christian Conversation.* Maryknoll, N.Y.: Orbis Books, 1990.

Cooey, Paula M., William R. Eakin, and Jay B. McDaniel, eds. *After Patriarchy: Feminist Transformations of the World Religions.* Maryknoll, N.Y. Orbis Books, 1993.

Corless, Roger, and Paul F. Knitter, eds. *Buddhist Emptiness and the Christian Trinity: Essays and Explorations.* New York: Paulist Press, 1990.

Crossan, John Dominic. *The Historical Jesus.* San Francisco: HarperSanFrancisco, 1991.

Daly, Mary. *The Church and the Second Sex, With an Autobiographical Preface and Postchristian Introduction by the Author.* Boston: Beacon Press, 1973.

Davis, Winston. *Dōjō: Magic and Exorcism in Modern Japan.* Stanford, Calif.: Stanford University Press, 1980.

D'Costa, Gaven, ed. *Christian Uniqueness Reconsidered: The Myth of a Pluralistic Theology of Religions.* Maryknoll, N.Y.: Orbis Books, 1990.

Denny, Frederick M., and Rodney L. Taylor, eds. *The Holy Book in Comparative Perspective.* Columbia: University of Southern Carolina Press, 1985.

de Silva, Lynn A. *Buddhism: Beliefs and Practices in Sri Lanka.* Colombo, Sri Lanka: Wesley Press, 1974.

Deutsch, Eliot, trans. *The Bhagavad Gita.* (Lanham, Md.: University Press of America, 1968.

Dillard, Annie. *Holy the Firm.* New York: Harper & Row, 1977.

———. *Living Fiction.* New York: Harper & Row, 1982.

———. *Pilgrim at Tinker Creek.* New York: Harper & Row, 1974.

———. *Teaching A Stone To Talk.* New York: Harper & Row, 1982.

Donohue, John J., et al., eds. *Islam in Transition: Muslim Perspectives.* New York: Oxford University Press, 1982.

Dumoulin, Heinrich. *Christianity Meets Buddhism.* Trans. John C. Maraldo. La Salle, Ill.: Open Court, 1974.

Dunne John S. *The Way of All the Earth.* South Bend, Ind.: University of Notre Dame Press, 1978.

Eisley, Loren. *The Unexpected Universe.* New York: Harcourt, Brace, Jovanovich, 1969.

Fiorenza, Francis Schüssler. *Foundational Theology: Jesus and the Church.* New York: Crossroad, 1984.

Gergen, Kenneth J. *The Saturated Self: Dilemmas of Identity in Contemporary Life.* New York: Basic Books, 1991.

Gilkey, Langdon. *Reaping the Whirlwind: A Christian Interpretation of History.* New York: Seabury Press, 1981.

Gilson, Etienne. *The Christian Philosophy of Saint Augustine.* New York: Random House, 1960.

———. *The Christian Philosophy of Saint Thomas Aquinas.* New York: Random House, 1956.

Grant, Robert M. *A Historical Introduction to the New Testament.* New York: Harper & Row, 1963.

Griffin, David Ray, and Thomas J. J. Altizer, eds. *John Cobb's Theology in Process.* Philadelphia: Westminster Press, 1977.

Griffiths, Paul J., ed. *Christianity Through Non-Christian Eyes.* Maryknoll, N.Y.: Orbis Books, 1990.

Gross, Rita M. *Buddhism After Patriarchy.* Albany: State University of New York Press, 1993.

Guisso, Richard W., and Stanley Johannsen, eds. *Women in China: Current Directions in Historical Scholarship.* Youngstown, Oh.: Philo Press, 1981.

Guiterrez, Gustavo. *A Theology of Liberation.* Maryknoll, N.Y.: Orbis Books, 1973.

Habito, Rubin L. F. *Healing Breath: Zen Spirituality for a Wounded Earth.* Maryknoll, N.Y.: Orbis Books, 1993.

Haddad, Yvone Yazbeck. *Contemporary Islam and the Challenge of History.* Albany: State University of New York Press, 1982.

Hakeda, Yoshihito S., trans. *Kūkai: Major Works.* New York: Columbia University Press, 1972.

Harvey, Van A. *The Historian and the Believer.* New York: Macmillan, 1966.

Hassan, Riffat. "Equal Before Allah? Woman-Man Equality in Islamic Tradition." *Harvard Divinity Bulletin* 17 no. 2 (January–May 1987): 2–20.

Heick, Otto W. *A History of Christian Thought*, vol. 1. Philadelphia: Fortress Press, 1965.

Hevener, Ivan. *Q: The Sayings of Jesus*. Collegeville, Minn.: Liturgical Press, 1987.

Hick, John. *Death and Eternal Life*. Louisville, Ky.: Westminster/John Knox Press, 1994.

———. *God and the Universe of Faiths*. New York: Macmillan 1973.

———. *God Has Many Names*. Philadelphia: Westminster Press, 1980.

———. *An Interpretation of Religion*. New Haven: Yale University Press, 1989.

———. *The Metaphor of God Incarnate*. Louisville, Ky.: Westminster/John Knox Press, 1993.

———. *The Second Christianity*. London: SCM Press, 1968.

———, ed. *The Myth of God Incarnate*. Philadelphia: Westminster Press, 1977.

———, ed. *Problems of Religious Pluralism*. New York: St. Martin's Press, 1985.

———, and Brian Hebblethwaite, eds. *Christianity and Other Religions*. Philadelphia: Fortress Press, 1980.

———, and Paul F. Knitter, eds. *The Myth of Christian Uniqueness: Towards a Pluralistic Theology of Religions*. Maryknoll, N.Y.: Orbis Books, 1989.

Holmes, Charles M. *Aldous Huxley and the Way to Reality*. Bloomington, Ind.: Indiana University Press, 1970.

Horner, I. B., trans.. *The Collection of Middle Length Sayings*, vol. 1. London: Pali Text Society, 1954.

Huxley, Aldous. *The Perennial Philosophy*. New York: Harper & Row, 1945.

———. *Time Must Have a Stop*. 1944. First Perennial Classic Edition, New York: Harper & Row, 1965.

Ingram, Paul O. *The Dharma of Faith: An Introduction to Classical Pure Land Buddhism*. Washington, D.C.: University Press of America, 1977.

———. *The Modern Buddhist-Christian Dialogue*. Lewiston, N.Y.: Edwin Mellen Press, 1988.

———. "Nature's Jeweled Net: Kukai's Ecological Buddhism." *The Pacific World* 6 (1990): 50–73.

———. "The Power of Truth Words: Kukai's Philosophy and Hermeneutical Theory." *The Pacific World* 7 (1991): 14–25.

———, and Frederick J. Streng, eds. *Buddhist-Christian Dialogue: Mutual Renewal and Transformation*. Honolulu: University of Hawaii Press, 1986.

James, William. *The Varieties of Religious Experience*. 1912. New York: New American Library, 1958.

Käsemann, Ernst. *Perspectives on Paul*. Philadelphia: Fortress Press, 1971.

Kato, Banno, trans. *Myōhō-Renge-Kyō: The Sutra of the Lotus Flower of the Wonderful Law*. Revised by W. E. Soothill and Wilhelm Schiffer. Tokyo: Kosei Publishing Company, 1971.

Katz, Steven T. "Is There A Primordial Philosophy?" *Journal of the American Academy of Religion* 55 (Fall 1987): 553–66.

——, ed. *Mysticism and Philosophical Analysis*. New York: Oxford University Press, 1978.

——, ed. *Mysticism and Religious Traditions*. Oxford: Oxford University Press, 1983.

Keenan, John P. *The Meaning of Christ: A Mahayana Theology*. Maryknoll, N.Y: Orbis Books, 1989.

King, Sallie B. "Toward of Buddhist Model of Interreligious Dialogue." *Buddhist-Christian Studies* 10 (1990): 121–26.

King, Winston L. *In Hope of Nibbana*. La Salle, Ill.: Open Court, 1964.

Knitter, Paul F. *No Other Name? A Critical Survey of Christian Attitudes Toward the World Religions*. Maryknoll, N.Y: Orbis Books, 1989.

Küng, Hans. *On Being a Christian*. New York: Pocket Books, 1978.

Lefebure, Leo D. *The Buddha and the Christ*. Maryknoll, N.Y.: Orbis Books, 1993.

Leopold, Aldo. *Sand Country Almanac*. New York: Oxford University Press, 1949.

Lopez, Donald S., Jr., trans. *The Heart Sutra Explained*. Albany: State University of New York Press, 1988.

Mack, Burton L. *The Lost Gospel of Q: The Book of Christian Origins*. San Francisco: HarperSanFrancisco, 1993.

McDaniel, Jay B. *Of God and Pelicans: A Theology of Reverence for Life*. Louisville, Ky.: Westminster/John Knox Press, 1989.

McFague, Sallie. *Models of God: A Theology for an Ecological, Nuclear Age*. Philadelphia: Fortress Press, 1987.

Mernissi, Fatima. *Beyond the Veil*. Cambridge: Schenkman Publishing Company, 1975.

Mitchell, Donald W. *Spirituality and Emptiness*. Mahwah, N.J.: Paulist Press, 1991.

Moltmann, Jürgen. *The Church and the Power of the Spirit: A Contribution to Messianic Ecclesiology*. Translated by Margaret Kohl. New York: Harper & Row, 1977.

Neihardt, John G. *Black Elk Speaks*. New York: Washington Square Press, 1932.

Nikhilananda, Swami, trans. *The Bhagavad-gita*. New York: Ramakrishna-Vivekananda Center, 1944.

——. *The Gospel of Sri Ramakrishna*. New York: Harper & Row, 1952.

——. *The Upanishads*. New York: Harper Torchbooks, 1963.

Oakman, Douglas E. "Ruler's Houses, Thieves, and Ursurpers: The Beelzebul Pericope." *Forum* (September 1988): 109–23.

Oberman, Richard H. *Evolution and the Christian Doctrine of Creation*. Philadelphia: Westminster Press, 1967.

O'Flaherty, Wendy Doniger, trans. *The Rig Veda: An Anthology*. New York: Penguin Books, 1981.

Organ, Troy Wilson. *The Hindu Quest for the Perfection of Man*. Athens, Oh.: Ohio University Press, 1970.

Panikkar, Raimundo. *The Silence of God: The Answer of the Buddha*. Maryknoll, N.Y.: Orbis Books, 1990.

———. *The Unknown Christ of Hinduism.* Maryknoll, N.Y.: Orbis Books, 1981.

Pannenberg, Wolfhart. *Metaphysics and the Idea of God.* Trans. Philip Clayton. Grand Rapids, Mich.: William B. Eerdmans, 1988.

———. *Theology and the Philosophy of Science.* Trans. Francis McDonagh. Philadelphia: Westminster Press, 1976.

Parriskar, Vasudeva Laksmana, ed. *Srimad-Valmiki-Maharisi-Punith Yogava'-sistha.* Bombay: Tukaram Javaji, 1978.

Petry, Ray. *Francis of Assisi.* New York: AMS Press, 1964.

Pieris, Aloysius, S.J. *An Asian Theology of Liberation.* Maryknoll, N.Y.: Orbis Books, 1988.

Plaskow, Judith. *Standing Again at Sinai: Judaism from a Feminist Perspective.* San Francisco: HarperSanFrancisco, 1990.

———, and Carol P. Christ, eds. *Weaving the Visions: New Patterns in Feminist Spirituality.* San Francisco: HarperSanFrancisco, 1989.

Prebish, Charles, ed. *Buddhism: A Modern Perspective.* University Park, Penn.: Pennsylvania State University Press, 1975.

Pye, Michael. "Skillful Means and the Interpretation of Christianity." *Buddhist-Christian Studies* 10 (1990): 17–21.

Radhakrishnan, Sarvepalli, and Charles A. Moore, eds. *A Sourcebook in Indian Philosophy.* Princeton: Princeton University Press, 1957.

Rahman, Fazlur. *Islam.* Chicago: University of Chicago Press, 1966.

Rahner, Karl. *Theological Investigations,* vol. 5. Baltimore: Helicon Press, 1982.

Reimer, Jack, ed. *Jewish Reflections on Death.* New York: Shocken Books, 1975.

Rhys, C. A. F., and T. W. Davids, transs. *Dialogues of the Buddha (Digha and Magghima Nikayas),* vol. 2. London: Oxford University Press, 1938.

Ridderbos, Herman. *Paul: An Outline of His Theology.* Grand Rapids, Mich.: William B. Eerdmans, 1975.

Rochelle, Jay C. "Letting Go: Buddhist and Christian Models." *The Eastern Buddhist* 22 (Autumn 1989): 27–47.

Rogers, Minor L., and Ann T. Rogers. *Rennyo: The Second Founder of Shin Buddhism.* Berkeley, Calif.: Asian Humanities Press, 1991.

Rolston, Holmes, III. *Environmental Ethics: Duties to and Values in the Natural World.* Philadelphia: Temple University Press, 1988.

Rorty, Richard. *Philosophy and the Mirror of Nature.* Princeton: Princeton University Press, 1979.

Ruether, Rosemary Radford. *Sexism and God Talk: Toward a Feminist Theology.* Boston: Beacon Press, 1983.

Sagan, Eli. *At the Dawn of Tyranny: The Origins of Individualism, Oppression, and the State.* New York: Alfred A. Knopf, 1985.

Sanday, Peggy Reeves. *Female Power and Male Dominance: On the Origins of Sexual Inequality.* London: Cambridge University Press, 1981.

Santayana, George. *Interpretations of Poetry and Religion.* New York: Harper Torchbooks, 1957.

Schimmel, Annemarie. *The Mystical Dimensions of Islam.* Chapel Hill: University of North Carolina Press, 1975.

Schuon, Frithjof. *The Transcendent Unity of Religions.* New York: Harper & Row, 1975.

Segundo, Juan Luis. *The Liberation of Theology.* Maryknoll, N.Y.: Orbis Books, 1976.

Sharma, Arvind, ed.. *Women in World Religions.* Albany: State University of New York Press, 1987.

Singer, Peter. *Animal Liberation: A New Ethics for Our Treatment of Animals.* New York: Avon Books, 1975.

Smith, Huston. *Forgotten Truth: The Primordial Tradition.* New York: Harper & Row, 1976.

———. "Is There a Perennial Philosophy?" *Journal of the American Academy of Religion* 55 (1987): 553-66.

———. *The Religions of the World.* News York: HarperCollins, 1991.

Smith, J. M. Powis, and Edgar J. Goodspeed, transs. *The Complete Bible: An American Translation.* Chicago: University of Chicago Press, 1948.

Smith, Wilfred Cantwell. *Belief and History.* Charlottesville: University of Virginia Press, 1977.

———. *Faith and Belief.* Princeton: Princeton University Press, 1979.

———. *The Faith of Other Men.* New York: New American Library, 1965.

———. *Islam in Modern History.* Princeton: Princeton University Press, 1957.

———. *The Meaning and End of Religion.* New York: New American Library, 1964.

———. "Participation: The Changing Christian Role in Other Cultures." *Religion and Society* 18, no. 1 (1979): 56-73.

———. *Towards A World Theology: Faith and the Comparative History of Religion.* Philadelphia: Westminster Press, 1981.

Snodgrass, Adrian. "The Shingon Buddhist Doctrine of Interpenetration." *Religious Traditions* 9 (1986): 88-114.

Stace, Walter T. *Mysticism and Philosophy.* Philadelphia: Lippincott, 1960.

Streng, Frederick J. *Emptiness: A Study in Religious Meaning.* Nashville: Abingdon Press, 1967.

———. "Mutual Transformation: An Answer to a Religious Question." *Buddhist-Christian Studies* 13 (1993): 121-26.

———. *Understanding Religious Life.* Belmont, Calif.: Wadsworth Publishing Company, 1985.

Suzuki, D. T. *Manual of Zen Buddhism.* New York: Grove Press, 1960.

Swartz, Merlin L., ed. and trans. *Studies on Islam.* New York: Oxford University Press, 1991.

Swidler, Leonard, ed. *Toward a World Theology of Religions.* Maryknoll, N.Y.: Orbis Books, 1987.

———, John B. Cobb, Jr., Paul F. Knitter, and Monika K. Hellwig. *Death or Dialogue?* London: SCM Press, 1990.

Taiko, Yamasaki. *Shingon: Japanese Esoteric Buddhism*. Boston: Shambala Publications, 1988.

Taylor, Mark Kline. *Remembering Esperanza: A Cultural-Political Theology for North American Praxis*. Maryknoll, N.Y.: Orbis Books, 1990.

Thich Nhat Hanh. *Zen Keys*. Garden City, N.Y.: Anchor Books, 1974.

Thompson, Laurence G. *Chinese Religion: An Introduction*. Belmont, Calif.: Wadsworth, 1989.

Tillich, Paul. *Dynamics of Faith*. New York: Harper & Row, 1957.

———. *Systematic Theology*, vol. 1. Chicago: University of Chicago Press, 1951.

Toynbee, Arnold. *An Historian's Approach to Religion*. New York: Oxford University Press, 1956.

———. "What Should Be the Christian Approach to the Contemporary Non-Christian Faiths? In *Christianity Among the Religions of the World*. New York: Scribner's, 1957.

Tracy, David. *Dialogue with the Other: The Inter-Religious Dialogue*. Grand Rapids, Mich.: William B. Eerdmans, 1990.

Underhill, Evelyn. *Mysticism*. New York: Meridian Books, 1955.

van Buitenen, J. A. B., trans. *The Bhagavad Gītā in the Mahābhārata: A Bilingual Edition*. Chicago: University of Chicago Press, 1981.

Waley, Arthur, trans. *The Analects of Confucius*. New York: Random House, 1939.

———, trans. *The Way and Its Power: A Study of the Tao Te Ching and Its Place in Chinese Thought*. New York: Grove Press, 1958.

Warren, H. C., trans. *Buddhism in Translation*. Cambridge, Mass.: Harvard University Press, 1922.

White, Lynn, Jr. "The Historical Roots of Our Ecological Crisis." *Science* 155 (1967): 1203–7.

Whitehead, Alfred North. *The Concept of Nature*. Cambridge: Cambridge University Press, 1971.

———. *Process and Reality*. New York: Macmillan, 1929. Corrected edition. Ed. David Ray Griffin and Donald W. Sherburne. New York: Free Press, 1978.

———. *Religion in the Making*. New York: World Publishing Company, 1967.

———. *Symbolism: Its Meaning and Effect*. New York: Capricorn Books, 1927.

Woolf, Virginia. *A Room of One's Own*. New York: Harcourt, Brace, Jovanovich, 1957.

Yagi, Seiichi, and Leonard Swidler. *A Bridge to Buddhist-Christian Dialogue*. New York: Paulist Press, 1988.

Yang, C. K. *Religion in Chinese Society*. Berkeley, Calif.: University of California Press, 1967.

Index of Names

Index of Subjects

ātman (Self), 83, 88, 189, 200-201, 219
Allah, 58, 76, 82, 149, 167, 181, 215
androcentrism, 136-38
anonymous Christianity, 21, 43, 170
Arjuna, 48, 66-68, 72, 189
asceticism, 164
avidyā (ignorance), 83-84

balance, 98, 114, 122, 126, 129, 193, 220-21
belief, 16, 32-33, 51, 59-60, 71, 170, 181
Bhagavad-gīta, 48, 66, 69, 72, 81, 83, 189
Bodhisattvas, 69, 76, 78, 167
Brahman, 48-49, 58, 60, 67-68, 76, 82-84, 88, 189-90, 215, 218-19
Buddha, 1, 36, 48, 62, 75, 77-78, 84-85, 90, 167, 178, 181, 190-91, 218, 230
Buddhism, 10-11, 34, 36, 52, 54, 58, 61, 71-72, 77, 86, 90-91, 96, 98, 102, 106, 110, 112, 131, 138, 141, 143, 155-57, 160, 170, 179-80, 182, 185, 202, 206, 230
  Hua-yen, 35, 102-3, 106-7, 109, 112
  Mahayana, 36, 86
  Theravada, 77

Cartesian objectivity, 13, 213
  See also Descartes
christocentrism, 46, 48
communication, 108, 172, 210
Confucianism, 54, 72, 143, 156
creativity, 23-24, 43, 81, 101, 104-6, 152, 216-18
culture, Western, 4, 22, 56, 97, 116, 152

darśan (seeing), 39-40, 52, 56, 84, 190, 209

death and dying
  Buddhist tradition, 2, 26, 36, 42, 78, 85, 102, 141, 162, 178, 180, 190
  Chinese religions, 192
  Christian tradition, 17, 26, 36, 42, 46, 95-97, 103-4, 137, 145, 197, 199, 203, 211, 216
  Hindu tradition, 88, 147, 162, 189, 201, 213
  Jewish tradition, 151, 195-96, 202-3
deconstruction, 149, 221
dependent co-origination, 14, 23-24, 84
Descartes, 97
destruction, environmental, 127, 155
Dharma, 24, 28, 58, 60, 67, 76, 78, 85-86, 165, 180, 215, 218
dharmakāya, 78
dialogue, 5-6, 14-27, 30-36, 38, 44, 49, 53-54, 58, 70-72, 90-91, 109-10, 134, 153, 160-63, 168-77, 179-81, 185, 210-2, 215-16, 218, 221
  Buddhist-Christian, 35-36, 38, 71, 91, 180-81
  interreligious, 5, 14-18, 21-23, 25-27, 30-34, 36, 38, 49, 162-63, 168-69, 171, 173-75, 177, 210, 216, 221
diversity, religious, 29, 31-32, 53-54
doctrine, 6, 22, 24, 29, 69, 84, 102, 107, 111, 157, 169-70, 198
duḥkha (suffering), 84, 190, 201
Durgā, 76, 148

ecology, 95, 110-11
ecosystem, 98, 119, 129
egoism, 75, 84, 86-88, 114, 209, 223, 227-28
Emptiness, Emptying, 7, 24-26, 32, 36, 84-87, 158-59, 178-81, 192, 215, 218